Welcoming a New Brother or Sister Through Adoption

of related interest

Reparenting the Child Who Hurts
A Guide to Healing Developmental Trauma and Attachments
Caroline Archer and Christine Gordon
Foreword by Gregory C. Keck, Ph.D.
ISBN 978 1 84905 263 4
eISBN 978 0 85700 568 7

Attaching in Adoption
Practical Tools for Today's Parents
Deborah D. Gray
ISBN 978 1 84905 890 2
eISBN 978 0 85700 606 6

Toddler Adoption
The Weaver's Craft
Mary Hopkins-Best
ISBN 978 1 84905 894 0
eISBN 978 0 85700 613 4

Adoption is a Family Affair!
What Relatives and Friends Must Know
Patricia Irwin Johnston
ISBN 978 1 84905 895 7
eISBN 978 0 85700 619 6

The Mulberry Bird
An Adoption Story
Anne Braff Brodzinsky
Illustrated by Angela Marchetti
ISBN 978 1 84905 933 6
eISBN 978 0 85700 720 9

Creating Loving Attachments
**Parenting with PACE to Nurture Confidence
and Security in the Troubled Child**
Kim S. Golding and Daniel A. Hughes
ISBN 978 1 84905 227 6
eISBN 978 0 85700 470 3

ARLETA JAMES

FOREWORD BY GREGORY C. KECK, PH.D.

WELCOMING A NEW
Brother
OR Sister
THROUGH ADOPTION

Jessica Kingsley *Publishers*
London and Philadelphia

Permission has been granted by Josh Kroll, of NACAC, for use of "What Am I Willing to do?" chart in Chapter 4.
Permission has been given by Dr. Wayne Deuhn for use of "Family sexual policies" list in Chapter 5.
Permission for the charts in the Appendix has been obtained from Zero to Three: National Centre for Infants, Toddlers, and Families, the Child development Institute and *Toddler Adoption: The Weaver's Craft* by Mary Hopkins-Best (London: Jessica Kingsley Publishers).

First published in 2013
by Jessica Kingsley Publishers
116 Pentonville Road
London N1 9JB, UK
and
400 Market Street, Suite 400
Philadelphia, PA 19106, USA

www.jkp.com

Copyright © Arleta James 2013
Foreword copyright © Gregory C. Keck 2013

Front cover image source: iStockphoto®. The cover image is for illustrative purposes only, and any person featuring is a model.

Library of Congress Cataloging in Publication Data
James, Arleta M., 1960-
  Welcoming a new brother or sister through adoption : from navigating new relationships to building a loving family / Arleta James ; foreword by Gregory C. Keck.
      p. cm.
  Includes bibliographical references and index.
  ISBN 978-1-84905-903-9 (alk. paper)
  1. Adopted children--Family relationships. 2. Adoptive parents--Family relationships. 3. Brothers and sisters--Family relationships. I. Title.
  HV875.J364 2013
  362.734--dc23
                            2012041428

British Library Cataloguing in Publication Data
A CIP catalogue record for this book is available from the British Library

ISBN 978 1 84905 903 9
eISBN 978 0 85700 653 0

Printed and bound in the United States

This book is dedicated to my family: my father—resting in peace, my mother, and my two sisters.

Contents

Foreword

When Jessica Kingsley Publishers asked me to write the foreword for *Welcoming a New Brother or Sister Through Adoption*, I felt honored and privileged—honored to be acknowledged by JKP as a person whose voice might help promote this book and privileged to be able to do this for my colleague and friend, Arleta James. Arleta has helped so many children and families address the challenges that they face as they transcend the adoption process on their journey to becoming a family, and by writing this excellent book, she is continuing her efforts to help every person who is involved in the adoption arena: parents, children, adoption and mental health professionals, extended family members, school personnel, etc. Adoptive families interface with world as do all families; however, some of the issues unique to these families are either not understood, misunderstood, ignored, not acknowledged, or simply minimized to the point that the child and family do not get what they need to help them move from unfamiliar and unconnected to closeness and securely attached.

There are books that are primarily theoretical in their orientation. There are books that are comedic for the reader. Other books are seemingly practical but not written with an underlying theoretical framework. After I have read some books, I say, to myself, "AND?" James has produced an extremely practical, theoretically based book which will have many parents laughing and, sometimes, crying. So, in one book she has successfully integrated many components which offer readers an intimate view of what occurs with children who have been traumatized, separated from their birth families, and united with a family who has taken on the task of loving a child or adolescent who may not have any understanding or experience of being loved or of loving, of being tolerated or being tolerating, of being respected or of being respectful. The insiders, that is, adoptive parents, those people very close to adoption, and some older adolescent or adult adoptees, will immediately recognize the issues illuminated in *Welcoming a New Brother or Sister Through Adoption.*

What struck me as I read each page of this book was how frequently the author encouraged families to share information with all of their children—HONESTLY and COMPLETELY. James' suggestions about how to deal with tough issues, that is, sexual abuse and sexual activity, will be helpful to families as they ask themselves, "How can I share_____? When should I share_____? How old should my children be when I tell them_____?" I believe that the reader will find nearly every issue that they face addressed in this book. James leaves no stone unturned, and she provides hundreds of examples of how to approach the sensitive issues that confront families.

Throughout the book, James discusses the impact of bringing a traumatized child into a family with children already living there. She goes into great detail about how to prepare the children in the family, whom she refers to as resident children, for things previously unknown and foreign to them, such as sexual abuse, sexual activity, stealing, lying, aggression, chronic dysregulation, and the chaos that they see their parents endure as the new brother or sister joins their family. Her pre-placement suggestions will help immunize, if you will, all existing family members from the trauma that the new sibling may bring into the home environment. As I read her explicit discussions of what may occur with the resident children, I thought of what one adopted adolescent told me about his other adopted siblings, "I think that this adoption thing is a good idea gone bad." Perhaps, had this book been available at this time, his parents would have been better prepared to help every member of the family.

Whether you are interested in pre-placement issues, post-placement concerns, disruption/dissolution, sexual acting out, blending siblings, or marital stress, *Welcoming a New Brother or Sister Through Adoption* will have something to offer you in 14 information-rich chapters. I believe that every adoptive family will be better able to deal with difficulties that their children and family may be experiencing. Adoption agencies should consider making this book mandatory reading as a component of their pre-placement training program, and anyone who works with adoptive families will appreciate the deep insight that Arleta James has shared with us.

Gregory C. Keck, Ph.D.
Founder/Director of the Attachment and Bonding Center of Ohio
Co-author of Adopting the Hurt Child *(2009),* Parenting the Hurt Child *(2002), and author of* Parenting Adopted Adolescents *(2009)*

Acknowledgments

My first thanks go to the many adoptive parents, brothers, sisters, and adoptees who contributed to this book. Your lives are busy, yet you eagerly took the time to personally write or to allow me to portray your experiences. You did so out of a strong desire to help those who will read this book. Over time, I have been privileged to learn from you, and now others will reap that same benefit.

Pat Johnston—you initiated my first book on this topic, *Brothers and Sisters in Adoption*, after attending a workshop I conducted. This work allows *all* children in adoptive families a voice that might otherwise have gone unheard. So, thank you for the nudge I needed to speak on behalf of the brothers and sisters in adoption. You are now retired, but I also want to thank you for your long-standing commitment to the field of adoption. I entered the field of adoption almost 17 years ago, and feel I "grew up" as a professional as a result of many Perspective Press books you published.

Stephen Jones and Jessica Kingsley Publishers—you came along just when I needed a new publisher. Thank goodness! The opportunity to write this new book is indeed a gift to the parents and children that will benefit from its content.

Greg Keck and Tom Collins—my mentors—thank you for the knowledge, patience, guidance, and opportunities you have offered me over the past 17 years. You gave me my professional foundation. This work is built from that secure base. It reflects you, and, as you look at it, I hope you are pleased with your images.

My human foundation came from my mother and family members. Because of my family, I am able to achieve, thrive, and enjoy life. You gave me the gift of a healthy beginning that, in turn, has given me a present and future filled with endless possibilities.

Certainly, I have also been influenced by the work of a significant number of other professionals, foremost among whom are Barbara Holtan, Daniel Hughes, and Regina Kupecky. Thank you for helping me along my journey through adoption.

Anne-Marie—you are the sister extraordinaire and the most remarkable personal assistant! Thank you so much for taking care of so many things so that I could work on this one book!

Nancy G.—no matter where I live or what endeavor I take on, you are always there to help me. Thank you for being a friend and colleague.

Introduction

Why was this book written?

Many families coming forward to adopt are already parenting children—children born to them and/or children they have adopted. Certainly, adding a child or children to the family carries visions of chuckles and fun! There are also images of one child teaching another to build with blocks, to utter words, to read, to play games, having a snowball fight, jumping on the trampoline in the back yard, riding bikes together, shooting hoops in the driveway, and so much more. Ample cuddles and kisses will be shared as well!

Yet the arrival of an adopted sibling can—unexpectedly—adversely alter the lives of these children already in the family as well as their parents' lives. This is especially true if the adoptee enters the family with a history of trauma—abuse, neglect, abandonment, pre-natal drug and/or alcohol exposure, and so on—as have a large majority of waiting children, infants to adolescents, intercountry and domestic.

Trauma can have long-lasting deleterious effects that are inadequately represented by the phrase *special needs*, which is so commonly used to depict the children waiting for a place to call home. *Complex trauma* offers a more realistic portrait of the damaging imprints that traumatic experiences embed, in children, in their aftermath. *Complex trauma* better describes the potential for the newcomer, from orphanage or foster care, to arrive with issues that may not simply fade away with time and love.

Thus, *Welcoming a New Brother or Sister Through Adoption* is put forth as a guide. It is designed to help siblings flourish in spite of challenges that may arrive with the newcomer. It is intended as a plan to facilitate the types of close, connected relationships that mothers and fathers want for themselves and all of their children.

Which families will benefit from this book?

Much of this book is about integrating traumatized children into families whose composition already includes typically developing children. However, families that adopt and then give birth, adopt for a second time, or blend step-children into the family will benefit from the advice as well.

I've also written this book to help professionals, extended family, family friends—anyone who desires to help brothers, sisters, mothers and fathers, and adopted children pre- and post-placement—so they can find the information and tools to fulfill this aspiration.

The book concentrates on the growing-up years of children who are raised from infancy to the age of majority and who, whether by birth or adoption, are those children whose development is proceeding on track through predictable stages.

Socially, emotionally, cognitively, and physically, these children already in the family at the time of the adoption are thriving. They are able to learn, explore their environment, make and keep friends, express and accept affection, participate in extracurricular activities, and, overall, simply enjoy and happily absorb what life has to offer them. They are already residing in a family that adds a child who has complex trauma. Within the book, I refer to these children variously as "brothers and sisters," "birth-" and/or "previously adopted children," "resident children," "typical children," "age-appropriate children," "healthy children," "appropriately developing children," or "children who are on track developmentally." It is worth stressing that they may have been born to the family or they may have been adopted, as certainly there are many adoptees who enjoy appropriate development.

As there are many other excellent books written on understanding and meeting the needs of the adopted child, within this book I take as my primary focus the needs of appropriately developing children. However, the content also includes an introduction to the types of trauma that newcomers experience pre-arrival, and this book is full of parenting tips to better manage behavior, facilitate grief, talk with children about being adopted, and so on.

What does this book address?

Navigating relationships between sons and daughters who are growing well and those who are struggling is rewarding and yet presents various challenges. Frequently, parental time and family resources shift to caring for the "ailing" family member—the adoptee. The needs of the healthy brothers and sisters, as well as the parents, are often put on hold until the adoptee heals. Once in this pattern of focusing so much of the family's resources on the child with a history of abuse, neglect, or abandonment, parents find it difficult to rectify the situation—to strike a balance and to meet the individual needs of all of their children.

Parents begin to question themselves, often asking:

"Did we make the right choice by adopting?"

"How is this affecting our typical children?"

"What can we do for our resident kids?"

"Will our adopted son or daughter heal?"

"Will our family ever be the same as it was before we adopted this child?"

The brothers and sisters might start saying things like:

"It's annoying. When my new brother moved in, I didn't think he was going to have any problems. When I figured out he did have problems, I just wished he had been born to my mom and dad. Then he would be okay. I don't like it when we go somewhere and he starts acting bad and then Dad starts yelling."

"Prior to the adoption, someone could have told me how attention-needing she was. Someone could have explained to me that having a little sister was not going to be all fun and games. The changes she brought to the family have affected me. I have had the loss of a peaceful household, the loss of parental time, and the loss of privacy. She, at age ten, knows much more about 'bad words' and what they mean on TV shows than I did at her age, or anyone at her age should."

"I get really mad at my brother. I also feel like I can't go anywhere without him right behind me breaking something of mine or making fun of me, copying me, or touching something of mine that he shouldn't be touching."

Welcoming a New Brother or Sister Through Adoption responds to these questions and issues in an honest and forthright manner—and with a lot of optimism! The content, stories, and the writings of the resident children themselves feature within "Sibling Talk" boxes, sprinkled throughout the chapters, which highlight the "common challenges" that the adoption-built family faces as it works to weave the needs of a child with complex trauma into its fabric, accompanied by abundant solutions!

When helped, brothers and sisters do shift their perspective, as is exemplified by this young man who moved from "stuck in feelings" to "love and happiness" for his brother-by-adoption:

"Since we adopted my brother, seven years ago, my household has not had many peaceful moments. I've lost a lot of parental attention. This makes me jealous and angry. For a while, I had to share a room with my new brother and I lost a sense of privacy and space in the process. I was angry that I couldn't have my own room. I also had to lock a lot more things up after my brother started stealing from me. I lost a lot of material possessions. I didn't get as much as I used to and the things that I did have were often broken by my sibling. This angered me once again because some of the things had sentimental value to me. I definitely lost a peaceful household and fun activities.

"Eventually, my parents and I started to talk a lot about the situation. I learned to ignore the things that my sibling was doing. I do have to admit that sometimes I still do explode and my parents have to remind me that my sibling does things to push me away because he is scared of being loved.

"To tell the truth, in the beginning, I was mad, sad, jealous, and embarrassed. I learned (and am still learning) that feeling and being 'stuck' in those feelings doesn't do any good for you. And now my feelings have now changed to love and happiness toward my brother. I don't know what I would do if he wasn't in my life."

The more education this young man received, the better able he was to cope and to navigate positive relationships with his sibling. It is so unfortunate that this took seven years! Certainly, an intended goal of this book is to reduce the amount of time family members spend engaged in an unhealthy emotional climate.

How is the book structured?

The book is organized from pre- to post-placement. Chapter 1 describes the types of expectations that brothers and sisters develop when they learn their family is adopting; Chapter 2 offers an overview of complex trauma; Chapter 3 suggests ways for mothers and fathers to conduct pre-placement preparation with their sons and daughters. Chapter 4 is for moms and dads. There are parental qualities that contribute to enhanced success when combining typical and traumatized children, tweens and teens, so this chapter is for parents who want to hone and expand their strengths.

Finally, the child moves in and Chapter 5 is there to guide international or domestic families with this part of their journey. Chapter 5 discusses the pros and cons of traveling—with the children already in the family—to the newcomer's homeland. This chapter is rich with ways to transition the new son and daughter sensitively and by including the brothers and sisters. This phase of the adoption process is really the time to plant the seeds that eventually grow post-placement attachments.

Next, Chapter 6 covers the "common challenges" that arrive with the son or daughter with complex trauma. "Common" means that these issues emerge with frequency in the family that expands by adoption. Most families will learn to cope with these daily dilemmas. Yet Chapter 7 is offered for those parents who feel the challenges are too great for their particular family composition. Chapters 8 to 13 are packed with solutions, solutions and more solutions! Hope and healing—for each member of the family—abound in these pages! We end on a positive note in Chapter 14.

The full details of any books, websites, movies, or useful organizations mentioned in the pages of this book will be found in the "Resources" section at the end of the book.

As a prelude, a healthy sibling offers us her sentiments:

"There are so many positive aspects of adoption! Yeah, it's scary as hell to bring a total stranger into your home who may not want to be there, but the positive aspects outnumber the negative aspects so greatly. I enjoy playing with, talking to, and teaching my younger brother a lot of things. Even though the siblings act like they don't love me, they do. Also, adopting forces you to look deeper into people and to have a better understanding of why people act the way they do. The greatest of *all*, though, is that I know that I partook in giving two children a home."

Brothers and sisters—from diverse backgrounds—can learn to navigate relationships when joined by adoption!

1

"I'm Getting a Brother or Sister!"

KIDS DEVELOP EXPECTATIONS PRE-ADOPTION

Parents come to the adoption process along many avenues. Some are moved by the stark images of orphans across the globe. Others intersect with a child along their career path—a teacher or coach learns that a student or team member needs a "forever" family. Perhaps a foster child or a relative's child unexpectedly becomes available for adoption. A single adult comes to adoption out of a desire to become a parent. No matter the route the parents take to make a decision to adopt, brothers- and sisters-to-be develop a set of expectations about the sibling who is to come and join their family. This chapter will provide an overview of the expectations of the kids residing in the family prior to the arrival of the adoptee. We'll look at parental and professional contributions to these expectations as well.

It is important to note that brothers, sisters, and parents present pre-adoption with expectations that are ideal and optimistic. Certainly, these attitudes, feelings, and beliefs are wonderful for the newly arrived son or daughter to experience. Frequently, children available for adoption haven't always been welcomed so wholeheartedly into a family or haven't had the opportunity to live with a family at all. Yet forming realistic expectations increases the family's ability to accept the new family member with all of his needs and to integrate him into the existing family system.

Kids' expectations include...

"I will have a playmate!"

When asked, many children state, "A new brother or sister will be so much fun!" In fact, this is the most prominent expectation with which the appropriately developing children approach the pending adoption. They perceive that they are getting a playmate with whom they will ride a bike, toss a football, share their dolls, play dress up, or totally defeat at video games.

> "I was excited and even ecstatic. I had bothered my parents all my life to adopt again. I was adopted as a baby. I was an only child and very lonely. When I heard that my parents were adopting, I thought I was finally going to have play partners. Siblings will be fun and we could help kids have a better life at the same time."

> "I thought having a brother would be a lot of fun. I thought my brother would be so much fun to play with. Since we adopted my brother, it has been really noisy at our house. Whenever he gets mad, he will scream and cry. Also, when he doesn't get something he wants, he will scream and scream!"

"I will have someone to teach!"

Some believe that they will get a younger brother or sister who will seek out and benefit from their help with homework or who will be open to absorbing their knowledge. "I can hardly wait to teach her to read!" "I bet he'll be really impressed with my iPod® playlists. I can teach him everything about music!"

"Great! I'll have help with chores!"

Other children may be excited by the prospect of a sibling who will share in the chores. "We can take turns loading the dishwasher!"

Such expectations make sense, especially if there is a healthy sibling relationship in the family prior to the arrival of a brother or sister by adoption. Simply put, siblings are socialization agents. The sibling relationship provides a context for social development.

Through ongoing, long-term interactions, siblings teach each other how to play and how to make and keep friends.

As they become tweens and teens, brothers and sisters share advice about clothing, hair, dating, driving, and everything else that comes along with growing up. They help each other and teach each other. Brother–sister relationships provide opportunities for the expression of feelings, sometimes intense feelings like those that go along with sibling rivalry! They are there for each other to share the excitement of a first date or the devastation of the subsequent break-up. They learn the art of competition, the fun of board games, or touch football in the back yard. Then they cheer each other on at sporting events. They offer a support system that continues through adulthood (Powell and Gallagher 1993).

Given that the birth- and/or previously adopted children are routinely excluded from pre-adoptive education efforts—which would challenge their expectations—it makes even more sense that siblings-to-be enter the adoptive process from a positive perspective.

Parent's expectations include…

"I want my children to have more siblings"

Erick and Marianne adopted Peter as a toddler. They were concerned that Peter would be alone at some point in his life. They felt adoption offered him the opportunity to have "company" now and later. When Peter was age nine, they adopted Mark and Mike, ages ten and six respectively.

"Prior to the adoption, I was not so keen on the thought of bringing another child or children, in my case, into an already settled home environment. I was 16 years old. Of course, I knew that since I had gone my entire life without having siblings it would take some getting used to. My parents had looked at many children and we were under the impression that they would adjust well to our home. We were so naive. We expected them not to have problems and not to have been abused. We expected that these were basically normal healthy children."

The decision by parents to have more than one child is sometimes a desire to offset loneliness in the first-born or adopted, a hope to create opportunities for healthy competition, and a wish to provide their children with the "gift" of a ready-made playmate or companion. Mothers and fathers often envision that their children will magically become close, affectionate, and mutually responsive and may even remain lifelong friends—a parental legacy expressed in the phrase "After we're gone, you'll always have each other" (Bank and Kahn 1997).

Sibling relationships are important

The above expectation is quite understandable because the brother and sister relationship is taking on greater importance in light of changes in family structure:

- The average number of siblings is currently one.

- The sibling relationship is our longest relationship. Longer lifespan means that we may become dependent on our siblings, rather than our partners, throughout the course of our lives.

- An increase in divorce and geographic mobility may cause us, young and old alike, to cling tightly to the constancy and permanency a brother or sister can provide.

- The absence of parents due to stress, employment obligations, and divorce invites brothers and sisters to band together as a mutual support system (Goetting 1986).

These facts make clear that positive sibling relationships are of great value. It is no surprise, then, that parents expect and want to create intimate bonds between their resident children and the sibling they add by adopting.

The expectation of close sibling ties is created by other factors as well. These factors are explored on the following pages. It should be noted that the content of this book focuses on sibling relationships from birth through late adolescence—the time in which siblings are growing up together.

Expectations inherent in developmental tasks

Siblings have three primary developmental tasks in childhood and adolescence. First, and most important, siblings provide companionship, friendship, comfort, and affection for one another. Siblings are social agents.

Second, brothers and sisters are a primary means of child care. It is probably true that single-parent families, families in which both parents work, large families, and families overwhelmed by a child with a disability are more likely to delegate care-taking responsibilities to their sons and daughters.

Lastly, siblings benefit each other by managing relationships in various ways between parents and siblings. A child can protect a brother or sister from a confrontation with the parent by distracting Mom or Dad from the potentially explosive situation. Brothers and sisters can join forces with one another against the parent to strengthen resources for negotiation (Goetting 1986). For example:

> "If you bought us all bikes, you could save a lot of driving time and gas!"

As a second example:

> Melanie, age seven, was under the care of her 16-year-old sibling, Carol, for the summer. Melanie, adopted at age two from Belarus, has a limited sense of danger and lacks comprehension of the consequences of her actions. While Carol was babysitting, several of her friends stopped by. A television commercial regarding drugs caused the older children to make what they thought were some humorous comments about drug addicts. Melanie's interpretation of their remarks was "I would be cool and likeable if I took drugs." And, indeed she did. She swallowed almost a whole bottle of a prescription medication. Melanie's vital signs stabilized with the assistance of a 911 team. Carol explained to her very upset parents that Melanie's behavior was the result of the conversation with her friends. Carol intervened on Melanie's behalf and quite nicely diffused the situation. Melanie's parents were able to calmly discuss this situation with each other and Melanie. Since this incident, Carol's friends no longer stop by while she cares for Melanie. All medications have been placed in

locked containers. Melanie's grandmother visits more frequently while Melanie's parents are at work.

Expectations abound within these developmental tasks. Visions of siblings playing games, ganging up on Mom and Dad to obtain privileges, and assisting with household responsibilities are the types of experiences families want to facilitate, as well as experience for themselves. Carol and Melanie help us understand that blending children—typically developing and traumatized—may or may not play out as dreamed about pre-adoption. Chapter 2 will expand on the types of difficulties the child with a history of trauma may bring to the adoptive family.

"I would tell other kids not to assume anything. That's what I did, and it was totally the opposite."

Expectations derived from roles

Who were you in the family? Were you the "peacemaker"? Were you the "responsible one"? The sibling relationship can be a major determinant of both identity formation and self-esteem (Cicirelli 1995). Think about the following questions as you read this segment:

- What are my expectations of sibling relationships?

- Did I always get along with my brother or sister?

- Did I willingly share friends with my close-in-age sister?

- Did I willingly babysit my younger brother?

- Did I feel resentful or angry when my sibling "got away with" a behavior for which I was certain that I would have received consequences?

- How are my sibling relationships at the present time?

- What was my role in the family?

- Do I have expectations about what roles my appropriately developing children will assume once I become an adoptive parent?

- Do I have expectations as to what role my child by adoption will assume once she enters my family?

- What experiences have I had in which my expectations were not met? How did I feel in these situations? How did I cope with these situations?

- What are my expectations of my spouse?

- Are we united about adopting?

- About child-rearing?

- About the division of household responsibilities?

- Are my expectations about adopting changing as I am provided with information from my agency's pre-adoptive training program, readings, surfing the Internet, and networking with families already parenting an adopted child?

- What are my typically developing children's expectations of a new sibling?

- Have I talked with them?

Birth order

Place in the family—oldest, youngest, middle child—figures prominently in adult perceptions of sibling relationships as well. Birth order contributes to role identification, and as adults we often carry out the roles learned as children—"the helper," "the baby," "the older responsible one." Thus, our role becomes a large part of our identity.

There exists a bias within the child welfare system to avoid placements that move a typically developing brother or sister out of his or her role as oldest child.

When Mike and Nancy added Patty and Dave to their family, their birth son, Ryan, age 11, became the second oldest. Patty was ten months older than Ryan. Ryan's difficulty adjusting to Patty and Dave had nothing to do with the birth order. In fact, Ryan continued to receive all of the privileges usually ascribed to the oldest child as his development was in accord with his chronological age.

Patty's development, on the other hand, because of the pre-adoptive trauma she had experienced, resembled that of a child about five or six years old. Therefore, her freedoms and the possessions provided to her were doled out based on what she could handle in light of her developmental delays. Ryan's adjustment was related to the behavioral problems Patty and Dave brought into the family. Patty, who had an extensive history of trauma, had experienced 11 placements prior to coming to live in Mike and Nancy's home. Throughout her residences, her place in the family had changed repeatedly. Sometimes she was the oldest. Sometimes she was the youngest. Sometimes she was the middle child.

Parents know their children best. If mothers and fathers feel strongly that one of their sons or daughters needs to retain his or her place as oldest or youngest, then the newcomer should arrive at the according age. And, vice versa, if a mom and dad know that their kids can handle a shift in position, then the newcomer can arrive at any age within the parameters set by the parents-to-be. As the example of Patty and Ryan makes clear, birth order isn't always the biggest factor when the family expands via adoption. Later, we'll explore an array of "common challenges" an adoptive family can face after the child with a history of trauma arrives.

Ascribed roles

Roles in the family may also be ascribed due to qualities—for example, "the brain" or "the beauty." When parents extend and elaborate these differences over the years, these assigned traits may become a person's lifelong and satisfying identity. However, a negative role such as being a "fool," "the bad seed," or the "black sheep" can become a yoke around a son or daughter's neck; it may begin innocently, but once set in motion it remains fixed and even grows with terrible consequences for a lifetime (Bank and Kahn 1997).

Referring back to Patty, her moves were the result of negative behaviors. Foster family after foster family refused to deal with Patty's aggression, lying, and bed-wetting. Patty's ascribed role was that she was "bad" and "difficult." Her ascribed role caused her to act poorly. She defined herself as "too bad for anyone to keep." The worse she acted, the more she moved. And the more she said to herself, "See I am 'bad!'" It was a six-year endeavor to assist Patty to see herself in a more positive light.

The roles learned in a child's family of origin lend themselves to creating expectations of the roles parents believe the adopted child will assume. As Patty makes clear, adopted children may have little experience with roles or they may have taken on a role that is not beneficial to themselves or the adoptive family.

Time as an expectation

One year seems to be a marker frequently put forth as an adjustment period. It seems that there is a belief that in about a year the newly adopted child will be established in the adoptive family and the adoptive family will be settled and moving forward. Yet, as we'll learn later in this book, the child's traumatic past may take years to overcome. Two other factors that may further exacerbate the time it will take to integrate a child into an adoptive family are psychological fit and shared history.

Psychological fit

Psychological fit relates to the interplay between parental experiences, expectations, desires, and wishes and the child's capabilities and performance (Trout 1986). Psychological fit is also applicable to the brothers and sisters in the family built by adoption. Let's exemplify this concept:

> Peggy and Cameron had four children by birth, ranging in age from seven to 14. Their children were all healthy, excelled academically, and had terrific musical and artistic talents. Evenings were spent singing and playing the piano, flute, trombone, and cello. The family was fortunate financially. They decided to share their blessings by adopting an orphan. Eight-year-old Owen joined the family from Columbia. Owen struggled academically. He preferred baseball, soccer, and swimming to reading and math. He also had no interest in singing or playing an instrument. His lack of "fit" affected everyone in the family.

Peggy stated, "We simply cannot relate to him. He is not like us at all. We certainly expected that he would choose to do well in school. We thought that he would accept our interests as his own. We have attended his sporting events and have disliked every moment spent as spectators."

Peggy and Cameron ultimately made the decision to dissolve their adoption of Owen. They felt that trying to blend Owen into their family was comparable to putting a round peg into a square hole— Owen would never "fit." A new family was located for Owen. This family enthusiastically enjoys watching Owen score home runs and goals.

As a second example:

Donna is the youngest of three female adolescent birth children. Several years ago, her family adopted Maggie, currently age nine. Maggie is clumsy. It seems that every time she enters a room she breaks something. She has little knowledge of personal boundaries. She enters Donna's bedroom without knocking. If she sees something she likes, she takes it. She constantly interrupts conversations. She is "busy"—she walks or runs around the house constantly. Sitting still is difficult for Maggie.

Donna expected a sister who would enjoy dressing up, painting her nails, and having her hair styled. These were all things she enjoyed with her birth sisters. Maggie would have none of this. Maggie preferred toy trains and cars. She liked noisy toys that she could move around the house. Donna and her sisters were quite compliant children. They wanted to please their parents. Maggie, on the other hand, wanted to do things her way. Donna couldn't comprehend this type of disobedience. Daily conflict erupted due to Maggie's insolence. Donna wrote the following:

"I found it increasingly hard as the years went on to bond with Maggie. I felt most of my family's arguments and problems were her fault. I resented her a lot for the problems that began to arise in my family, especially the constant arguments. It became really hard for me to be nice to her and even to think about getting close to her. I was mean to her.

I yelled at her for not doing anything. I hated to be in the same room with her. I blamed everything on her.

"I have had to work hard to overcome my feelings of resentment towards her. I no longer get irritated by her as much or as quick. I try to do fun things with her that I know she will like and that will be fun for her. When I look back at how mean I used to be to her, I feel terrible about it. I never want to act that way towards her again. It made me sad to think how much I could have been hurting her feelings and her views about herself. I now know she isn't the whole reason my family gets into arguments. I am able to handle being around her and playing with her without getting frustrated, angry, or annoyed by her. I was able to become closer to her and know she was going to be my sister forever if I liked it or not. I would have to make it work without hurting her or myself."

Donna's poignant account helps us understand the personal struggle that she underwent in order to attain a level of "fit" with her sister. Maggie did not live up to Donna's expectations or experience of a sister. Maggie entered the family with her own unique interests, abilities, temperament, strengths, weaknesses, values, and attributes. Initially, Donna focused on all of the things Maggie didn't have. Ultimately, Donna realized that there were some areas the two could share. She went about connecting—"fitting"—with Maggie in those areas. At present, Donna and Maggie can sometimes be found laughing together!

"I knew it was a mistake. I mean you have to figure we already had kids. We had two girls and two boys. We didn't need another person and we didn't have room for another person. You're dealing with a person whose ways are different. You're dealing with a teenager who's basically set in their ways. They have different values to you and your family. So you're trying to put them in a new system and they're used to doing what they want to do. I didn't expect anything. I just didn't want him to come. I didn't care if he was going to be difficult or great. I had a brother and two sisters. What else do you need?"

Many adoptive families will have to follow Donna's lead. Experiences, expectations, desires, and wishes will have to be tailored to "fit" with the unique characteristics of the adoptee. This will be a process for each member of the adoptive family—parents, the children already in the family, and the child about to move into the family.

Shared history

Almost all of us have had the experience of being the "new person." For example, when you started your job, how long did it take to get to know your co-workers, the workplace dynamics, the formal and informal rules, where supplies were located, and so on? Learning all of this and assimilating into the workplace probably took time. Learning about a family and incorporating into a family will most likely take longer. The formation of relationships between parents, brothers, and sisters will occur gradually for the new arrival and over a long period of time—perhaps years.

Psychological fit is further complicated as the toddler or older adopted child is someone who is not initially a "true" sibling. He is placed into the sibling role but does not know the rules by which the other children (whether born into the family or adopted into it years before) have grown up (Ward and Lewko 1988). For that matter, he also does not know the family history, the likes and dislikes of family members, the inside jokes, the holiday traditions, birthdays, and so forth.

Parents and professionals alike must curb their expectations and their internal calendars for when change is expected. Having high expectations that must be achieved within a certain period of time and attempting to assimilate the child into the family within that time period may only lead to disappointment for all involved.

Parental and professional contributions to kids' expectations

"I am supposed to have a positive attitude about my new sibling"

Parents and professionals often unknowingly contribute to the resident children's expectations. One common method of preparing brothers and sisters for the arrival of an adopted sibling is to emphasize that the child is unfortunate and needs parents and a permanent home. Brothers- and sisters-to-be are admonished to make the adoptee feel at home and to help atone for the past deprivations experienced by the newcomer (Poland and Groze 1993; Ward and Lewko 1988).

Such post-adoption sentiments continue when parents encourage the resident children, "Put yourself in his place—he hasn't had what you have had," "We need to be more understanding," "We need to be more sensitive to how she feels." Such statements cause birth and/ or previously adopted children to believe that they must maintain a positive attitude about the adoptive child and thus the experience overall. The typically developing children often believe a positive attitude is expected of them. Therefore, resident children keep questions and concerns to themselves.

Expectations and reality often clash

Subsequent content will demonstrate that children arriving from institutional care and/or after abuse, neglect, and abandonment are not always capable of being good playmates, nor do they always readily accept help with their homework. They may have a preference for attempting to manage their own needs rather than seeking assistance from a parent or sibling. Their traumatic pre-placement experiences have left them with fragmented development and as such their actual skills are in discord with their chronological ages.

The following statements made by typically developing children, ages six to 15, will offer an indication of what may happen when expectations do not match with reality. These sentiments were expressed in interviews I conducted with resident children several years after an adoption had taken place in their family.

> "I expected children who were like my sister and me. I thought I could teach them the fun things I did when I was younger, like dolls, sidewalk chalk, and sewing. At first, there was a nice period. And then they basically started terrorizing the house—running around, breaking things, fighting. So it turned into a mess. I expected a lot different from what we got."

"Well, I wasn't really prepared for the big change. I had two sisters and a brother before he came. We got along and played a lot. I thought he would be the same. I didn't think that he would be the way that he was. I thought he was going to be like us, more civilized."

"I wanted a sister who would like to play games and use her imagination with me. I thought it would be pretty fun having her here. Her behavior has not been very good. We have to do a lot more work helping her than we used to. My dad has more gray hair now. Our house isn't as much fun because she takes up most of our time. It kinda upsets me. I thought we were going to get a baby. It does make me happy that I can see what she does that's wrong so I can keep from doing that myself."

"He was staying with one of our friends. I met him for like two minutes at a fair. I figured it wouldn't matter; just someone to hang around the house and play with and stuff. I was wrong. I am eight months older and I expected to just have another brother to hang out with. He's a pain. He isn't as bad as he used to be, but he's still so annoying."

Chapter summary

- Before the adoption, birth and/or previously adopted children develop positive expectations about the sibling joining the family. They look forward to passing on knowledge, playing, and sharing chores. Parents and professionals— unknowingly—contribute to these positive, enthusiastic expectations.

- Parents frequently envision a family comprised of children engaged in playful, enjoyable relations. Yet the adoptee who has previously been neglected, abandoned, and/or abused may arrive with a host of issues. Family members may struggle to maintain the peace, joy, and harmony that satiated the family prior to the adoption. Time will be needed to restore the emotional climate of the home.

- Birth order, ascribed roles, psychological fit, and shared history contribute to how quickly or gradually the post-adoption adjustment of typical and traumatized siblings may occur.

- Expectations and reality clash post-adoption. Yet families armed with knowledge can rebuild. Brothers, sisters, mothers, fathers, and the adoptee will adjust their expectations. Each family member will begin to accept the other's unique qualities and strengths as well as their warts and blemishes! Kids and parents will learn to "fit" with one another.

2

"My New Brother or Sister Experienced Trauma"

WHAT DOES THAT MEAN?

Complex trauma: "Think younger"

Many folks will adopt a child who has suffered complex trauma—multiple traumas that are simultaneous or occurring in a sequence, are chronic, and begin early in childhood (Cook *et al.* 2003). The institutionalized child arrives after inadequate care-giving—neglect—due to the modest caregiver-to-infant ratio found in orphanage settings. This son or daughter has also suffered abandonment, the move from homeland, loss of culture, loss of orphanage friends, and possible loss of siblings. There may be the trauma of pre-natal drug/alcohol exposure. Child welfare and infant adoptees undergo similar experiences. Sadly, there will be those children who join their families after the traumas of emotional abuse, physical abuse, and/or sexual abuse.

Complex trauma interrupts development. The newly chosen child presents as "younger" than his or her chronological age. Let's take a look at this concept of "social and emotional age" as opposed to "chronological age." It is really a key matter when blending siblings that have arrived in the family along different avenues—birth and adoption.

The Vineland Adaptive Behavior Scales offers one way to test the actual age at which a child is functioning—in four main areas—in comparison to the child's chronological age:

TABLE 2.1 THE VINELAND ADAPTIVE BEHAVIOR SCALES

Communication domain	Daily living skills domain
RECEPTIVE How the individual listens and pays attention, and what he or she understands. EXPRESSIVE What the individual says, how he or she uses words in a sentences to gather and provide information. WRITTEN What the individual understands about how letters make words, and what he or she reads and writes.	PERSONAL How the individual eats, dresses, and practices personal hygiene. DOMESTIC What household tasks the individual performs. COMMUNITY How the individual uses time, money, the telephone, the computer, and job skills.
Socialization domain	Motor skills domain
INTERPERSONAL RELATIONSHIPS How the individual acts with others. PLAY AND LEISURE TIME How the individual plays and uses leisure time. COPING SKILLS How the individual demonstrates responsibility and sensitivity to others.	GROSS How the individual uses arms and legs for movement and coordination. FINE How the individual uses hands and fingers to manipulate objects.

Source: Sparrow, Cicchetti, and Balla 2005

On the following pages are two sets of Vineland scores. We can see the impact of trauma on these children's development in a very simple, concise way. Subsequently, we will discuss the most pertinent ways these types of developmental delays affect sibling relationships when these kids with histories of complex trauma are introduced to age-appropriate brothers and sisters.

Robert

Robert was adopted from Eastern Europe when he was six months old. His complex trauma included abandonment, pre-natal alcohol exposure, and neglect.

Robert's current chronological age is 11 years, one month. Robert's actual abilities are:

Communication	
Receptive	1 year, 9 months
Expressive	5 years, 11 months
Written	9 years, 2 months
Daily living skills	
Personal	5 years, 11 month
Domestic	7 years, 7 months
Community	8 years, 11 months
Socialization	
Interpersonal relationships	1 year, 11 months
Play and leisure time	3 years, 2 months
Coping skills	2 year, 3 months
Motor skills domain	
Gross	Age equivalent
Fine	Age equivalent

Robert, at the chronological age of 11, has development that is scattered. In interpersonal relationships he functions at one year, 11 months. He plays like a pre-school age child—three years and two months old. His ability to get dressed, complete chores, and behave out in the community are more in accord with children about ages six to eight. Robert is "young" when we compare his chronological age to his social and emotional age. Brothers and sisters expecting Robert to play like an 11-year-old will quickly learn that he cannot perform to this level. Taking out the trash, vacuuming, and feeding the pets are all chores that Robert may require help or supervision to carry out correctly.

Betty

Betty is a domestic adoptee. In foster care she experienced abandonment, neglect, separation from three older birth siblings, and three foster care placements. She finally arrived in her adoptive home at age 14 months. Betty's current chronological age is four years, four months. Betty's actual abilities according to her Vineland score are:

Communication	
Receptive	1 year, 3 months
Expressive	2 years, 6 months
Written	4 years, 5 months
Daily living skills	
Personal	3 years, 1 month
Domestic	4 years, 6 months
Community	3 years, 1 month
Socialization	
Interpersonal relationships	1 year, 1 month
Play and leisure time	0 years, 4 months
Coping skills	1 year, 10 months
Motor skills domain	
Gross	2 years, 1 month
Fine	3 years, 6 months

Betty, like Robert, is not performing at her chronological age of four years, four months. Her receptive skills—what she hears, her capacity to pay attention, and what she understands—lag three years behind. There is an almost two-year gap in her ability to express herself— four years, four months as opposed to two years, six months. She struggles to form relationships, to play, and to move forward with rudimentary coping skills.

Betty and Robert are not unique or "worst case" scenarios. They offer the opportunity to recognize that the child arriving may be "younger" than expected. Social, emotional, physical, physiological, and cognitive domains of development are not proceeding within the parameters expected for the child's age. Let's now look more fully at some of the issues this presents when attempting to navigate close sibling relationships.

Complex trauma: The types of delays created
Attachment

Touch is critical to human development. Loving touch sets in motion a healthy attachment. Attachment, in turn, is the context in which all development—cognitive, social, emotional, physical, and neurological—becomes possible. In essence, our attachment to a nurturing caregiver sets in motion all facets of our human development.

Attachment, in family life, is also the blueprint for all subsequent close relationships. Attachment is a relationship (Gray 2012). If you have parented (or cared for) an infant, stop for a moment and think about the hours you spent holding, stroking, touching, rocking, caressing, kissing, and hugging the baby. As your child grew, touching and holding continued—hugs and kisses before getting on the school bus or while bandaging a cut knee, snuggling while watching television or reading books, pats on the back for accomplishments, stroking hair as a gesture of affection, and lots of kisses and caresses just out of love.

As a result of consistent and predictable parental nurture and support—the cycle of needs—this child develops a *secure attachment*. The child trusts his parents to meet his needs: "My parents are always there for me." He feels good about himself: "I am worthwhile." He seeks out his parents when he needs help or comfort: "I can rely on my parents." He has absorbed the skills to navigate life. He can develop solutions, handle stress, regulate emotions, follow directions, complete tasks, and the list goes on.

He demonstrates empathy and remorse: "I have hurt Mom's feelings. I need to make this right." He strives to have fun. He explores his environment. He seeks parental praise for a job well done: "I want to please my parents." He enjoys intimacy. He seeks out companionship: "I want to be around others." He can do all of these things within relationships with parents, his brothers and sisters, peers, teachers, coaches, neighbors, and so on. His blueprint is "I am safe within relationships." He applies his secure model of attachment to all human interactions.

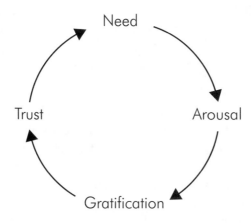

FIGURE 2.1 CYCLE OF NEEDS

In adulthood, this secure attachment will allow him to continue to have close interpersonal relationships. He will feel love and give love. He will understand that his past—emotional baggage—will not interfere with his capacity to interact in his marriage, with his children, in his career, and so on.

Inopportunely, many adoptees arrive in the family having been deprived of *enormous* amounts of emotional and physical nurturing in the months or years prior to their adoption. Or their sense of touch, love, and affection may have become skewed because abuse has taught them that affection is sexual or that being beaten is the way touch is administered from a parent to a child. Their style of attachment and their ability to navigate relationships reflect their traumatic experiences and is *insecure*. Of course, parents want their son, daughter, and sibling-to-be to have the capacity to give and receive affection and to know that their mom, dad, brother, and sister are reliable. Yet adoptive family members need to understand that there might not be "love (attachment) at first sight!"

Attachment is a process that takes Mother Nature 18–36 months to complete! In that time period, the healthy parent works at forming that attachment—feedings at 3 a.m. are work—albeit pleasurable work! The child with a history of complex trauma may not simply move into the home and form an attachment. Trauma has distorted the blueprint! In some instances, the relational template was fractured hours or days after the abandonment, or even pre-natally by drug and/or alcohol exposure. We aren't just talking about the older arrivals. Even infants can enter a family with attachment interruptions. Therefore, forming an attachment to your adopted son or daughter, and between your resident sons and daughters, may take work—a lot of it!

> Clay was adopted from India at age two and a half. He entered his adoptive home with a view of adults as uncaring because of his pre-adoptive abandonment and institutional deprivation. He felt as if there was something wrong with him and that this inherent defect caused the lack of nurture he received in the orphanage. He also thought this had led his birth mother to abandon him. So he sought to make himself unlovable to his new family. He refused to shower. He hoarded food that would spoil in his bedroom. Foul odors would permeate the home. He would often wear the same clothes day after day. He spent long periods of time in his room away from the family. He refused to participate in family fun such as watching movies or playing cards.

Clay's parents sought years of professional services to help Clay form meaningful relationships with them and their younger birth son. Finally, when he was age 13, a successful course of therapy was implemented. Today, Clay seeks interaction with the family. His sense of self has improved significantly. He no longer keeps bologna under his bed and he bathes daily! Board games are becoming a weekly event for Clay and his little brother.

This example illustrates that attachment difficulties impact each member of the family. Clay's parents were sad that he could not enjoy being with the family. They lamented the child they had hoped for when they traveled to India. There was anger as well for the negative behaviors that daily affected the running of the family. He was unable to reciprocate affection. He cringed each time he was hugged by his mother, father, or brother. Overall, he paid very little attention to his younger brother, who desperately wanted Clay to play with him. Clay and his family lived under these circumstances for approximately ten years before finding an effective treatment. In essence, they worked for ten years to develop a relationship with their son and between their sons!

Insecure styles of attachment

Four main styles of insecure attachment develop when a caregiver and an infant don't attune well. Newcomers arriving with a pattern of insecure attachment will adversely impact parents and the children already present in the family at the time of the adoption.

"Adopting a sibling into the family can be fun but also can be stressful. When you first meet your new brother or sister, you will probably feel very happy and good about helping a little child out. But, as they grow up and possibly turn out having attachment issues like my sister, it can get hard. I started feeling as if my life was never going to get back to normal again. It made me want to get rid of my new sister."

AVOIDANT ATTACHMENT

This child's model of relationships is that parents or others are not all that useful in meeting needs. So there is no point in seeking assistance. Connecting is limited; this adoptee refrains from engaging in meaningful interactions. There is little willingness to explore the environment or to play. The desire—early in life—to have an emotional connection was so frustrating that this child learned to tune out in order to survive the rejecting, neglecting relationship. Family members of children with avoidant attachment commonly report:

"He never asks for any help."

"He takes what he wants without asking."

"He stares when he wants something. He won't ask."

"He never asks politely. It is always a demand. 'I'm thirsty.'"

"He is always bored. He can never think of anything to do."

"She doesn't play."

"We came home from our birth son's band concert. He didn't even act like he noticed we had been gone."

"He can be alone in his room so long that we forget he is there."

"As soon as someone starts talking, she glazes over."

"He's always where the family isn't. If we're watching a movie, he's in his room. If we're in the front yard cleaning up, he's behind the house."

"She wanders off when we are shopping or she walks way ahead of us."

AMBIVALENT ATTACHMENT

This attachment style has two subtypes. One is demonstrated by a child who is anxious or "clingy." This child fears the parent may disappear at any moment. This child displays considerable distress when separated from parents, although she often isn't comforted when the parent returns. In fact, the returning caregiver may be met with anger and a rejection of efforts to reconnect with the adoptee. The focus of this child is on the parent. She wants to dominate the parent's time and attention. Parents of ambivalently attached children may arrive at therapy saying:

"I can barely go to the bathroom. She is at the door wondering if I am in there!"

"We try to go out with friends and he acts so 'bad' the babysitter or our other kids call. We have to return home."

"She follows me throughout the house. If I turn around, I practically run into her."

"She can't sleep in her own bed at night. She has to get in bed with us, or we find her on the floor next to our bed."

"He won't go to sleep until my husband, who works second shift, gets home from work. He has to know we are both in the house before he will go to bed."

"She can't go to a sleepover."

"She has to be with us at church. She won't stay in the Sunday school class."

"She interrupts when any of my other children try to talk with me."

"If I am trying to help one of the other kids, he'll create such a disturbance that I have to tend to him."

A second type of ambivalent attachment is seen in the child who appears to "push" and "pull"—"I want you." "I don't want you." These children had birth parents or caregivers who exhibited inconsistency in responding to his needs: sometimes they were unavailable or unresponsive; at other times they were intrusive. The caregiver misread the child's signals. Thus, internally, this youngster is uncertain as to his own needs and emotional state. This is a child who may not soothe easily, even when Mom or Dad is providing exactly what is necessary to aid in calming him. A parent of this type of ambivalently attached child may state:

> "She asks for help with her homework, and when I come to help her she tells me I am doing it wrong: 'That isn't what the teacher said.'"

> "When I have bananas, he doesn't want one. If I don't have a banana, look out, there will be a huge fit."

> "Getting dressed for school is so difficult. We pick out an outfit and a few minutes later it isn't right. He is screaming and shouting that he can't possibly wear the red shirt! It is so hard to help my son and daughter get ready for school with all of his chaos."

> "She asks for a hug and when I give it to her, she pinches me or hugs so tight I have to ask her to let go because she is hurting me."

> "We have a great time making brownies, and then she won't eat any with us."

DISORGANIZED ATTACHMENT

Disorganized attachment is a mix of the attachment styles discussed above. These boys and girls lacked the ability to be soothed by their birth parents because these early caregivers were a source of fear or abuse. These children must cope with the loss of their birth parents on top of resolving the terrifying events that most likely led to the separation from the birth parents. Children with disorganized attachment have been found to be the most difficult later in life, with emotional, social, and cognitive impairments (Siegel 2001).

These parents report many of the themes as pointed out in the ambivalent and avoidant attachment descriptions. Yet these parents also report, "He can do something that just incenses me or his brother. There is a big fight. Then, five minutes later, he asks me what we are having for dinner. It's like nothing happened! He can't figure out why we are still angry!" Or: "When once of us is infuriated with him, he smiles. We all struggle to control ourselves!" Many abused children utilized smiling or hugging the past perpetrator as a defense against further abuse. They thought, "If my abuser is happy with me, maybe he won't hit me today." When triggered, this coping mechanism appears again in the adoptive family. These styles of attachment defy and defeat an overarching family goal—fun, happy family interactions, and close, loving family connections.

Separation from siblings further complicates attachment

Don, Betty, and Mary were removed from their birth parents early one morning. By evening, each was placed in a separate foster home. In one day they lost the only parents they had ever known as well as each other. Can you imagine losing your entire family in one day?

Sergei came to America at the age of nine. During his years in Russia, he moved through three orphanages. His older brothers continue to reside in institutional care in Russia.

Luis resided in an orphanage in Mexico for almost six years. He developed a close tie to another boy who was in the orphanage. He refers to this boy as his brother to this day. Luis has ongoing guilt regarding the fact that he now has a rich life full of food, toys, and family members while this brother remains in residence in grim conditions. Luis has a profound sense of sadness over the loss of this brother.

Pam resided with her three brothers in their birth home, and then the four siblings resided in a foster home for several years. Unfortunately, the foster mother was diagnosed with multiple sclerosis. She decided not to proceed with her plans to adopt the children. The news of her medical condition and the need to move to a new home caused the children's mental health to deteriorate. The end result was that all four children were placed separately. Pam, now age 11, has come to terms with the loss of her birth parents. She was able to process their acts of neglect, abuse, and abandonment and conclude that she is "better off" being adopted. However, the loss of her siblings is an ongoing struggle. She continues to create fantasies of the four children reuniting and living together again. This is not possible as two of her brothers were adopted, while the other aged out of foster care. This brother's whereabouts are unknown.

The stories above are included to demonstrate the types of scenarios that lead to sibling separation in countries across the continents. Kids separated from brothers and sisters aren't always easily able to accept their new siblings. For example, Pam resides in an adoptive family in which she has two brothers and three sisters. She has been reluctant to form any type of relationship with any of these children. In fact, she regularly plays by herself. She resents the fact that these children have had the opportunity to grow up together. She wants to know, "Why didn't I get to grow up with my brothers and sisters? They get to."

Further, Pam and the other children above—international and domestic—are frequently convinced that as they mature, they will be reunited with the brothers and sisters from whom they were split. Kids with this type of reunification fantasy see no reason to make connections with the resident children in their adoptive homes. "I don't want 'new' brothers and sisters. I want my 'old' family back."

Luis's and Sergei's cases alert us to an issue that plagues international adoptees. Children who reside together develop ties to each other. They think about the children left behind at the orphanage. They have difficulty comprehending that they can be happy while these children—birth or perceived brothers and sisters—reside in conditions far less plentiful than what their adoptive family has to offer. Such survivor guilt is difficult for these adoptees to overcome. It impedes integration into the new family system.

Emotional development

This realm of development includes the ability to identify, express, and regulate feelings. These skills create the capacity to enter into reciprocal emotional relationships. There is currently much information available regarding traumatized children and emotional development. The emphasis is on *emotional dysregulation*—dissociation and hyperarousal, more commonly known as flight or fight.

Each time a healthy parent picks up a baby who is wet, hungry, or craving attention, the youngster calms. Repetition of this dance (cycle of needs) helps the brain, as it matures, to learn the skill of self-calming. As kids move through pre-school and into grade school, they can express and manage their own feelings. The skill of emotional regulation has transferred from parent to child. Brain growth is "user-dependent." It needs repetition of experiences to develop the skills necessary for the individual to function (Perry and Szalavitz 2006).

Children with histories of trauma lacked a nurturing adult to lead the dance. The orphanage setting or chaotic birth home isn't able to soothe the crying infant with the consistency needed to develop regulatory capacities. In fact, the stress of living in a chaotic and/or neglectful environment creates a brain—a human being—more vulnerable to stress (real or perceived). The infant or toddler traumatized prior to adoption arrives in the family with an overactive stress response system. So she will enter the states of flight (dissociation) or fight (hyperarousal) easily and long after placement in a healthy family system. Again, brain growth is user-dependent. Early developed patterns will continue to have disproportionate importance to how the brain functions (Perry and Szalavitz 2006). Repetitive experiences during infancy and the toddler period will continue to influence the way the brain causes the person to respond long into adolescence and perhaps adulthood.

Thus, traumatized children are analogous to deer. Deer flee in an instant when frightened. Deer are hypervigilant—always wary of their environment. Traumatized children operate in a similar fashion. They are physiologically in a state of alarm, of "flight" or "fight," even when there is no visible threat or demand. So a stressor arises. Perhaps there is an argument with a sibling or a firm parental request to sit down and complete homework. This over-reactive child feels stressed. He quickly moves to fight—yelling, stomping, slamming doors, etc.—or flight—staring off into space, withdrawal to a bedroom, biting his lip, playing with his fingers, or providing no response as to whether his mom's request was even heard. We have all experienced dissociation while driving the car. We arrive at our destination with no memory of steering the car! We were immersed in a deep, internal thought process which typically defies memory as well.

I have worked with many children with histories of complex trauma who spend a majority of their day moving in and out of dissociative states. These kids miss large chunks of information. They aren't hearing their parents, brothers, sisters, peers, or teachers. This phenomenon affects every aspect of their interaction with people inside and outside of the family. Dissociation and hyperarousal are excellent methods for surviving harsh and overwhelming experiences. They are poor coping skills when utilized in a fun, loving family or in the classroom.

In describing Gina, their now 13-year-old daughter whom they adopted, John and Nancy stated:

> "We never know what is going to set her off. Everything can be calm and off she goes—shouting, swearing, running up and down the stairs. This can go on for several hours. Just the other night, we decided to play board games. We popped popcorn and made hot chocolate. The whole family sat down and she started screaming. We tried to ignore it. However, it was hard to ignore someone screaming while we were trying to have fun."

Nancy went on to say that incidents like this are particularly disruptive to the whole family, which also includes their two birth children, Joshua, age nine, and Carol, age 11. She continued by discussing that she expected that their lives would be more hectic with three children. She expected there would be more transportation issues, more homework to help with, more laundry, and so on. To Nancy, what the adoption of Gina brought to the family was chaos. Plans often had to change based on her hyperarousal. Promises of activities or one-on-one time to Joshua and Carol were broken.

It is also important to point out that neglect causes other problems. As pointed out previously, children need nurture and acknowledgment in order for cognitive, social, physical, neurological, and emotional development to proceed along a healthy path. If this psychological stimulation is not provided, the brain's pathways that were ready to grow through experiences with caregivers wither and die.

- If babies are ignored, if their caregivers do not provide verbal interaction, language is delayed. It is difficult to express feelings with this deficit.

- If a child does not receive kindness, he may not know how to show kindness.

- If a child's cries go unheard, he may not know how to interact positively with others.

(Child Welfare Information Gateway 2001)

This additional information related to neglect is especially important for the family adopting internationally. Again, the ratio of caregivers to babies and toddlers in institutional settings is often poor. Review of countless hours of orphanage video clearly demonstrates five or more infants with one caregiver. This would be the same as a family having quintuplets—except that, in an institutionalized setting, a mother, mother-in-law, sisters, church members, and neighbors aren't available to help out.

Cognitive development

A part of *intellectual* or *mental development*, cognitive activities include thinking, perception, memory, reasoning, concept development, problem-solving ability, and abstract thinking. Language, with its requirements of symbolism and memory, is one of the most important and complicated cognitive activities.

In her book *Toddler Adoption: The Weaver's Craft* (2012), Mary Hopkins-Best describes rudimentary cause-and-effect thinking and problem-solving skills as developing between 12 and 18 months of age.

It is quite common when a family enters our agency for services that they proclaim, "He is so smart!" And indeed it is usually true. Intelligence tests confirm that many traumatized children have a good level of overall intelligence, which is often translated into being bright. However, without the capacity to reason or generate solutions to problems, the smart child is impaired.

Alice is age nine. She was adopted when age four. Her adoptive family includes a 12-year-old birth son. One evening, at age one and a half, social workers had arrived at her birth home and removed her. Her birth mother did not participate in reunification efforts and so Alice never saw her again. Her perception of her removal is that she was "stolen." This is certainly understandable. What else would a toddler think when women come into your home, take you, and then give you to another family? Alice has stolen on a regular basis since coming to reside with her adoptive family. Jewelry, video games, pens, and pencils disappear routinely, despite consequences much to Alice's dissatisfaction.

Alice lacks basic cause-and-effect thinking. She repeats the same behavior over and over. She does not learn from her mistakes or consequences. She is deficient in creating solutions to solve her problem of feeling stolen. The only way she is able to demonstrate her confusion for the loss of her birth mother is to re-enact the event of stealing.

Imagine the problems this may pose for Alice's family. It will be difficult to instill morals and values into the older birth son while Alice continues to steal. He questions, "Why can't my parents make her stop stealing?" He becomes angry when she steals from him. Then he feels guilty for the constant conflict in their relationship. At different times, Alice has stolen from relatives' homes. This is a cause of much embarrassment.

Another area of cognitive development that poses difficulty for adoptive families is that of concrete thinking. The concrete thinker sees the world as black or white. There is no gray. There is limited or no abstract thinking. The concrete-thinking child often appears defiant.

> Cody, age 11, has been stealing since he was placed with Dan and Rita seven years ago. Dan stated, "Cody, you have sticky fingers and it needs to stop!" Cody, puzzled, began to feel his fingers. He replied, "Dad, I washed my hands a few minutes ago. My fingers aren't sticky." Dan, annoyed, said, "Cody, you know what I mean." Cody replied, "No, really, I washed my hands just a few minutes ago." Dan then stated, "Enough. I don't want to hear anymore."

Actually, Cody had no idea what his father was talking about. His immature thought processes only allow for literal interpretations.

Because of this, arguments frequently occur due to the child's exacting manner. The rule "no running in the house" is taken as fact. Kids like Cody do not understand that implied in the rule about running are similar behaviors such as hopping, skipping, and jumping across the living room. A once peaceful household may become teeming with anger and frustration. Exasperation permeates the home. The family's ability to relax and have fun gradually diminishes.

Lastly, many traumatized children, due to their cognitive delays, receive labels as being learning disabled (Perry 1997). Tutoring and special education services require time to locate, negotiate with a school district, and monitor, as well as time if travel is involved or meetings need to occur. The child with special needs begins to dominate the family's time.

Social development

This domain of development includes how the child interacts with other people—individually and in groups. The development of relationships with parents, brothers and sisters, and peers, assuming social roles, learning the values and norms within groups, internalizing a moral system, and eventually assuming a productive role in society are all social tasks.

The development of social skills is emphasized in today's society. Parents spend much time involving their children in a variety of organized sports. There are also martial arts, dance classes, band, camps, and play dates. It is with good reason that we strive to teach children social skills:

- Children have a high probability of being at risk unless they achieve minimal social competence by about age six. The risks of inadequate social skills are many: poor mental health, dropping out of school, low achievement, other school difficulties, and poor employment history (Peth-Pierce 2000; Katz and McClellan 1991; McClellan and Katz 1993).

- Indeed, the single best childhood predictor of adult adaptation is *not* school grades and *not* classroom behavior, but rather the adequacy with which the child gets along with other children. Children who are generally disliked, who are aggressive and disruptive, who are unable to sustain close relationships with other children, and who cannot establish a place for themselves in the peer culture are seriously at risk (Hartup 1992).

Social skills begin to advance in early infancy. Infants only months old watch and imitate others, are sensitive to social approval and disapproval, are interested in getting attention and creating social effects, and enjoy simple games such as peek-a-boo and bye-bye. The 12- to 23-month-old likes to lug, dump, push, pull, pile, and knock down. She also likes to climb and kick. During this time period, there is pleasure in stringing beads, learning to catch a large ball, looking at pictures in books, nursery rhymes, and interactive games such as tag. By 24 to 35 months, there is lots of physical play such as jumping, climbing, rolling, throwing and retrieving objects, and pushing self on wheeled objects. This is also the age of developing first counting skills, as well as the time children begin to draw and mold with clay. Children of this age enjoy matching objects, sorting objects by size, and playing with patterns. Imaginative play increases. The main interest is still in parents; however, there is the beginning of cooperative play with others.

This last sentence is a key point for any family wanting all of their children to play and get along. Social skills develop early and they develop within the parent–child relationship. Later, at about age three, kids are more inclined to participate in group play with other children including their own brothers and sisters. In effect:

- Social competence is rooted in the relationships that infants and toddlers experience in the early years of their life. Everyday experiences in relationships with their parents are fundamental to children's developing social skills (Peth-Pierce 2000).

- In particular, parental responsiveness and nurturance are considered to be key factors in the development of children's social competence (Casas 2001). Children who have close relationships with responsive parents early in life are able to develop healthy relationships with peers as they get older (Peth-Pierce 2000).

Consider the chosen daughter who was confined to her crib in her orphanage, or the child who resided in a birth home wherein he was neglected and abused and was consumed with his own survival. Toys there were minimal, as was quality adult interaction. This child enters an adoptive family with limited ability to play. The expectation that the adoptee will make a playmate for the birth and/or previously adopted children is immediately shattered. In fact, it is not uncommon that neglected children chronologically ages eight, ten or 12 years old are still parallel playing. They have not developed the skills to know how to enter a group. They are unable to take turns, lose graciously, or play a game according to the rules. Frequently, they move from toy to toy. They are unable to choose an item and sit for a period of time to enjoy the item. Other children simply sit among their toys not knowing exactly what to do with them. Their play is often filled with themes of their life experiences.

> Tammy is currently age six. She joined her adoptive family four and a half years ago. She enjoys playing house. However, Jean, her mother, states, "When she plays house, she lines up many dolls— five to ten dolls. Then she goes from doll to doll, offering each a bottle or a diaper change. Really, she is playing orphanage."

> Paula, the adoptive mother of two female siblings, described that doll after doll had been purchased. "One by one, their clothes disappeared, and their arms and legs were removed. It was as if they were breaking the dolls in the same manner they felt broken by the sexual abuse they had sustained at the hands of their birth father."

Such social lags create a variety of difficulties in the adoptive family. The resident children lose interest in playing with their new brother or sister, as do children in the neighborhood. Invitations to parties and play dates, for the adoptee, may be rare. This area often leads typically developing children to make statements such as "I don't want to play with him. He's no fun." "I want to go to my friend's house alone. He is embarrassing to have around my friends." "Do we have to adopt him?" "Why can't we send her back to China?" Frequently, the brothers and sisters will begin spending more time at the neighbor's house than at home.

"My friends and I have to always go into my room and lock the door so that my brother doesn't keep bothering us. He'll scream and pound on the door until Mom or Dad calm him down. Whenever we offer to have him play with us, he goes crazy. He only wants to play what he wants to play, and he will scream until he gets his way. No one wants to play with him because we always have to play what he wants or else he will throw a big fit and cry and scream. It gets really embarrassing when he throws fits in front of my friends."

Delayed moral development also impacts adoptive family interactions. Moral development is the capacity to control one's own behavior internally (Santrock 1995). We can all most likely recall a childhood situation in which our peers wanted us to do something that would definitely lead to parental disapproval and consequences. Instantly, the following thought popped into our heads: "My mother would kill me if I did that!" Our moral system went into effect and we were able to make a decision about how to best handle the situation. Mom and Dad were with us—internally. Everywhere we went and in all situations, their voices resonated as a guide to our conduct.

Moral development is a process that involves acquiring and assimilating the rules about what people should do in their interactions with other people. The process requires reasoning skills and the ability to feel a wide range of emotions—empathy, sympathy, anxiety, admiration, anger, outrage, shame, and guilt. When models who behave morally are provided, children are likely to adopt their actions (Santrock 1995). Many adoptees lacked moral models while in residence with their birth families or in institutional settings. They witnessed violation after violation of principled behavior while experiencing and witnessing abuse, neglect, and drug use. Therefore, they enter the adoptive family with a system of morals and values in direct contrast to that of the parents, brothers, and sisters.

Moral development consists of three stages. In pre-conventional reasoning, moral thinking is based on rewards and self-interest. What is right is what feels good and what is rewarding. Conventional reasoning sees children adopting their parents' moral standards, seeking to be thought of by their parents as a "good girl or boy."

Post-conventional reasoning is the highest stage at which the person recognizes alternative moral courses, explores the options, and then decides on a personal moral code (Santrock 1995). Adoptive parents may find that the child they adopt displays pre-conventional reasoning well into adolescence or beyond. They may not internalize the parent's moral standards—or at least not quickly.

> Grant, age 16, removed a chocolate cream pie from the refrigerator and sat down at the kitchen table. He ate almost the entire dessert. Made earlier for the church bake sale, the pie was not for consumption by the family. This had been made quite clear by Sarah, Grant's mother. Sarah was livid when she came into the kitchen. Grant, adopted by Sarah and her husband at age three, violated rules and boundaries daily. If he wanted to use a tool, he simply took it, never returning it. If he wanted money, he took it from Sarah's purse. If he wanted his brother's stereo, he took it. If he wanted his sister's CD player, he took it. The list could go on and on. Locks had not worked; he would find ways to remove them. Door alarms offered no solution either; he dismantled them.

The end result of Grant's lack of morals was a family in emotional turmoil. On the one hand, each family member was angry with Grant for ravaging through their personal possessions for years. On the other hand, each had concerns for his future. If he did not stop this behavior, what kind of a life would he have? Would he be able to work? Would he go to jail?

Complex trauma: Special focus on orphanage life

Institutional settings have a "culture," as do families. Institutionalized children spend a bulk of time with other children. They reside in a group environment wherein interaction with peers is dominant. The child adopted internationally has learned about group living, not about family life. Children learn this group philosophy at very early ages. Certainly, it is not uncommon to see children adopted at 12 months old and up (and in some cases younger) operating in a family as if the parents only exist to provide food, clothing, and toys. These children seek little adult interaction beyond that which is essential. In essence, the child feels as if he has been moved to a different orphanage. Your family may have more food, better-quality food, a softer bed, nicer clothing, and an abundance of toys, yet the adults are looked at as caregivers rather than parents. Sibling relationships are skewed as well. In some cases, the adoptee attempts to use siblings to meet his needs. The adoptee is more comfortable with children. It is the sibling who approaches the parents for snacks, drinks, new toys, and privileges on behalf of the adoptee. In other instances, the adoptee may avoid forming relationships with siblings if he is uncertain as to whether or not the siblings will remain in the family. After all, he thinks, many orphanage friends left the orphanage to be adopted, to move to another orphanage, or because they were ill.

This situation may be compounded by the use of professional child care soon after the adoptee has arrived in his new family. A room full of children and staff resembles an orphanage to the formerly institutionalized child. Depending on the number of hours the child is in a child care program, the child's integration into the family may be inhibited.

TABLE 2.2 ORPHANAGE CULTURE VS. FAMILY CULTURE

Orphanage culture	Family culture
SURVIVAL/SELF-RELIANCE Poverty, governmental policies, lack of staff education, lack of medical care, etc. may cause an atmosphere in which the meeting of physical needs prevails. Meeting psychological needs not a priority.	**RECIPROCITY/TRUST** Parents desire to have and raise a child within an environment of caring and sharing. This meets the child's physical and psychological needs.
UNCERTAINTY Caregivers may not provide nurturing. They change shifts, leave to pursue other employment, or may be a source of abuse. Peers leave as a result of adoption, a move to a different orphanage, illness, or death. The child learns that people go away. "Those who should provide me affection do not. Those who should protect me do not always do so." Often, there is little or no focus on the child's future due to the demands of meeting the day-to-day basic needs. The child internalizes a one-day-at-a-time attitude as tomorrow everything may be different.	**PREDICTABILITY** Parents instill trust and safety by consistently meeting the child's needs. The child learns that parents behave in predictable ways. "I can rely on my parents." The child transfers this knowledge to other spheres of life such as, "I can rely on my teacher." There is emphasis on the child's future. Parents provide education and experiences essential to carry out career goals, marriage, family life, friendships, etc. The child internalizes the family's values. The child views investment in the future as valuable and worthwhile.

ROUTINE	INTERNAL REGULATION
Orphanages utilize a regimented routine to provide for children. Children eat on a schedule, go to the bathroom on a schedule, sleep on a schedule, and so on. This schedule is based on a timeline created by the staff. The child may not learn to regulate bodily functions. The child does not learn to express his needs. The child may determine that he meets his own needs. For example, "I hold my own bottle. I provide my own food."	Families also utilize routines to carry out daily tasks. However, the routines are more flexible and take into account individual needs. For example, an infant is fed as the infant expresses a cry of hunger. An older child may be provided three meals per day and snacks on request. The family accommodates its members, rather than the members totally accommodating the routine. The child learns many valuable life skills from this: reliance on parents, delaying gratification if parents are involved in meeting the needs of another family member, internal regulation of bodily functions, interdependence, cooperation, etc.

Complex trauma: Special focus on sexual abuse

Sexual abuse is a difficult topic to think about. Speaking with kids about sexual matters is hard too. Many youngsters adopted via the child welfare system will arrive after suffering the atrocity of sexual abuse as well. Clinical experience with boys and girls adopted from institutional settings makes clear that such settings are not immune to sexual abuse. The arrival of a sexualized child is shocking.

> Five-year-old Jeffrey arrived from Bolivia. Present in the family were two parents and their two children by birth, ages ten and 12. Motivated to adopt by a desire to provide a child a loving home, the family was surprised by Jeffrey's perpetual stealing, hoarding of food, and destruction of household items. However, the family was devastated when Jeffrey sneaked into their female birth child's bedroom during the middle of the night and attempted to "get on top of her." In therapy, Jeffrey talked of the chronic sexual activity between children in the orphanage. The institutionalized

children, lacking adult nurture, utilized sexual gratification as a means to offset their fears and loneliness.

Julie and Robert, the adoptive parents of two typically developing adolescents, decided to adopt five-year-old Lori as a result of strong religious convictions to give to someone less fortunate. The family received little information regarding Lori's pre-adoptive history. However, they felt little concern. They believed their experience as parents would ensure that Lori would do fine in their home. Lori's arrival was met with several welcoming parties attended by supportive extended family members as well as friends from their church and community. At one point in therapy, Julie stated, "She received 16 Barbie dolls, two Ken dolls and a Barbie Dream House. We were trying to teach our older children that sex outside of marriage was not acceptable. Yet, in Lori's play, Ken was always in the hot tub with five naked Barbies. Everything became sexual with Lori."

Shelia and Wendell have one child by birth. Staci is 14. She is attractive and smart. Their second child, Yvonne, joined the family via adoption at age two. She is now 12 years old. Recently, condoms have been turning up in her back pack, purse, jeans' pockets, and her bedroom. The family's home is located within walking distance of the school. When Yvonne was late in arriving home from school one day, Shelia began canvassing the neighborhood looking for her. When she could not spot Yvonne, Shelia began knocking on neighbors' doors asking if anyone had seen Yvonne. Indeed, one mother reported that Yvonne had come home with her 13-year-old son. The two were "upstairs listening to music." This parent went upstairs to let Yvonne know that Shelia was waiting for her. There was quite a rustle on the other side of the boy's bedroom door as the two attempted to put their clothes on.

Subsequently, Wendell and Shelia presented this situation to their family physician. After much discussion, Yvonne was placed on birth control. The family has increased their supervision of Yvonne. Shelia and Wendell have also engaged in extra conversations about sex with Staci. They became fearful that Staci would be influenced by Yvonne's behavior.

John is 14 years old. He was adopted by Marcy and Dan when he was age ten. The couple also has two birth children, presently ages 11 and eight. Marcy and Dan have made great efforts to monitor their children's use of the Internet as well as the music they listen to and the movies they watch. However, John always seems to find ways around their parental controls. Each time he obtains access to the Internet, he downloads pornography. Pornography turns up in the bedroom he shares with his younger brother, in the bathroom, in his backpack, and once it was left, in plain sight, on the dining-room table!

Eventually, the couple sought professional assistance. Over time, John described sexual abuse by several men and his birth grandfather. It became clear that the pornography was his way of attempting to let Dan and Marcy know that he had been sexually abused. He was also verifying that seeing men having sex with women made him feel heterosexual. As long as he was "excited" by what he considered "normal" sex, he did not feel as if his sexual experiences with men had "caused him to be gay."

The vignettes above show that adopting a child—young or older—may mean dealing with pornography, masturbation, homosexuality, sexual identity confusion, pre-marital sex, birth control, the sexual abuse of one child by another, and so on. Being proactive about sex and sexuality may not come easily to some adoptive parents, but, as the above stories indicate, proactivity is an invaluable tool for families adopting children coming from traumatic backgrounds. I'll revisit this topic in Chapter 12 to provide tips that will ensure the safety of each child in the family.

Complex trauma: Special focus on domestic violence/physical abuse

Physical abuse and domestic violence are also traumas affecting both domestic and intercountry adoptees. Here are some examples:

Dustin and Kristen entered their pre-adoptive family at ages five and four. Shortly upon their arrival into this family, Dustin became angry with a neighbor child and immediately located a plastic bag. He then attempted to place the bag over the child's head. Fortunately, an adult intervened. When asked why he had done it, Dustin was quite clear that his birth father often "beat me with a belt" and "tied bags over my head" when he was angry. It was certainly a long time before Dustin was able to play without adult supervision.

Mark, a four-year-old, arrived into his adoptive family after a four-year stay in a Ukrainian orphanage. Attempts to discipline Mark were often met with his running to cower in a corner or a closet. Frequently, he would cover his face and shout, "No, please don't hurt me!" Bewildered by this behavior, the family sought mental health services. Over time, Mark described that some "orphanage ladies" would hit the children with sticks for behavioral infractions. He assumed the adoptive family would do the same.

As our examples make clear, children who were physically abused or who witnessed domestic violence in their birth or foster home or a foreign institution may move into the adoptive home and hit, shove, push, kick, and so on. The intensity and frequency of this behavior is well beyond "normal sibling rivalry." Traumatized adoptees will repeat the patterns of behavior they learned in a dysfunctional birth home or orphanage until they learn a new way to act. Aggression can be a behavior resistant to change.

Infants and toddlers who have experienced deprivation may become aggressive as they mature. This latter group wasn't shown love in infancy. So their moral development will lag behind. They may not be able to show affection, empathy, and remorse until parents have the right tools and therapy to help teach these skills. These kids have distorted thoughts in addition to their immature development. They may think that aggression is a means to solve problems. The strongest person gets his way or gets more of his wants and needs met.

A child who has been a victim of unpredictable physical abuse learns that if this abuse is going to happen, it is far preferable to control *when* it happens. As a result, children who have been physically assaulted will frequently engage in provocative, aggressive behavior. They believe that the adoptive home operates as did their orphanage or birth home. This means that the child is soliciting anger—from parents and siblings. He believes it is easier to provoke a "beating" than to wait for one to occur. Indeed, in my clinical work with adoptive parents they report, "I never thought I could be so angry!"

Brothers and sisters also report, "I get so angry with him that I hit him back." "She makes me so mad that I get in her face and scream at her. I just can't help myself!" "Once he made so mad, I pushed him onto the couch!"

Complex trauma: Conclusions

Interwoven into the content of this chapter are examples of some of the behavioral difficulties presented by children adopted through intercountry programs and from the child welfare system. The behaviors presented thus far are in no way exhaustive.

"When they first came, we played like regular brothers and sisters. Later, that period ended. I expected to have some fun brothers and sisters to play with. It's not fun at all. Sometimes my brother plays with me, but my sister and I don't even talk most of the time. I expected a happier family. I ended up with a family that isn't so happy. I am mad about that. I am mad at my brother and sister, but mostly I am mad at my parents because they made a decision that changed my life."

These behaviors stem from an inability to form a healthy, loving attachment, or due to the adopted son or daughter feeling the need to avoid attaching to his or her adoptive parents, brothers and sisters. The heartache of abandonment is a pain the child fears re-experiencing. Subsequent losses of foster families, a favorite orphanage caregiver, an orphanage mate, classmates, foster siblings, pets, neighbors, church members, and so on only serve to reinforce that relationships lead to hurt. Provoking the family with negative behaviors leads to anger. Anger creates distance in the relationships. The adopted son or daughter thinks, "Distance is safe. My heart won't break again." Fear of intimacy and grief for past losses and traumatic insults cause the child to act out to self-protect.

The behavior stems from fractured development. The child is one age chronologically and a younger age socially and emotionally. The new son joining the family at the chronological age of four may actually function as a one- or two-year-old. He is a much "littler" child than expected. Or the newly arrived daughter may not meet age-appropriate developmental milestones as she matures.

The developmental interruptions are most prominent in the areas of cause-and-effect thinking, problem-solving skills, abstract thinking, moral development, delayed gratification, the ability to identify, express, and regulate emotions, accepting responsibility, sense of future, initiative/interest in environment, play and social skills, and reciprocity.

In essence, the child with a history of complex trauma arrives with all major foundational skills ruptured or cracked. Like a house with faulty foundations, the structure falters. This is true also for human development. New growth cannot occur at a "normal" pace when the foundation isn't solid and stable.

Readers can also glean that trauma contributes to how a child thinks. Remember Pam? She didn't want to form relationships with her adoptive family's typical children. She wanted to return to her "old" family and her birth siblings. Thus, she rarely engaged with her brothers and sisters. She felt no need to form positive relationships with these "new" kids. Thus, her thought process drove her behavior.

The negative behaviors of the child joining a family through adoption often become a major source of frustration, anger, and despair for parents and typically developing children. In fact, the child-by-adoption becomes the identified problem in the family. His temper tantrums, lying, inability to enjoy outings, poor table manners, poor hygiene, destruction, and so on are blamed for the entire state of the family. Life begins to revolve around "fixing" the problem—the adoptee—so the family can resume life in the same manner as prior to the adoption. Time, energy, and financial resources are devoted to the child with complex trauma issues.

The fallout from this scenario has many facets. Valuable time with the birth and/or previously adopted children is lost. The resident children perceive that the way to get attention is to act out or overachieve. Or, observing the stress their parents are already under, they harbor their thoughts and feelings. Anger and resentment build. The children in the family, prior to the adoption, begin to dislike the adoptee. Then they feel guilty for having these feelings about their sibling.

In essence, the arrival of the child with complex trauma may create a complex family system. As this book unfolds, readers will be offered an in-depth look at these "common challenges" that arrive when a child with a traumatic past joins the family. Then I'll offer an array of solutions to offset the long-term impact of importing a traumatized child into a healthy family system. Each member of the family—adoptee, parents, and the children already in the family—can flourish and thrive. There is a path to navigate to connected relationships in your family!

This is pictorially presented in Figure 2.2.

Child arrives with unresolved emotions

Child acts out behaviorally

Parents' own unresolved issues are triggered

Child and parent engage in negative emotional interactions

Typically developing children flee to their bedrooms
or a friend's house OR engage in the conflict

A negative emotional climate is created

FIGURE 2.2 COMPLEX TRAUMA AND THE CREATION OF A
NEGATIVE EMOTIONAL CLIMATE

Chapter summary

- The son- or daughter-to-be may arrive with a social and emotional age much "younger" than his or her chronological age. Or the adoptee may mature at a pace slower than what is considered to be within "normal parameters." The new sibling's social, emotional, physical, and cognitive delays can present challenges for brothers, sisters, mothers, and fathers.

• The adopted child may struggle to form a secure attachment to her parents and siblings. Her past relational model is skewed. She may present with an insecure attachment that is avoidant, ambivalent, or disorganized. She fears re-experiencing the pain that comes with the loss of past caregivers, birth parents, previous brothers and sisters, orphanage mates, classmates and so on. The family built by adoption won't forge strong connections upon first sight. Navigating satisfying relationships with parents and between brothers and sisters will take time.

• A special focus must be placed on those children arriving post-institutional living, as well as after the atrocities of sexual and physical abuse. Each of these traumas presents its own unique concerns. The child arriving from the orphanage understands group living, not family life. The sexualized child may present safety issues and may hasten the need for parents to provide sexual education to their birth and/or previously adopted children. The aggressive child believes that hitting, kicking, pushing, and shoving are the way to get wants and needs met. He seeks to elicit anger from moms, dads, brothers, and sisters. Such behavior is shocking to the family that previously enjoyed peaceful, fun, loving interactions.

• Fallout—post-adoption—is normal. Although offering a home to a child in need extends untold positive benefits, it may also bring frustration, exasperation, aggravation, sorrow, jealousy, woe, despondency, despair, unhappiness, and more. Negative feelings afflict adults and kids alike. Knowing this in advance helps moms and dads circumnavigate such conditions. Prepared for the rough patches, the family quickly finds the alternate route to a contented state.

3

"Yes, We Brothers and Sisters Need Information"

PRE-ADOPTION PREPARATION

"Experienced" sisters and brothers tell us that parents must be proactive in offering information (Meyer and Vadasy 1994). Advice from adolescent age veteran siblings includes:

> "Get all the information on the new kid that you can! Keep communication open. Tell your kids what's going on and what you're doing about it. To other kids, 'Don't assume anything about your new brother or sister.'"

> "If people are thinking of adopting, they need to get as much background information on the child before they make a final decision just so that they know exactly what they're going to be dealing with. And I know sometimes they won't get that information. Go to classes to be prepared, so that you would know the child could be disruptive and you know how you would handle it, and the child could not be disruptive and then you will have a nice family. I would also tell them that they should adopt if they really want to because every kid deserves a home."

So, based on these children's expert advice, in this chapter we'll explore the nuts and bolts of preparing the children already in the family at the time of the adoption for the newcomer's arrival. "Family Talk" boxes are also included. These are examples of talking with your resident children about the new child. As you come across these

Family Talk blurbs, think about actually having such conversations with the children you parent now.

"FAMILY TALK" ABOUT A SIBLING-TO-BE ARRIVING WITH COMPLEX TRAUMA

"We received some information about a girl named Renee. She is seven. It seems that her birth parents hurt her in several ways, like we read about in *Zachary's New Home*. Do you remember that book? She was often hungry and left alone. Her birth parents fought so bad the police were called to her birth home. She must have been so scared.

"She enjoys some of the same things we do like singing and reading. She also has some problems. She has temper tantrums and she throws things.

"We do have some ideas about how to help Renee with these tantrums. We will also be getting some help from a therapist, a person who helps kids like Renee, and from the social worker whom you already met.

"Do you have any thoughts about having a sister who yells and throws things?

"When we go to the matching meeting, we would be happy to ask any questions you may have. Write them down and give them to us."

This introductory conversation would work well with school-age and pre-adolescents. If the resident child is young, emphasize the potential safety issues involved with Renee and let the child know that you will be teaching him or her to go to a "safe spot" during Renee's tantrums in the event that Renee turns out to be the child the family adopts.

If the prospective brother or sister is a teen, it might make sense to include him or her in the information-sharing meeting at the adoption agency. He or she needs to know as much about the new sibling as possible in order to prepare for the changes in the family. He or she especially needs information about the new sibling if he or she will be providing any child care.

Sharing information: Influence on adjustment

Research is clear that how a family handles the dissemination of information about the adoptee's history, behavior, academic skills, and so on will greatly influence the adjustment of the children already in the family. Some parents seek to shield their children from the reasons for their adopted siblings' actions and issues. Certainly, the desire to protect the innocence of childhood and to allow children to be carefree is understandable. Yet the child arriving has experienced some of the worst atrocities that exist. This book's previous examples make clear that age-appropriate sons and daughters do need to be ready for the potential safety issues, questions, stares and comments of neighbors, peers, and strangers, the unusual behaviors, and so on that come along with the new brother or sister who has a history of complex trauma.

Traditional information—books, articles, community trainings, videos—is usually geared toward parents. Siblings are usually excluded from other avenues of information too—the teacher, guidance counselor, pediatrician, psychiatrist, therapist, social worker, and others providing services to their traumatized brother or sister.

The isolation, loneliness, and loss some siblings experience will be complicated by a lack of information about their sibling's residual trauma issues. In some families, appropriately developing brothers and sisters receive a clear signal that the problems are not to be discussed, leaving them to feel alone with their concerns and questions. However, even when parents are happy to answer questions, some typical sons and daughters will keep their questions and concerns to themselves. These resident children feel their parent is too stressed or saddened by the adopted child's needs. So they keep quiet in order to try to be helpful to their parents. Some parents are unaware that their children actually desire information. Parents may assume everything is fine if their birth and/or previously adopted children do not present with their issues.

Sharing information: "When do we tell our kids that we're planning to adopt?"

A reasonable time to inform your existing siblings that you have decided to proceed with the adoption is at the time you have made the commitment to actually move forward with a home study. This most often occurs when parents have completed the required pre-adoption coursework conducted by their selected agency. In my experience, prospective parents often determine to forego an adoption or put adoption plans on hold once they complete the educational classes. The information gleaned at the preparation program is such that mothers and fathers decide to wait until the kids already in the family are older. The interval between the home study and the arrival of a son or daughter offers plenty of time to quell existing children's concerns and to prepare these siblings-to-be for the newcomer.

Sharing information: Recommendations

In their book *Sibshops: Workshops for Children of Siblings with Special Needs*, Meyer and Vadasy (1994) make the following (paraphrased) recommendations for sharing of information. Overall, a good "rule of thumb" for mothers and fathers to keep in mind is that the birth and/or previously adopted children's need for information will parallel that of the parents.

- Keep the sibling's needs an open topic.

- Answer resident children's questions about the condition in a forthright manner.

- Provide brothers and sisters with written materials.

- Include siblings in visits with social workers, therapists, physicians, etc.

- Determine the sibling's knowledge of the adoptees' difficulties (i.e. What do you know about why your brother-to-be needs a "new" family? Why do you think your sister is living in an orphanage? Why do you think we will be taking your brother to therapy? Do you know any kids at school who go to therapy?) Provide the information necessary to fill in gaps or misperceptions.

"FAMILY TALK" ABOUT A SIBLING-TO-BE ARRIVING FROM AN ORPHANAGE SETTING

"Your new brother is coming home from Peru. He has been living in the orphanage. What do you remember from the pictures of children in orphanages we looked at online?

"That's right. There are a lot of babies and only a few ladies to take care of all of the babies. So your new brother may not know much about a mom, a dad, or a brother or sister. We will have a lot to teach him. He may not know how to play or how to eat correctly. He may cry a lot or have trouble sleeping. We will have to be patient. He will be scared. He will be moving to a new country and a house with a family. This will all be new. We will have to understand that while we are all happy to be getting him, he will have feelings of sad, mad, and scared. We will have to be patient.

"Let's look at some of the books about adoption and the ones about having a new brother or sister that we have read. Would you like to start with *A Pocket Full of Kisses?*"

Sharing information: Age-appropriate considerations

Pre-schoolers

- Very young children often do not even refer to their brother's or sister's special needs when they describe them to others. Rather, at a young age, siblings focus on the actions, appearance, and their own gut emotional reactions. These youngsters usually recognize that the child has problems and acknowledge that there are more disruptions in their family plans and routines (Lobato 1990).

- Young children who have been exposed to pre-school, play dates, organized activities, Sunday school, and so on have most likely had positive peer interactions as well as negative peer interactions. As such, they have more experiences than we think. So they can comprehend some of the difficulties a traumatized sibling may have.

- Pre-schoolers have egocentric thinking. They believe they are the cause of their newly arrived brother's or sister's difficulties. They need reassurance and facts so as not to take responsibility for any problems occurring in their adoption-built family.

- It is quite a common practice for parents to compare their children to one another. It is also common for siblings to do the same. The young child looks for similarities and differences between herself and her adopted brother or sister in order to determine whether they are well and able themselves (Lobato 1990).

- Young children ages two to six are very concrete thinkers. Explanations of complex trauma should therefore be as clear as possible. Children as young as age three can recognize some of their brothers' and sisters' problems, especially when they have had contact with other children and when their siblings are older than they are. Three years old is not too early to share comments about an adoptee's difficulties.

Cora is two years old. She was adopted after her brother, Steven. Steven exhibits very difficult behavioral issues. The most serious negative behavior is his frequent aggressive temper outbursts. Cora's parents have taught Cora to go to a "safe spot" when Steven escalates. One day, while reading *One Fish, Two Fish, Red Fish, Blue Fish* by Dr. Seuss, Cora associated her brother with the "very, very BAD fish" which is depicted as hitting and slapping another meek fish. Cora's mom reported being speechless that Cora was so intuitive at such a young age.

School-age children

- During their grade school years, siblings need information to answer their own questions about their sibling's problems as well as questions posed by classmates, friends, or even strangers. More so than pre-schoolers, school-aged children may have more specific questions (Meyer and Vadasy 1994). They may ask, "Why does he take medication?" "Why did he live in an orphanage?" "What happened to her birth parents?" "Why does a country only let people have one child?" "Where would I live if something happened to you?" "Why can't he act right?" "When will he act right?" "When will he be able to play nicely?" "What should I say when my friends ask me about adoption?" "How do I explain why she steals other kid's snacks at school?"

"FAMILY TALK" ABOUT PLAYING WITH THE NEWCOMER

"The social worker said your new brother loves to play baseball and soccer. You two seem to have some things in common. The social worker also said he can be really competitive. He is known to push and shove other kids to get the ball. We want to talk about some of the ways you could handle this. We know how important your friends are to you. So we want to help keep your friendships going okay."

Or:

"We learned today that your new sister sometimes likes to play house. Isn't that great! You know, sometimes kids who didn't have good parents play house differently. They play that there is no food or water. They play that the mommy isn't home and so the baby dolls are alone. They may also want the dolls to fight and hit each other. If this happens, we want you to come and get one of us right away. Your new sister isn't doing anything bad. We just want to be able to come and teach her the right way to play so you two can have fun. How does this sound?"

- School-age children most likely have peers who reside in families where there has been a divorce. They may have experience with death, and therefore grief and loss. They have been presented the Drug Abuse Resistance Education (D.A.R.E.) program. They may be assisted to apply this knowledge to the thoughts and feelings of the child with complex trauma issues.

- School-age children may hold beliefs about the cause of the difficulties that places blame on the child with complex trauma.

- Information needs to be relayed to school-age children in short segments, perhaps 20–30 minutes in length.

- "Fantasy flourishes where facts flounder" is a very good expression to keep in mind. Lacking information, grade-school-age boys and girls tend to create their own ideas about a sibling's difficulties. Usually, what they compose is far worse or quite off base from the reality. A "just the facts" parental approach helps this age group rein in their vivid imaginations with regards to the adopted brother or sister.

- School-age children may have experience with other children who have been adopted.

Adolescents

- Even adolescents may have misconceptions about their siblings' problems. Some may assign a psychological or metaphysical (i.e. "God brought my brother in to bring the family closer") reason for the issues that present from the adoptee's background of complex trauma (Meyer and Vadasy 1994).

- Like school-age children, adolescents have specific questions about their brother's or sister's traumatic experiences and the way the trauma residue plays out in the family.

- Adolescents have more exposure to the issues which bring children into foster care and adoption, or at least to similar issues. They have witnessed peers involved with drugs or alcohol. They may have personal knowledge of suicide or suicidal ideation. It is likely they have experience with death. Certainly, they have familiarity with sex and sexual behaviors. Thus, they have the capacity to handle an array of topics with a depth of content.

- Adolescents have the capacity to attend informational presentations of a length similar to adults.

- Adolescents may also have experience with children who have been adopted.

"FAMILY TALK" ABOUT A SIBLING-TO-BE ARRIVING WITH A MENTAL HEALTH DIAGNOSIS

Children of all ages can most likely equate a mental health disorder with a medical problem. You might talk to your children about mental health issues like this.

"Do you remember when you were sick and we took you to the doctor? He gave you some medicine. You stayed home for a few days and felt better. Well, your new sister has some mental health problems. She didn't get the care and love she needed in the orphanage. She is sad a lot. She is all mixed up about parents and living in a family. She doesn't feel very good about herself. She needs medicine to help her think better. We will be going to therapy with her. She will talk with the therapist and this will help her realize that we are a good family and we do love her. This is going to take time. Let's see, you are nine now. She may be better when you are ten or 11. It may even be longer.

"The actual name of her problem is Posttraumatic Stress Disorder (PTSD). These are some of the ways she may act. She may get really sad and then really happy. Sometimes she will be cranky. She may forget things. She may sleep a lot. Sometimes she won't want to play with you. This has nothing to do with you. She may also have a hard time sitting still. She may not be very good at sharing or taking her turn. This may make watching a movie, getting homework done, or playing a game difficult.

"We are reading and going to a support group for parents who have children with PTSD. So we will be learning ways to handle this. We will be passing on what we learn to you.

"Do you have any questions? What do you think? If you think of any other questions, let us know. Let's talk about this again in a couple of days after you have had time to think about this."

Sharing information: A menu of suggestions

Recognizing that each brother or sister is a unique individual, the following baker's dozen of pre-adoption preparation ideas are presented as a menu. Parents can pick the items they feel will most benefit their sons and daughters.

- Books are a great way to relay information! Consider sharing this book with your older kids. Imagine your family dealing with the types of issues presented in the vignettes—these stories are a wonderful impetus for conversations about the impending changes adoption may bring to the family. Younger children can benefit from the infinite array of children's books available today. Peruse the Resource section at the end of this book. Schedule a trip to the local book store with your son or daughter. Journey through everything from orphanage life— *Borya and the Burps*—to *The Lapsnatcher*—a great tale about adjusting to the arrival of a younger sibling—to *The Colors of Us*—celebrating the delicious colors of diverse peoples.

"FAMILY TALK" ABOUT BECOMING A MULTICULTURAL FAMILY

"Dad and I have been reading up on adopting a child of a different culture. We are realizing that we must look at our family and our community. We thought we could make this a family activity. We thought you could start checking out your school. Your older brother is going to do the same. Are there any children or teachers from Ethiopia? How many are of a different culture? What about your after-school program?

"I thought you and I could go to the library and start doing some reading about Ethiopian culture. We can learn about the religion, food, holidays, and customs. All of these things will be important to your brother and our family as he grows up.

"I found a great book for you—*If the World Were Blind*. Dad and I are going to help you learn more about prejudice and discrimination.

"We'll have more of these talks before and after your brother arrives. What questions do you have so far?"

- Pop some popcorn and watch a movie—*Martian Child*, *Pinocchio* or *The Blind Side* accurately portray the types of issues adoptive families may face. *Toy Story 3*, *Anne of Green Gables*, *Tarzan*, *The Lion King*, and *The Lost and Found Family* also nicely depict themes of abandonment, adjustment, and moving on. In terms of documentaries, *Wo Ai Ni Mommy*, *First Person Plural*, and *"I Wonder…" Teenagers Talk about Being Adopted* offer real-life examples of the thoughts and feelings of adopted persons.

- Do you prefer electronic means of gathering information? "Friend" or "Like" members of the adoption community on Facebook™. "Suggest" your favorites to your resident adolescent. Parents and teens can share the daily adoption- and trauma-related articles and quips.

- Piggybacking on the above suggestion, if you have a son or daughter who loves to surf, the Internet is a wealth of information about trauma, post-institutionalization, and adoption. See what he or she can find! Share the information. Siblings love competition—see which typical child can find the most websites, articles, and so on!

- Visit my website www.arletajames.com. You and your typical kids—of all ages—can view the video *Supporting Brothers and Sisters*. This movie includes 14 birth and/or previously adopted kids (and their parents)—ages six to 20—talking about the challenges and positives that adoption brought to their families. Two of the adoptees offer their perspective of joining a family as well.

- Join an adoptive parent support group. Network with veteran adoptive families. It is likely that they'll have children who can have a play-date or sleep over with your kids. Pre- and post-adoption, navigating relationships will definitely go more smoothly with experienced guides! There are also support groups designed for specific populations. For example, Children and Adults with Attention Deficit/Hyperactivity Disorder (ADHD) (CHADD) is available to families with children diagnosed with this mental health condition. The incidence of ADHD is higher among adopted children than the general population. Brothers, sisters, moms, and dads will benefit from networking with such organizations pre-adoption. As you receive information about a potential adoptee, don't shy away from what I call "alphabet soup"— acronyms that describe mental health diagnoses, medical conditions, special education services, and so on—ADHD, PTSD, IEP, ARND, RAD, and more. Use Google to guide you to the meaning of these acronyms and to the community resources you'll need post-placement.

- Share any materials provided by your adoption agency with your birth and/or previously adopted children. Ask if your adolescent can attend pre-adoptive education classes. Arrange for your social worker to meet with your age-appropriate children. He or she can share information and provide examples to you and your sons and daughters. Brainstorm a list of topics and resources with your social worker. While you wait for your new arrival, work your way through the list.

   Conferences are a great way to acquire a lot of information! They are also a way to meet veteran adoptive parents and the top professionals in the field of adoption. If you're based in the US, consider planning a family vacation around the North American Council on Adoptable Children (NACAC) conference or the Association for Treatment and Training in the Attachment of Children (ATTACh) conference—you'll be glad you did! If you live outside the US, most other countries will have equivalent organizations and events, so check out what is happening in your locality. You can use these opportunities to enjoy a fabulous city and to learn more than you can believe about adoption, attachment, trauma, speech development, children's mental health, parenting tools, special education services, Sensory Integration Dysfunction, Fetal Alcohol Spectrum Disorder, and more! Conference workshops are often recorded and available for purchase. Pop them in the car CD player. The family that rides together learns about adoption together!

- Dovetailing with the above, your local hospital, community mental health center, child welfare agency, and/or public school offer continuing education seminars. Call today and ask for their current schedule. Make sure you add your family to their mailing list. Keep in mind that older kids make great companions at workshops! Events close to home help identify professionals and agencies that may offer needed services post-adoption.

- Plan a field trip to a neighborhood that offers a culture different to that of your family's. Let brothers, sisters, and yourselves experience new foods, a language unlike your own, the feeling of being among people that look different, and so on! We live in a society that remains plagued by prejudices, discrimination, and the stereotyping of various groups of people based on their race, religion, sexual preference, citizenship, and socioeconomic status. It shouldn't be surprising, then, that adopting transculturally adds another complex layer to the experience of adoption. Preparation for the arrival of a family member that forever alters the cultural composition of the family begins prior to the adoption.

- Kids will need coping skills post-adoption. Before the new brother or sister arrives is a wonderful time to bolster ways of solving problems and generating solutions. Workbooks and websites abound with ideas to enhance such abilities. Sons and daughters also benefit from strengthened capacities in the areas of stress management, expressing feelings, and communication.

- Offer to babysit for friends who have children similar in age to the child you plan to adopt. Or volunteer to help out in the church nursery. Typically developing children who have not had the experience of sharing their parents with a young child are often blind-sided by the parental time consumed by a little one. Parents can offer some preparation for the changes about to occur because of the addition of a baby or toddler. As you care for this youngster, point out the tasks it involves. "Oh my, it's time to the change the baby again" or "The baby needs another bottle." Of course, caring for a young child who has resided in a healthy family environment will be different to caring for the institutionalized infant. Yet your resident children will at least gain an understanding that their new brother or sister will require sharing Mom and Dad's time—perhaps much time!

- Search your Yellow Pages or ask your social worker for a list of agencies/organizations that specialize in adoption-trauma competent services, adoption medical care, speech therapy, occupational therapy for Sensory Integration Disorder, and so on. Schedule a visit for the whole family. Understanding what the service offers, meeting your future post-adoption guides, learning why a brother or sister may need different therapies or medical interventions, the travel time involved, co-pays or out-of-pocket expenses, and so on all lend to a more successful post-adoption experience.

Remember to organize information as you gather it. Post-adoption you'll have a wealth of material at your fingertips. When a problem arises, an article, book, website, blog, support group, or professional can be quickly located. Right away you'll have guidance to keep your family on course!

"FAMILY TALK" ABOUT POTENTIAL BEHAVIORS THE NEW ARRIVAL MAY PRESENT

"Your new brother, Eric, may act very different from you. Remember, he didn't have a mom and dad who were there to teach him all the right things.

"We learned from his social worker that he has temper tantrums. Sometimes when he is mad, he uses bad words. Sometimes he throws things.

"He wets the bed—do you know what that means? Sometimes, he hides the wet clothes in the closet. This may make his room smell and even the hallway. We will be checking his room and helping him remove any wet clothes or sheets. This will help with the odor.

"In the other homes he lived in, he blamed other children for the mistakes he made. We are expecting this to happen here too. We know you and how you act. We will be able to decide who is telling the truth.

"We also want you to know that all the rules are staying the same. We expect that you will follow the rules even when he doesn't. We know that doesn't seem fair. We will certainly be working to change the way he acts. In the meantime, you still need to act correctly.

"What do you think about these things? Keep asking us questions as you think of them. We'll be talking more about this before he moves in and after he moves in."

Sharing information: Anticipate questions

Shannon and Ed adopted Taylor as an infant. The family felt it time to pursue a second adoption when Taylor was about a year away from entering kindergarten. They believed that their second child would arrive just as Taylor started school. Shannon would have days free to care for the baby. Guatemala was their sending country.

Baby Amelia arrived pretty much on schedule. During the year wait, Taylor kept asking, "Why can't we just go get her?" "Why is this taking so long?" "Who is taking care of her?" "What if I never get a sister?"

Additionally, thinking about the pending adoption caused Taylor to begin to ponder his own adoption. He asked, "Why don't some moms keep their babies?" "Where is my birth mom?" "Why didn't she keep me?" "What would happen to me if something happened to you two?" "Where would I live?"

Shannon and Ed did their best to console Taylor regarding his questions and confusion about the arrival of the new baby. They had not expected so many adoption-related questions at age five!

Whether you are parenting a birth child or an adopted child, anticipate questions! Entering the adoption process sets off a host of thoughts! Expect basic questions such as "Where is he going to sleep?" "Are we getting a boy or a girl?" "Will she speak English?" Count on tougher questions like Taylor's above. The array of queries is likely to be endless!

"FAMILY TALK" ABOUT THE SIBLING-TO-BE, SCHOOL, AND LEARNING

"Dad and I want to talk to you about your new sister. She may not be able to learn as well as you. She will have to learn a new language when she moves here and she may have learning disabilities. These are problems that make it hard for her to understand what the teacher is saying.

"She may get very frustrated. Sometimes we will have to put her homework away and work on it another day, even though our rule for you will be to finish your homework before you go out with your friends.

"We may have to give her a lot of extra help with her homework. We may have to take her to tutoring. Sometimes you may have to find rides to football practice. We may not be able to play as much as we do now.

"If there are specific ways you can help us, we'll let you know. Mostly, this is our problem. Your job is to be a kid.

"What do you think about the changes that may happen? Let's sit down and figure out the things we do as a family. Which of these are most important to you? We want to continue the ones most important to you, even if your sister takes up a lot of our time."

Chapter summary

- Parents must determine when to tell the typical children about their adoption plans. This news is best delivered when mothers and fathers have committed to expanding their family via adoption.

- Brothers' and sisters' need for information parallels that of their parents. Sharing knowledge among family members contributes to the adjustment of parents and all the sons and daughters. Education is the key to success for the family built by adoption.

- Children—ages pre-school through adolescence—have life experiences. This knowledge can be utilized as a springboard to "family talks." Parents take the lead in imparting learning on the resident kids. Parents initiate follow-up conversations as well. Extend plenty of opportunities for questions. Offer honest responses to your birth and/or previously adopted kids' queries.

- A menu of ways exists to help your children (and yourselves) prepare for the arrival of the new child. Devour each method of pre-adoption education. Your journey will be better if full of information!

- Anticipate lots of questions from your resident sons and daughters. If your family composition includes an adoptee, a second, third, or fourth adoption will act as a trigger. That is, these kids will likely enter a process of rethinking the circumstances that led to their own adoption. Contemplate, in advance, the types of queries your sons and daughters might put forth. Formulate some responses.

4

"I Am a 'Quality' Parent!"

REVIEWING AND REFINING YOUR PARENTING STRENGTHS

After a careful reading of preceding content, prospective adoptive mothers and fathers are likely coming to recognize that the adoptive family will be providing an environment in which the adoptee can heal from past hurts. Within this healing environment for the newly adopted child, parents must maintain the well-being of the children they parented prior to the adoption as well as their own emotional stamina. Various qualities are beneficial in achieving this delicate balancing act. This chapter looks at the parental strengths believed to underlie successful adoption-built families.

Moms and dads may want to think in terms of the fact that they will be helping the adoptee, themselves, and their resident children form relationships. The son or daughter, arriving with a traumatic past, displays difficulties in intimate relationships. Many of the skills presented are those utilized daily to form and nurture relationships—there will be some familiar territory in this chapter. However, conducting rewarding family life which includes a child who arrives after abuse, neglect, and/or abandonment will require implementing these skills with greater frequency and over a long period of time. Adoptive parenting may also require learning a few new skills too. As you read, use current relationships as a context. Assess the quality of each of your life's important relationships—marital, parent–child, friend-to-friend, sibling-to-sibling, with extended family and so on.

Ask:

- Overall, are your relationships satisfying? Why are they satisfying?

- How is each satisfying or dissatisfying?

- Have you experienced relationships that were not fulfilling? What was missing?

- What did you contribute to this situation?

- How often do you see your parents and siblings?

- Do you harbor unresolved feelings for past events that occurred in your family of origin? If so, how do these issues impact your current relationships? How does this impact your parenting?

- How often do you get together with friends?

- Who can you depend on? How has this person demonstrated this?

- How many long-term relationships do you have? If there are few, what are the reasons for this situation?

- What do you enjoy most about parenting? What do you enjoy least?

- Have you been disappointed by a child you are currently parenting? What was this like?

- When have you been proud of your resident children? What was this like?

- Are you currently a step-parent? If so, what types of issues has this presented? What difficulties emerged in blending children from two families? How long was the transition process or is it still ongoing?

- Did you previously adopt? If so, were there challenges integrating the adoptee into the existing family system? Are there ongoing hurdles?

- How easily do you build new relationships?

- Are you able to ask for help?

Qualities for successful adoptive parenting
The strength of time management

Work, grocery shopping, yard work, laundry, driving the kids to piano lessons, arranging play dates, meeting friends for dinner, completing homework, spending time alone with your partner, birthday parties, visiting extended family—where does the list end! Add to the already long list therapy, psychiatric appointments, tutoring, school meetings, and occupational, physical, and/or speech therapy. All children need time. The child with a history of trauma may require extensive time. Below are comments made by typically developing children, ages 11 through 19, after their family's special addition arrived:

> "I lost a lot of attention because I was the only child until they came. My parents told me I would lose attention, but I never thought it would be as much as it has been."

> "Since the adoption, things have changed a lot in our household. After my adopted sibling was brought into our lives, Mom and Dad switched to focusing more on my adopted sibling. They started seeing signs of irregular behavior around the age of three or four and took her to multiple doctors' offices to try to understand what was going on.
>
> "That was only the beginning. As my sibling grew older and older, the problems got worse. She would have a fit when she couldn't get one of the many things she wanted. She also started lashing out for the simplest of things, such as making noise in her play area, asking her to get off of the computer, etc.
>
> "My parents started paying a lot more attention to her, and therefore less on my brother and me. It has gotten to a point where they spend almost 100 percent of their time on her. This has really discouraged me, because it makes me feel like I'm not really important."

> "I've lost a lot of time with my parents. I remember my mom, me, and my sisters could just go out shopping like every weekend. Now, I don't want to be in the house. I go out and find things to do. I do anything to get out of the chaos of the house."

Prospective families often recognize that adding another child to the family will increase the grocery list, the pile of laundry, the transportation duties, and so on. Prospective moms and dads do not always recognize that time will also be diverted to the newly adopted child due to the parental attention and professional services this child may need to improve his physical, emotional, cognitive, and social well-being. Prospective parents may benefit from asking themselves the following questions:

- How will we make time to accommodate another person and his needs, interests, and talents into the family?

- What areas of time can decrease if necessary?

- How flexible is my job? If I need to attend school meetings or mental health appointments during the day, will I need to use sick time or vacation days? What is the impact on other family members of consuming vacation days to meet the new child's needs? Can I use Family Medical Leave Act time? FMLA provides certain employees with up to 12 weeks of unpaid, job-protected leave per year. It also requires that their group health benefits be maintained during the leave. It is designed to help employees balance their work and family responsibilities by allowing them to take reasonable unpaid leave for certain family and medical reasons, such as the placement of a child for adoption. (www.dol.gov/dol/topic/benefits-leave/fmla.htm)

- What sacrifices might I have to make to ensure that all of my children benefit from my time and attention? Am I willing to make these sacrifices?

- What time do I need for myself so that I can maintain the emotional health needed to parent effectively?

Again, reflect on your relationships. Who can you rely on for help?

Stress management: Maintaining a healthy emotional climate

An adoptive mom to two typical daughters and two traumatized daughters stated:

"I eat under stress. I've gained 40 pounds. And I tell myself that I'm going to lose the 40 pounds, for health reasons, and then something happens with the adopted girls and I go eat something else just to feel better."

Stress! We've all felt it! It is a condition or feeling experienced when a person perceives that demands exceed the personal and social resources he or she is able to mobilize. In short, it is what we feel when we think we have lost control of events. People feel little stress when they have the time, experience, and resources to manage a situation. They feel great stress when they think that they cannot handle the demands put upon them. Table 4.1 compares everyday life between families with age-appropriate children and families parenting a blend of typical and traumatized children. The list of jobs is more than doubled in adoptive families! Talk about stress!

The last item in Table 4.1—hurt child's behavior problems— surely strains the family:

Jack is a member of the school board. Leah volunteers for many activities at church. Two-year-old Nathan joined this family along with his temper outbursts and many other unexpected negative behaviors. In second grade, Nathan rummaged through his classmates' lunches, eating their snacks. He stole an array of pens and pencils, threw books at the teacher, and had fits right in the classroom. The following year, he wrote profanity on the wall of the boys' bathroom. It was up to the school board to determine if this was a violation of the school's policy regarding defacing school property. If so, Nathan's consequence would be a ten-day suspension.

Rachel and Greg adopted six-year-old Amber. Originally from a South American country, she was placed with Greg and Rachel after the dissolution of her first adoption. Greg and Rachel reside in a small town. Greg is well respected for his work as a carpenter. One evening, the family was outside, landscaping. Rachel realized that she hadn't touched base with Amber for several minutes. She began looking for Amber. She located Amber etching a penis, with a key, on the side of Greg's work van.

TABLE 4.1 PARENTAL RESPONSIBILITIES: A COMPARISON

ALL families with children	Adoptive families parenting traumatized children
Money management. Time management. General parenting tasks and responsibilities. Household chores and tasks and repairs. Jobs. Child care. Dealing with schools. Illnesses, deaths in the family. Social endeavors for the family—vacations, general "fun." Social endeavors for the children—leisure activities, extracurricular activities, maintaining friendships. Social endeavors for the parents—leisure activities, maintaining friendships, volunteering. Holidays and vacations. Intra-family conflict (extended family).	Everything in the left column, plus … Infertility, step-family relationships, and/or other family building issues. "Uneven" motivation between partners about adopting. Lack of informed support—formal and informal—for adoption from family, friends, professionals. Lack of information about new child's history. Adoptee's mental health issues and developmental delays. Conflict between birth and/or typically developing adopted children and adopted children with special needs and issues. Managing openness in adoption (sibling visits, foster parent, or birth parent visits). Locating adequate child care, summer camps for children with "issues." School issues related to special education—negotiating IEPs, phone calls about misconduct, inadequate school performance. Learning how to talk to adopted children about birth histories. Understanding and dealing with triggers for adoption-related issues. Understanding and dealing with triggers for trauma- or neglect-related issues. Social conflicts outside the immediate family resulting from hurt child's behavior problems.

Based on but expanded from Ginther, Keefer, and Beeler 2003.

Imagine the embarrassment of your child searching for food in other children's lunches. Imagine being a member of the school board which is now meeting about your own son. Think about how you would go to work at a customer's home with a penis drawn on the side of your work vehicle! What type of reaction might this cause when taking the van to have the paint repaired? What will other people think of you? How do these behaviors cause conflict with your own values? What happens to the home environment with behaviors like these and the others described thus far in this book? Anger permeates the family's emotional climate. How do you explain such behaviors to your birth and/or previously adopted sons and daughters? How do others' opinions of your family impact those children? How are the brothers and sisters affected by a home environment sated with conflict?

Adoptive homes can become "stressed out," "absolutely frustrated," "over-stressed," "really stressed," "on edge," "on my last nerve," "over the edge," "under pressure," "just fried," "too stressed out," "so tense," "feeling pressured," "nerve-wracking," "too much drama" places! Once in a state of stress, we are excitable, anxious, jumpy, and irritable. This reduces the ability to interact with kids and grown-ups! With trembling hands and a pounding heart, we can find it difficult to execute a precise, controlled skill. We find ourselves more accident-prone and less able to make good decisions. There are very few situations in healthy family life in which this tense response is useful. Most situations benefit from a calm, rational, sensible approach.

Learning to put forth calmer interactions—maintaining a healthy emotional climate—in light of a laundry list of tasks, challenging behaviors, performing at work, fulfilling social obligations, and so on is an essential skill in the family that expands via adoption. Think about how you deal with stress by asking yourself the following questions:

- How do I manage stress? Do I become frustrated? Do I become angry? Do I become physically ill? Do I calm myself down and prioritize? Do I take breaks to relax?

- How do I express my emotions? Do I withdraw? Do I let things build up and then explode? Am I able to walk away and then return when I have calmed down? Have I learned to deal with my feelings in productive or unhealthy ways?

- How well do I communicate? Do I offer solutions before I have actually heard what the other person is saying? Do I interrupt? Do I think before I respond? Do I provide reassuring clichés? Do I have to have the last word? Am I able to listen with empathy and see the other's point of view? Do I actually face the person who is talking, or do I continue reading the paper or surfing the Internet?

Taking a proactive approach to sex and sexuality

Some folks will find themselves parenting sexualized children. Examples were put forth in Chapter 2. Curbing sexual behaviors, ensuring the safety of the children already in the home at the time of the adoption, instilling relational values, and so on require that parents be able to talk frankly and truthfully—proactively—with all of their kids. For parents raised in homes where sex was not discussed, or in which children were shielded from the realities of the world, open and honest dialogue about sexual matters may be uncomfortable or foreign. For parents who have experienced sexual abuse themselves, adoption may mean revisiting painful memories in order to be an effective parent. Pre-adoption is a good time to examine your thoughts and feelings regarding sex and sexuality. For example:

"Masturbation is considered a 'normal' activity in adolescence."

- Do you agree or disagree with this statement?

- How do you feel about masturbation?

- How would you react to a child masturbating?

- How might you respond when your birth and/or previously adopted child asks, "What's she doing, Mom?"

Or, what is your attitude toward birth control?

- Does placing an adolescent on birth control provide a license to be sexually active?

- What would happen if our adolescent experienced an unplanned pregnancy? Could the baby be placed for adoption? Would we want to help raise our grandchild?

- How do our plans to teach abstinence fit with the child's desires to engage in sexual behaviors?

- How does birth control mesh with our religious convictions?

- How do we balance supervising the sexually promiscuous child with the child's need to experience age-appropriate activities?

- How do we help a child who has experienced sexual activity understand that such activity should occur within a loving and kind relationship? The child who has experienced sexual abuse is often quite knowledgeable of the mechanics of sexual activity, yet, unfortunately, this child is unaware of the beauty of sex within a relationship wherein sex is a special and mutually satisfying part of that relationship.

- What is the impact of a sexually active child on the birth and/or previously adopted children? Will younger children use the adoptee as a model? Will resident adolescents think they can act as they see the adoptee acting?

How do we teach our typically developing children values and morals when we have a child who acts in ways that are incongruent with our belief system? Overall—whether the issue is pornography, pre-marital sexual relations, birth control, homosexuality, gender identity confusion, or sexually transmitted diseases—gaining clarification about your own sexual beliefs prior to accepting a new child into your home will be of benefit. In addition to the questions raised in preceding content, consider the following as well:

- What were you told about sex?

- How were you told about sex?

- When were you told about sex?

- Did you get enough accurate information about sex while you were growing up?

- Is whatever two consenting adults perform sexually their business? How about two consenting adolescents?

- What were your sexual experiences in early childhood, as an adolescent, and as a young adult?

- How much of your past sexual behavior would you change?

- How much of your past sexual behavior would you share with your child?

- In your family of origin, what was the family message regarding sex?

- In what ways have your sexual attitudes changed since age 18?

- How did you feel about the rate of your sexual physiological development?

- In what ways did your parents respond to your developing sexuality (wet dreams, masturbation, birth control, sex education, etc.)?

- How comfortable are you discussing the effects of puberty and sex?

- Have you ever had a negative sexual experience? If so, how have you dealt with it?

- Does your negative sexual experience impact your parenting? Does it impact other relationships?

- Are you willing to rework this trauma again if need be? The benefits of doing so are described below.

Entering and engaging in the parallel healing process

Brenda and Steve adopted two boys from Eastern Europe. Ron, adopted at age 18 months, entered therapy at age five. "Out of the blue" he would slap, punch, kick, or bite Brenda. Brenda stated, "Each time that he hits me, flashes of my abusive father instantly appear in my head."

Brenda is a very intelligent woman in her late 30s. She felt that she had resolved the physical abuse she suffered at the hands of her father. She was blindsided by the flashbacks Bryce's behavior triggered.

Becoming a parent, by any means, causes a life review. However, becoming a parent to a child who has experienced neglect, abuse, or institutionalization *intensifies* thoughts and feelings about childhood experiences and the type of parenting received while growing up. Like Brenda, many moms and dads are caught off guard when unpleasant memories resurface post-adoption.

Many adoptive parents will find that they must rework their earlier life circumstances while simultaneously assisting their adopted son or daughter in resolving his or her trauma. This is a *parallel healing process*—healing your son or daughter *and* yourself at the same time. The mental health of adoptive moms and dads is essential for their own sake as well as that of all of their sons and daughters.

> Tara and Danny parent their birth daughter, Mary Ellen, and their son, Chris, whom they adopted as an infant, and who are now ages 13 and nine respectively. Chris is obsessed with food. He hoards food in his room. A trail of wrappers from candy, granola bars, and cupcakes can be found in his locker, in his desk, under his mattress, in his backpack, and in his closet.
>
> While vacuuming, Tara found numerous wrappers and several empty yogurt containers behind the couch. She placed this trash on the kitchen counter. She stewed the entire afternoon. She was angry that Chris kept stealing food. "Why does he do this? We provide plenty of food. He gets plenty of snacks." She was also mad that he wouldn't put the packaging in the trash can.
>
> As soon as Chris entered the house from school, Tara confronted him. "Did you put this garbage behind the couch? Did you steal this food?"
>
> Chris said, "No, Mom. Really, I don't know how those got behind the couch."
>
> Tara responded, "You're lying."
>
> Chris again said, "No, Mom really, I don't know where they came from."
>
> Tara again stated, "You're lying!"
>
> The argument carried on for about 20 more minutes. Chris was sent to his room "until your father comes home."

In this midst of this argument, Mary Ellen went to a friend's house.

Tara, still fuming, also became guilty. She asked herself, "Why do I get so mad? I never used to be such an angry person. I didn't even know I could get this angry!"

Later in the week, Tara described this incident to the therapist. Together, the two clarified the event further. Tara's father had an affair that ultimately ended her parents' marriage. Her father's "lie" destroyed Tara's family. When Chris lies, it triggers Tara's anger about her father's actions. Chris receives this stored anger as well as the anger for the chronic lying he commits in relation to his food issues. Once Tara was helped to see this, she realized that she needed to work at moving beyond her father's affair—again! In the meantime, she was able to manage her reaction to Chris better because she understood why Chris's lying so enraged her.

Once Tara had gained insight into her own behavior, Chris was no longer able to *push her buttons* to so great a degree. Their home became more peaceful. Peace is a wonderful accomplishment in adoptive families!

So, if you are parenting a child with a history of trauma, enter a parallel healing process as needed. Make your parental mental health a priority. You and all of your children will benefit!

United we stand! "Complementing" your spouse

Six-year-old Hannah and her dad walked out of their home to run some errands, with Mom to follow in a minute. Hannah tried to open the door to a van that the family had just purchased. She was having difficulty. Dad, standing a few feet away, encouraged her to push the door button with both hands and to firmly plant her feet.

When Mom walked out the door, she saw that Hannah was struggling and said that she would help her open the door. Dad politely asked Mom to wait and let Hannah try to open the door herself. After a couple of tries, Hannah figured out how to open and close the door to the van. As they backed out of the driveway, Hannah stated, "Daddy, thanks for letting me do that myself."

In daily events in which a child confronts a frustrating situation, mothers generally are much more likely to intervene quickly, while a father is less likely to fix the situation, thus encouraging and strengthening the child's problem-solving skills. So Mom's response to the situation was not a bad or inappropriate one, but merely her maternal instinct kicking in. Dad's response was not better or worse than hers, rather his paternal instinct kicking in.

But how often do these types of occurrences create parenting adversaries instead of parenting complements? One parent feels contradicted or undermined. One parent scolds the other, "Why didn't you help her?" "Why don't you let her do more on her own?" It is as if mothers and fathers engage in a pseudo-competition to demonstrate that their parenting approach is superior to their partner's.

Day-to-day disagreements tend to increase in adoption-built families due to the phenomenon "splitting." Often, the newcomer is kind and respectful to one parent, usually the father. The mother experiences a child who is callous and uncooperative. The father begins to blame the mother for the problems the family is having with the adopted son or daughter. Because he does not see as many of the behavioral problems, Dad perceives Mom to be the problem. Criticism then follows: "You are too hard on him." "Why don't you lighten up?" "If you would just leave her alone more, she'd be better."

The mother is devastated by this lack of support from her spouse. She can't believe that her spouse "doesn't believe" her. In reality, the adopted child feels very let down and hurt by his birth mother. She was supposed to protect him and keep him safe, and she did neither. These emotions are vented onto the mother who is present— the adoptive mother. Mom really is receiving the daily troubles she describes when Dad arrives home from work. The damage "splitting" can cause to the marital relationship is obvious. Marital discord is like an oil spill. It spreads out, affecting whoever are in its path—all the children!

Marital quality affects the quality of parent–child relationships (Cummings and O'Reilly 1997). In particular, marital conflict has been associated with the quality of parenting practices and parent–

child attachment (Davies and Cummings 1994). This applies to all of the parent–child relationships in the family—birth and adoptive, whether having arrived at birth or at an older age. Marital relations can be a source of support for or can undermine the parenting role (Belsky 1984). Couples want to follow the lead of the dads below.

> "My relationship with my spouse was the key. Even when I was completely overwhelmed, just having someone there to listen and say 'I understand' meant everything. The ability to vent (sometimes loudly!) and still have your partner love and care for you really is the best coping mechanism of all. When we started to work as a team without the feelings of frustration towards one another, then the progress of our child moved at a steadier, but still slow, pace."

> "I have found it best not to set any expectation too high with the kids, or my wife for that matter. What doesn't work is coming home complaining to my wife about the normal things that just don't get done—dinner, keeping the house clean, or crabbing that she's in a bad mood or depressed and telling her to snap out of it. What does work is coming home, giving my wife a big hug, and then pitching in and having a united front where the children are concerned."

Pre-adoption is the time to investigate how fathers and mothers resolve conflict:

- Do such differences create conflict immediately?

- Are fathers and mothers able to step back and look at the outcome of a particular parenting intervention, and then decide that the child benefited and that this is what counts?

- How similar are parental goals for their children? Is each parent working on his or her own "agenda?" Is there one unified "agenda"?

- Is the child receiving a cohesive message about the values and expectations of the family? Is the child receiving "mixed messages"?

- Does the mother consider the father a "babysitter" or a full parenting partner? Does she allow the father to make his own mistakes, thereby navigating his own relationships with his children?

- Is the father authoritarian or controlling, superseding decisions made by his wife and thereby reducing the autonomy of, and respect for, his partner?

- Do fathers and mothers check with each other before assigning consequences and approving privileges?

Providing a nurturing environment

It might seem that it should go without saying that nurture would lead to a successful outcome. Children want and need hugs, kisses, and snuggling. Parents are happy to give this affection. Providing nurture to a child with a traumatic past goes beyond typical ways of expressing love. Nurturing the adoptee who has experienced abuse or neglect involves maintaining empathy and being tolerant in light of difficult and demanding behaviors and other trauma residue (Buehler *et al.* 2006).

The vignettes have highlighted various negative behaviors presented by children with histories of abuse, neglect, and/or abandonment. It is time now to start thinking about living with these behaviors.

Prospective adoptive parents may expect that the child they are adopting will have similarities and dissimilarities to the other family members. However, the family often anticipates that the differences will be more in the areas of food preferences, clothing and hair style, or hobbies. We all have relationships in which these contrasts exist. How often at the mall do we see the men sitting outside of the store waiting for their wives? Women want to look through the sales racks and men often do not. Or, during a shopping trip, the family splits up. Mom and the daughters proceed to the shoe stores. Dad and the sons go directly to power tools. Most families have more than one television. Everyone gets to watch their favorite shows.

Adoption brings with it such disparities. However, adoption may also mean attempting to form a relationship, obtaining a "psychological fit," with a person who has a very different value system. Over time, the child's behavior can be perceived as a direct affront to the mother's and father's good parenting and their efforts to help the child become a successful human being. Parents begin to make statements such as:

"He steals instead of asking."

"He hoards when we provide more than enough to eat. For Pete's sake, we aren't going to run out of food. We aren't his birth family!"

"I work hard and he breaks everything he gets his hands on. Who does he think is going to replace this stuff? Money doesn't grow on trees!"

"I can't believe he swears at me! I would never have talked to my parents that way!"

It is also not uncommon to hear, "I love him, but I really don't like him anymore," or "There are days I simply don't want to live with him any longer."

Empathy has turned to anger. Tolerance has vanished as well. Feeling that all of their good intentions have been rejected, the parents begin to withdraw from the child. What is the point in giving when it does not seem that it is received? Guilt heaps higher: "What example is being set for our resident children?"

"When we first met Jason, he was an infant, only eight months old. From his infancy to about age three, we had the same love for him as we had toward our birth daughter. Our love for him, at that time, was no different from the way we loved her. For the first few years, except for the screaming and the crying at bedtime and naptime, he seemed 'normal.' A 'normal' child is very easy to love regardless of the label of 'birth' child or 'adopted' child.

"But, after his behavior problems started to worsen, and as the years unfolded, our love for Jason started to change to anger, bitterness, and resentment due to the effect his behavior was having on the rest of the family. We gave unconditional love to him and received what seems to this day to be total rejection in return. We pray daily that the Lord will soften our hearts and teach us how to love him again as his heart heals from the pain of his childhood neglect. We have never totally stopped loving him. But it's almost like an obligatory love right now."

It is difficult to love *anyone* who rejects you—over and over—and has a very different value system. This includes your own child. It is also hard to be affectionate with a child whose daily rejection of your other children is breaking their hearts! Reflection in this area may include:

- What experience do you have with rejection? How did you handle such situations? What did it take to recover?

- Have your children been excluded from activities, turned down by a friend, gone through a romantic break-up? How did these incidents make you feel? How did you help your sons and daughters through these encounters?

- Have you served on a committee or in a community organization in which there have been value conflicts? Perhaps you have a co-worker with whom you find it difficult to engage for this reason.

- Perhaps you have an extended family member with whom you don't share beliefs. What is this like?

- How do you manage interactions in these instances?

Dealing openly with the adoptee's past

It seems that each time email is checked, there is an advertisement to find a classmate. Family gatherings are replete with siblings kidding each other about childhood events. Memories of deceased relatives permeate such get-togethers as well. How many times do we review photo albums? Or, for those old enough, how many times did you watch slides of the family vacation to Yellowstone or Niagara Falls? Our past is important to us.

The past is as important to the child who has been abandoned, abused, or neglected as it is to a member of an intact family. She has memories, thoughts, and/or feelings about her experiences just as we all do. Given today's climate of openness in adoption, she may have ongoing contact with her birth mother, birth siblings, and so on. Still, reflecting on her past is often painful and dismal, so families tend to avoid it for a number of reasons:

- Parents are frequently encouraged by various types of professionals to wait—wait until the child can handle it, wait until the child is old enough, or wait for the "right time."

- Families may hold on to the mistaken belief that children are resilient and will simply recover from their trauma.

- Realizing that discussing the adoptee's past is likely to generate grief for both child and parents, the desire to avoid this grief is often a reason that the child's history remains unspoken.

In reality, these situations force children to repress their normal curiosity about their roots. Lacking answers impairs their sense of security and self-esteem, and thwarts their expressions of their feelings of differentness. This scenario leaves the adoptee no room to express fears about loss, abandonment, and rejection. The adoptee cannot determine how past events influence present behavior. He is not able to work through his doubts about the adequacy of his bonds to his adoptive family (Kaye 1990).

> Marge contacted our office to request an assessment for her two daughters, Paulette and Kati, ages 15 and 16. The girls had been placed with Marge and her husband, Peter, when they were five and six years old. The children's history contained a vast amount of sexual abuse. It seems that their birth mother had prostituted them in order to support her drug habit.
>
> Marge reported that Paulette and Kati had brought the sexual abuse up time and time again. Marge stated, "Each time they talk about it, I tell them that it ended a long time ago and there is no need to think about it anymore. Daddy and I love them, and we make sure that nothing like that happens to them."
>
> Marge asks, "Why have I responded to my daughters that way? Why didn't I realize they were trying to talk to me seriously? Perhaps if I had listened all of these years, they would be better."
>
> Her reason for requesting services was that the girls had started running away several months ago. They were gone for hours. Marge and Peter's attempts to ask their daughters what

was going on were met with shouting and profanity. Paulette was failing school and Kati's grades had declined significantly. Boys—lots of boys—were calling their home at all hours of the late evening and early morning. Clothing, make-up, and jewelry that Marge and Peter did not approve of were turning up in their book bags, school lockers, and bedrooms.

Certainly, Kati and Paulette's inability to sort out their past is contributing to, if not totally responsible for, their current decline in functioning.

The truth is essential. Without the truth, children blame themselves for their abandonment, institutional placement, abuse, and so on. Lacking an ability to determine that the separation from the birth family was not their fault, they develop reunification fantasies which inhibit them from forming attachments to the adoptive family. Overall they may believe that they are "too bad" to be loved. They may assume that they will be returning to the birth family, so there is no need to form relationships with the adoptive parents, siblings, and peers. They resist forming friendships as they feel "different"—"If the other kids knew what happened to me, they wouldn't want to be my friend, so why bother?" They fear future abandonment based on the separation from their birth family. The concept of permanency or a "forever" family defies their experiences. They develop fears regarding whether they will develop medical or mental health issues.

Each member of the adoptive family benefits when the adoptee is able to integrate the past and the present. This process, which includes asking questions and receiving hard answers, struggling with painful facts and awful memories, and expressing intense grief, allows the adoptee to move beyond her past, and thus join the adoptive family. Thought-provoking questions include:

- How were losses handled in your family of origin?

- What is your experience of grief and loss?

- How do you respond to a loss?

- How do you include your children in the grieving process?

- How do you help your children grieve?

This section also raises the matter of discussing sensitive and painful topics with children:

- What are your views on telling children the truth about their past?

- Can you picture yourself discussing abuse, neglect, and abandonment?

- What might you need to do to prepare yourself for such conversations?

- What potential losses may such discussions trigger for you?

- What will be the impact of such discussions on your typically developing children?

Awareness of transcultural issues

An adoption is considered to be transcultural when any of the family members are of a different race to the others. This is often referred to as *transracial* or *interracial* adoption. Adoptions are also considered transcultural if children and their adoptive parents come from different countries but are of the same race. For example, if a white American couple adopts a white toddler from Eastern Europe, or an African American family adopts an Ethiopian child, these adoptions are not transracial, but they are transcultural. A majority of international adoptions are transcultural.

Identity formation is a difficult process for all of us. The transnationally or transracially adopted child must learn what it means to be biracial, or to be a Black-, Asian-, Latino-, Korean-, Chinese-, Peruvian-, Mexican-American, or to be a member of a multiracial family—a more complex process yet! Race, ethnicity, and culture can make identity formation even more complicated. In addition to adjusting to the cultural climate and values of yet another family, older arrivals may need to adjust to a new socioeconomic climate, and perhaps an entirely different language and/or religion.

The identity development of transcultural adoptees is influenced by the environment in which the child lives. Those of us in the dominant culture—the group that has power over the distribution of goods, services, rights, privileges, entitlements, and status, and those with access to education—develop confidence, self-esteem, and goals because we see others like us achieving in virtually any chosen endeavor (Crumbley 1999).

Children who are members of groups our society deems as minorities—groups subject to the power, control, discretion, and distribution of goods and privileges by another group—frequently observe others who are not like them. They observe or experience prejudice, discrimination, and stereotypical remarks, and thus may learn that they have more limited options and that their groups are somehow "not as good" as the prevailing cultural group. Thus a child's confidence, self-view, worth, self-respect, and goals may be negatively affected (Crumbley 1999).

Helping the transcultural son or daughter develop a thriving sense of self may require the entire family making some changes. Review Table 4.2, and ask yourself, "What am I willing to do to fulfill my newcomer's cultural needs? What impact would these changes have on my resident children?"

TABLE 4.2 WHAT AM I WILLING TO DO?

Child's challenges	How are you willing to change?
Transplanted from his birth country and placed with your family—a new country, a new home, a new family, a new neighborhood, etc.	Are you willing to move to a neighborhood that reflects the child's background? Visit your child's old neighborhood or extended relatives?
Expected to make friends with the children of your friends.	Are you willing to develop close, positive relationships with persons of your child's race or culture?
Expected to attend your place of worship.	Are you willing to regularly attend a religious institution familiar to your child? Join a religious institution with a diverse population?

Attend school, daycare, or a community center in your neighborhood.	Are you willing to participate in activities at a community center in a neighborhood that reflects the child's background? Find child care and/or educational facilities in which there will be others culturally similar to your child? Drive your child to a daycare center in the child's neighborhood?
Asked to eat food common to your culture.	Are you willing to include your child in the choice and preparation of ethnic foods for your family?
Endures prejudiced comments from neighbors, classmates and relatives.	Are you willing to respond constructively when you hear prejudiced comments from colleagues, acquaintances and loved ones?
Asked to take vacations with your immediate family.	Are you willing to plan trips to places that reflect the child's heritage or are familiar to the child?

Adapted from Bower (2012).

In addition to the parenting task of facilitating a positive cultural identity in their adoptee, moms and dads must also realize that they and their same-race resident children will be impacted by a transcultural adoption. They, too, will frequently find themselves the brunt of comments, questions, and criticisms, as well as being spotlighted by the stares of curious strangers.

> Danielle's birthparents were Latino and African American, but her adoptive family consisted of white parents and a white sibling who had also been adopted. The family lived in a small, mostly white town in Northern California. Danielle and her sister DeeAnne were well accepted at school and at synagogue and were active in scouting and sports during their elementary and middle-school years.
>
> When their father was transferred to a large city, the family moved to an integrated middle-class suburb and put the girls into public middle school and high school. Suddenly the earth shifted under Danielle's feet. Perfectly comfortable with white kids like those she had grown up with, she suddenly found herself the

target of black and Hispanic kids—especially the girls, who accused her of "talking white," "dressing white," and "acting white" as she drew the attention of boys of all races. After a year or so, she made a conscious decision to claim her black heritage and worked hard to model her dress, her behavior, and her talk on those of the group she wanted so much to be a part of. At the same time, DeeAnne began to complain loudly to their parents that Danielle's new behavior was an embarrassment to her.

Where did Danielle belong?

Before adopting transculturally, parents are encouraged to review materials pertaining to transcultural adoption. Parents must be aware that "isms" exist. They must prepare themselves and *all* of their children to handle this matter.

Linh's family "got" this need from the beginning. They had chosen to adopt from Korea partly because they lived in an upper Midwestern city with a large Korean community made up of first through third-generation families who had arrived in the US by immigration, as well as a large number of grown and still growing Korean adoptees. From the beginning, they chose to immerse their family in the city's Korean community—attending a Korean Presbyterian Church and enrolling all of their kids (including two born to them) in Korean culture camp and language classes.

Each family must embrace the culture of the adoptee by incorporating foods, holidays, traditions, music, and art reflective of the child's culture into their daily life. The son or daughter arriving by adoption must "see" that his or her culture is important to family members by actions and example. The adoptee must be able to answer the question "Who am I?" Each member of the family needs information to handle a vast array of queries, quips, gawks, criticism, racism, and more.

The capacity to identify, access, and utilize resources

The reading you have completed, or will do, and the pre-adoptive classes in which you have participated, or will participate, will help you to understand that assisting each member of your family adjust to the adoption experience may require seeking various types of support and services. Exploring this area prior to placement demonstrates that you are already experiencing the growth necessary to make your adoption journey as successful as possible. You are acknowledging that adoption will bring challenges, and you are preparing for these challenges. Overall, the acquisition of resources as early as possible has proven benefits:

- Learning and development are most rapid in the pre-school years. Timing of an intervention becomes particularly important when a child runs the risk of missing an opportunity to learn during a state of maximum readiness. If the most teachable moments or stages of greatest readiness are not taken advantage of, a child may have difficulty learning a particular skill at a later time.

- Earlier intervention has a significant impact on the parents and siblings of children with special needs. Early intervention can result in parents having improved attitudes about themselves and their child, improved information and skills for teaching their child, and more time for leisure and employment.

(KidSource 1996)

It is important, at this point, to examine your attitudes about accepting help. Mental Health America, the USA's leading nonprofit organization dedicated to helping people live mentally healthier lives, has concluded that Americans are more likely to view mental health issues as personal or emotional weaknesses rather than real health problems (Mental Health America 2007). Post-adoption, adopted sons and daughters often receive mental health diagnoses. Certainly, how the adoptee's problems are viewed affects how the condition will be treated. Think about the following:

- What are your views on individuals with mental health issues? Do you see a mental health disorder as a "health problem" or an "emotional or personal weakness"?

- Do you know anyone with a mental health issue (e.g. depression, anxiety, Posttraumatic Stress Disorder, Attention Deficit/Hyperactivity Disorder, alcoholism)? If so, what have you learned from this experience that would be applicable to parenting a child with special needs?

- Are you aware that children receive medication for various mental health issues (e.g. depression, anxiety, impulsivity attention difficulties)? Do you have a perspective on this?

- Are you willing to seek professional mental health services?

- What type of mental health coverage do you have through your health insurance policy?

- Do you know other adoptive families comprised of children with histories of trauma?

- Have you ever utilized therapy or support groups? Do you know if adoptive parent support groups exist in your area?

- Do adoption- and trauma-competent services exist in your community? Are any of these services community-funded or will they be out-of-pocket expenses?

- Do you have any experience with special education?

- Do you have the capacity to be assertive? Do you mind being persistent? Acquiring services is best described as being the "squeaky wheel getting the grease"—that is, parents often have to advocate for services.

- Who comprises your personal support system? Are they learning about adoption along with you?

- Are you involved in any organizations, such as a church, from which you may be able to obtain support?

- How well do you acquire information?

- If married, is your spouse participating in this learning process? Or is this endeavor one-sided?

In adoptive families, early intervention should start the moment the parents decide to proceed with the adoption process. Adoptive parents are *not* responsible for creating the difficulties their children have, but they *are* responsible for helping to correct them (Keck and Kupecky 2009).

Maintaining a sense of humor

Humor allows us to experience joy even when faced with adversity (Wooten 1996). The benefits of humor are amazing. Humor reduces stress, lowers blood pressure, elevates mood, boosts the immune system, improves brain functioning, protects the heart, results in a respiratory cleansing and leads to muscle relaxation similar to deep breathing, increases energy, gives us a sense of perspective on our problem—and is free!

Some events are clearly not occasions for laughter. However, most situations do not carry that type of gravity. Learning not to take ourselves and daily events too seriously is important. In other words, there will be times when lightening up is important. At these times, take a step back and put the situation in context and find the humor within the event.

> Gordon was 15 years old when he was arrested for vandalizing several cars parked at a local shopping mall. Gordon had been adopted internationally when he was 16 months old. This arrest was one more situation on a very lengthy list of negative behaviors. While at the police station awaiting his parent's arrival, Gordon decided he was thirsty. Spotting a vending machine, he attempted to stick his hands—which were handcuffed together—up the slot where a can of pop would drop out. Yes, his hands got stuck! Ultimately, a police officer heard his cries for help. Several officers worked to free Gordon's hands from the machine. However, the machine had such a tight grip that the paramedics had to be called. After removing many parts from the pop dispenser, Gordon was finally liberated from the machine's hold. Gordon's parents arrived just in time to witness the paramedics at work! Certainly, at the time, Gordon's parents weren't happy. However, later, Gordon's father couldn't help but laugh over the image of his son's attempt to steal—while at a police station—and get caught—by a machine!

Adoptive families would benefit from creating a "humor kit"—a collection of their favorite funny movies, books, CDs of their favorite comedians, comic books, anything that is guaranteed to generate a chuckle! Adoptive parents will be responsible for setting a positive and nurturing mood in their home. There will be days when this is difficult—very, very difficult. Humor will be a most important tool for carrying this out because when we laugh together, it can bind us closer together instead of pulling us apart (Lindeman, Kemp, and Segal 2012).

To laugh or not to laugh will be your choice!

Chapter summary

- Adoptive homes are a healing resource for the traumatized child. His healing will be crucial to his future, and it will contribute to the quality of the home environment. Parents must promote the new arrival's recovery while balancing their own needs and the needs of the children in the family at the time of the adoption.

- Once the newcomer arrives, parents take the lead in facilitating attachments between the members of their family. Parents want to assess the quality of their own attachments pre-adoption. All kids need strong attachment figures to flourish and thrive in today's society. The more vibrant the parental attachment capabilities, the more each child will mirror this most important skill. Connected children reflect their parents.

- Various parenting attributes—qualities—support the making of close family ties. Each of these strengths has been described in this chapter. Conduct a self- and marital inventory pre-adoption. Identify strong points as well as the areas in which there is room for improvement. Decide how best to grow yourself and your marriage as your prepare to grow you family. Refine and rework yourself as needed. Your journey as an adoptive family will be as good as the qualities you take along!

5

"Finally! My New Brother or Sister Is Arriving!"

PLANTING THE SEEDS THAT GROW POST-PLACEMENT ATTACHMENTS

Learning that your family has received a referral for the new child causes instant joy and excitement. The air simply crackles with delight! The long wait is over. Your new son, daughter, brother, or sister is coming home. Parents and the kids already in the family have all kinds of questions: When will we meet her? When can he meet our other children? Will it be "love at first sight"? What gift should we take on the first visit? What color should we paint the bedroom? How many visits or trips will there be until we can bring her home? Should we take our kids to the newcomer's homeland? How long will the trips be? What will she look like? Will he be walking? Talking? What will she like to play?

The purpose of this chapter is to look at the actual transition of the child into the family—to respond to the common queries above and more. We'll also look at ways to include the birth and/ or previously adopted children in this phase of the adoption process. Their involvement initiates the attachment parents want between all members of their family. Some of the ideas allow for gathering pieces of the newcomer's history. Post-adoption, this information will be important to healing the adoptee's past hurts. Helping the newly arrived son or daughter recover from his or her traumatic experiences is one way to navigate warm, earnest family relations.

This chapter includes "Adoptees Talk" boxes. Adopted kids were surveyed to find out what they thought about adoption—about the way they got adopted, about being an adopted person and whether or not that makes a difference at home or at school, and about what may be special about being adopted. The insight of these adoptees is quite interesting. Hearing their perspectives lends to furthering the understanding of adoption from each family member's point of view.[1]

ADOPTEES TALK

Best things about being an adopted person are:

- being part of an adoptive family
- having new things to do
- being loved/cared for
- feeling special
- having great adoptive parents
- feeling safe
- being different
- being someone your family chose
- having two families
- having fun
- making friends.

---

1   The information comes from the report *About Adoption*. Available online at www. rights4me.org/en/home/library/reports-about-adoption.aspx. The information was gathered by sending the adoptees question cards. Each card contained a question and a space for a response. The Adoptees Talk boxes contain the cumulative responses to these questions. The survey includes responses from 208 adopted children. The average age of the adoptees who responded was 11. The age range of the respondents was six to 22. The average age at which the children had been adopted was four. Just over one in ten, 11 percent, had been adopted when less than one year old. Nearly a quarter had been adopted before they were two years old. Nearly one-half had been adopted under the age of four. A quarter had been adopted when they were age seven or older. Only 6 percent of children had been adopted after they reached "double figures" in age at ten or older. The average time since being adopted was seven years.

Worst things about being an adopted person:
- not having contact with my birth family
- being teased or bullied
- losing contact with my birth brothers and sisters
- being different
- feeling left out
- knowing you are adopted
- other people talking about you being adopted
- complex emotions about it
- not knowing your heritage
- losing old friends
- being asked questions about being adopted
- feeling frustrated
- not being believed when you say you are adopted.

Eighteen percent of the respondents said there was no "worst thing" for them about being an adopted person.

Brothers and sisters of international adoptees

Parents expanding their family via intercountry adoption have much to consider before boarding the plane. The content that follows recognizes that each family is unique. Family members may select those ideas—traveling together or not, and pre-trip, during-trip, and immediate post-trip activities—which seem best suited to the particular needs of the family. The recommendations offer ways for each family member to participate in the process. Again, the information put forth is designed to help parents, the prospective adoptee, and the children already in the family to begin to facilitate positive interactions.

Traveling to the newcomer's homeland: Who should go?

A frequent question pre-trip is "Should we take our kids with us?" Moving a child via intercountry adoption means that parents need to take into account whether or not the family is traveling to the child's homeland, and whether or not they will be traveling with the children already present in the family. In some instances, country policies may prohibit taking resident children. In cases where the siblings may go, parents must decide who will go on the trip based on their resources and their knowledge of their typically developing children. Pros and cons that may be weighed in this decision-making process include the following.

Pros for siblings traveling to the homeland

- Experiencing the country gives a deeper understanding of what the adoptee's life was like prior to the adoption. In particular, visiting the child's orphanage makes clear the day-to-day living differences between such group life and family life. You can all begin to see the type of work you have ahead of you in teaching the newcomer how to learn to be a family member.

- Experiencing the child's culture contributes to raising the child in a culturally competent manner. As your family will be different from those around you, you can all see first-hand the type of cultural issues that may be experienced once you become a transcultural family. If feasible, families may want to consider staying in a family setting rather than in a hotel. This provides a realistic glance at what any child, but particularly an older child, will encounter upon changing countries. In a family setting, you would have to attempt to communicate, determine what you are eating, learn the family customs and routine, and try to understand social cues and emotional expression. Parents, brothers, and sisters would gain a depth of understanding of what the sibling-to-be will feel like upon moving to their home.

- Your family may experience culture shock. Adults and children may begin to feel uncomfortable or out of place in a country where nothing is familiar. This is positive, as it will evolve into empathy for the new arrival. He will likely have similar feelings once you bring him home to his new country.

- If you are traveling as part of a group, you and your resident children have the opportunity to form relationships with other families. These relationships may become a source of support post-placement.

- Brothers and sisters are more invested in the adoption process when they are present each step of the way.

- Older siblings may benefit from the travel to a foreign country. Certainly, there is learning value in experiencing the rich diversities the world has to offer.

- Older siblings may prove helpful. They can carry luggage, get diapers, make bottles, and keep you company. Your children are also good reminders of the fact that you can parent in the event that your new child's interactions are initially less than positive.

- Younger children, who lack a sense of time, may experience less separation anxiety if they accompany you on the trip.

- If your family already includes a child from overseas, depending on her age, the experience of returning to her homeland or visiting the country you have opted to adopt from this time around may be of great benefit. This is especially true if the child was too young at the time of the adoption to have memories of her own adoption process. Seeing another adoption take place fills in many of the blanks explaining how she joined the family. Again, this may also raise many questions or lead to an expression of grief for the loss of her country of origin, her birth family, or her orphanage mates. While comforting a grieving child is difficult for parents, active, healing grieving leads to long-term healthy emotional well-being.

  Cole and Becky parent a total of four daughters adopted from China. On each of their trips abroad, they have taken one child while the others stay with relatives and family friends. Becky arranged the travel so that the family had several days together before being joined by the new child. This allowed for sightseeing in the previously adopted child's homeland. It also allowed for some special one-on-one time for each of the children they already parent.

If you opt to take your birth and/or previously adopted kids along, keep in mind the following.

PLANS TO PREVENT "I'M BORED" SYNDROME

All parents have heard "I'm bored" at one time or another. (Actually, parents have probably heard this more times than they want to think about!) If you are taking siblings-to-be with you, it will be particularly important to investigate your accommodations abroad. What amenities are available? What activities can your children take with them for on the plane and while in the country? It is also important to think about how much you can pack. Veteran parents who have traveled abroad with their children are a great resource when it comes to helping you decide what to take and what will be available in the adoptee's homeland. In particular, search out parents who have traveled in the six months prior to your own trip. These families will have the most up-to-date information for the area and facilities in which you will be staying.

PLAN TIME WITH THE CHILD WHO CAME ALONG

The day-to-day activities may make for a busy trip, although some families report that there was much down-time. In any event, ensure that you devote time each day to the child or children making the trip with you. Even if you are busy, a few minutes goes a long way towards validating the typically developing child's feelings about being in a foreign country and sharing his parents with a new sibling.

EXPECT REGRESSION

The children you already parent may regress while traveling with you or post-placement. This is completely normal, especially if they are young. A parent's first instinct is to respond, "Honey, act your age!" Regression to earlier stages of development is a way for children to express the stress of a change in life. So allow the regression. Usually, this passes on its own. However, it is always a good idea to increase parental time with the youngster who has regressed.

Capturing the trip through the brother's or sister's eyes

Adopted children love to hear the story of how you got them—over and over! Today's tweens and teens are geniuses with technology! Let them help capture the sights and sounds of this journey to bring home the new child. Everything is always so interesting through the eyes of children! Here are some pointers:

- Photos and video of the child's actual living quarters, caregivers, and friends are important. The child needs to know where she came from and who was there. The child needs as many (or more) photos of the orphanage as she does of the well-known places of her country of origin. Make sure to get the names of the orphanage staff and your child's orphanage mates. The age-appropriate kids can label the pictures upon arrival on home soil.

- Take photos of yourselves and your family at the orphanage. If you are not in the photos, children adopted as infants or toddlers have difficulty connecting to the fact that you were actually at the orphanage.

- There are cases in which the family is unable to tour the orphanage. In these cases, have the typical kids capture photos of what is available—the outside of the orphanage, the grounds, the room in which you spend time with the child, the other children, the staff, the director, your interpreter, and so on.

- If you are close to the child's birth home town, make the drive! The child's birth parents are not going to recognize you. If you remain worried that they will identify the child, one parent and the siblings can make the trip while the other cares for the child in the city where you are staying.

- If your child is a toddler or older, the typical kids can frame some of the photos and display them in her bedroom after you get home. Just as familiar sights will be comforting to you while abroad, photos of familiar people will be comforting to your child as he adjusts to his new home.

- Make as much use of video as possible. It records the sights and the sounds.

- Audio taping is another consideration. One family recorded an orphanage caregiver singing a lullaby to their son while they were at the orphanage. This, combined with about 30 minutes of the normal sounds of the orphanage, allowed this child to fall asleep more easily in his new home. This was wonderful for this family's birth son who shared a bedroom with this younger brother.

- If the orphanage staff seem approving of the move, use the interpreter to gather a few sentiments about the newly arriving child. It is of great benefit to children to know they were cared about and that their move to the adoptive family was supported.

Once home, photograph the "new" family. The visual depiction of the change that has occurred in the family helps everyone begin to adjust.

CONS FOR PARENTS AND SIBLINGS
TRAVELING TO THE HOMELAND

- Completing an international adoption may be quite expensive. The family's resources may prohibit taking the children already in the family.

- Travel advisories for your chosen country may prove unfavorable. The US Department of State posts travel advisories.

- Parents and children alike may be affected by jet lag and time changes. If you are taking your birth and/or previously adopted children, especially those that are younger, you may want to arrive in the country a day or two early. This will provide some opportunity to adjust prior to initiating the steps necessary to bring your newcomer home.

- The flight is long and the trip may be long—longer if delays occur—and children may become affected by culture shock and by having access to limited activities.

- There are children who will have adverse reactions to an orphanage setting. The reality of children living without parents may be overwhelming to children with more sensitive temperaments. Parents need to think about the entirety of the trip. Depending on the adequacy and availability of child care, children who may suffer emotionally seeing an orphanage may be best left at home with a caring relative or family friend.

- If the process is demanding or the prospective adoptee experiences difficulties, families must determine if adequate time can be made available for the children along on the trip.

If you opt to leave the brothers- and sisters-to-be at home, consider the following.

STAY IN TOUCH WITH THOSE AT HOME

Use email or Skype™, wherever you can find these technologies, to send as many photos and videos home as you can. The brothers and sisters are eagerly waiting to see their new sibling!

Those at home will want to talk to their mom and dad as well. Call as often as possible. Investigate the cost of international phone calls in advance. Budget this expense into your journey to your new child's homeland. The children at home want and need to talk to you as frequently as possible.

ADOPTEES TALK

How important is it to be told about life before being adopted?

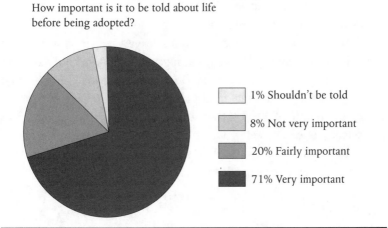

1% Shouldn't be told

8% Not very important

20% Fairly important

71% Very important

KEEP A JOURNAL

Again, adoptees love to hear the story of how you got them; they love to hear it over and over! Keep a journal of the sights, sounds, people, food, your reaction to being in a different country, what it was like meeting your child the first time—simply everything you can think to include. A journal in any medium—written, audio, or video—will do. This will be a gift to the adoptee of immeasurable value. In the event you experience culture shock, this will be a good exercise for you to process the thoughts and feelings of this experience.

Your resident children will want all these details too! They will want to know what you thought and felt. They'll want to know how often you thought about them!

DAILY REMINDERS

Parents who will be away can leave the siblings left at home a daily gesture to ensure that these children do not feel that they are forgotten. These daily reminders can include cards, notes, or small gifts. Provide a memento for each day you anticipate being gone. Leave a few extra in case of delays. Search Amazon® for *Stuck on You Love Notes, Stuck on You Laugh Notes, Love Coupons for Kids, Faith Notes: 100 Heavenly Ways to Say "I Care,"* and *Stuck on You—Warm, Witty, Wonderful Ways to Say you're Special.* Each book contains 100 notes. Kids just love these!

Another suggestion comes from the children's book *Seeds of Love: For Brothers and Sisters of International Adoption* by Mary Ebejer Petertyl and Jill Chambers. In this book, a mom and her daughter plant seeds. Mom tells her daughter that she and Dad will return home when the seeds begin to sprout. Their resident daughter places a daily sticker on the calendar to count down the days until her parents' and new sister's homecoming. This is a lovely story to read with children.

Children also benefit when parents leave them in charge of an item with sentimental value. One mom gave her 12-year-old daughter a quilt to use for the duration of Mom's trip abroad. The quilt had been handmade by the maternal grandmother. It helped this young adolescent feel as if her mother was with her every day. Whatever you select—a locket with your photo or a key ring with the family photo that is attached to the child's backpack—mementos and daily reminders lessen the impact of your absence.

Making the Trip Visual

Pre-schoolers and young school-age children are concrete thinkers. It is hard for them to picture Mom and Dad traveling to a foreign country, staying in a hotel, visiting an orphanage or foster home. The passage of time has little meaning. Remember how long it was to wait for Christmas when you were a pre-school or school-age child? This youngest group could benefit from a homemade booklet that visualizes the journey abroad. The Internet and clip art make it easy to locate a map of the sending country, as well as airplanes, hotels, orphanages, and the like. Simple captions complete this task. A calendar is also essential. Using stickers or markers, you can show your youngest siblings-to-be how long you will be gone, the date of that first very special meeting with the newcomer, and, of course, your intended return date! This pictorial portrayal of your journey will offer great comfort while you are away.

"Where will I stay?"

Children of all ages want to know where they will be staying during the time you will be away. Preferably, the children can remain at home and Grandma and Grandpa, an aunt, or a trusted family friend can come to your home for the duration of your trip away from your children. In this manner, they can continue school and their extracurricular activities with little to no interruption. Maintaining a routine lessens the impact of the life-altering transition for your resident children.

Of course, this may not be possible and alternative arrangements will have to suffice. In these cases, go over what the children may expect in their temporary quarters. For example, "I talked to Janie's mom and she is going to be able to get you to your soccer games while we are away. So, if there are any changes in your soccer schedule, you'll be talking to Janie's mom. I wrote her phone number down for you." Lay out all areas that are covered and by whom they are to be covered. Larger families may need to separate their typically developing children among more than one temporary caregiver. Make arrangements for them to communicate in your absence. Again, today's kids are technological wizards! Between Facebook™, cell phones, tablets, iPods®, and so on and on, the age-appropriate children should be able to talk frequently!

Older adolescents and young adult children might be able to stay at home with a trusted adult on call or looking in on them from time to time. Even they will miss you! Freeze some of their favorite meals and leave the cooking instructions. They will appreciate this thoughtfulness.

Leave a camera with the children at home. Encourage them to take photos of all the things they do while you are away. Reviewing these photos will make a great way to reconnect when you return home.

Brothers and sisters of domestic adoptees

Domestic adoption often includes a series of visits during which the family and the child joining the family can become acquainted. If the family and the child reside within driving distance of each other, the first visit may be brief. It may consist of a few hours with the child at the foster home, group home, residential treatment facility, or a neutral location that provides for a family activity. Subsequently, the family may take the child for an outing. Gradually, the child comes to the adoptive home for some overnight visits. Then the child moves in.

When the child is moving a significant distance—one state to another—that requires air travel, the overall visitation period may not involve as much transition time. The getting-to-know-each-other process may be carried out with a hotel or the child's current residence as a base. The child may or may not become acquainted with the adoptive family's home and neighborhood. Depending on expenses, there are cases in which the adoptee does not even get to meet his new siblings prior to placement. The family and the child's interactions are limited by the environment in which the visits take place. That is, the child does not get to see how the family operates on a daily basis and the family gains no insight as to how the child may interact with the family members.

Involving brothers and sisters in the pre-placement visits

This section presents activities that can be implemented during the pre-placement visitation process. Parents can select those suggestions that satisfy the needs of their particular family. These strategies offer ample opportunity for the children already in the family to participate in the transition of their new brother and sister, even in instances in which the visitation period is short or must be accomplished via technology. These ideas welcome the newcomer into the family and initiate the process of facilitating an attachment among all family members from the instant the match is made.

"OUR FAMILY" ALBUM

Prior to the start of visits, you might forward photos and information about your family. Many families opt to make a photo album of "Our family" for the child. This allows each member of your family an opportunity to participate in pre-placement activities. Let your children select favorite photos of themselves. Add some fun captions. Include photos of each family member, your home, extended family members, the school the new child will be attending, your community, and family pets. Other families decide to make a DVD containing this information. Allowing the adoptee the opportunity to "meet" you before you arrive is a great way to reduce her anxiety about what you look like, how many people are in the family, what type of home you have and what kind of neighborhoods he will be moving to.

ADOPTEES TALK

What do children most want to be told about their pasts?

- Why they couldn't stay with their birth family and so were adopted.
- Details about their birth family.
- Whatever they ask about.
- About their own life before they were adopted.
- Where they were born.

- If they have any brothers or sisters living someplace else, and why they were split up.
- Whether they can make contact with their birth family.

"THEIR PAST" PHOTOS

It never ceases to amaze me how few photos children have of their life prior to their adoption. It is very difficult to put your life together when you have so little information. The analogy we often use in therapy is that these adopted children are like a 500-piece puzzle missing 400 of the pieces. Photos are an integral part of healing the traumatized child. The more the newly adopted son or daughter recovers from past hurts, the more he or she can become a close, connected family member.

Make it a priority to obtain as many photos as you can. Give each sibling-to-be a disposable camera and let them snap away. Older kids can utilize their cell phone or tablet. If the foster family has any video, gather that up as well. Copies are easy to make if the foster family does not want to part with their originals.

If the child was in more than one foster home, gathering photos can be initiated pre-placement and then completed post-placement. Work with the social worker to identify these families, pressing if you must. The custodial agency has a record of where the children were in placement.

In return, when the adoptee visits your home, share your family photos albums and scrapbooks. These are, to a large extent, your already-resident children's lifebooks. This gives the adoptee a sense of the types of family fun he may expect. It also begins to give the adoptee a sense of your family history. Certainly, a review of family photos acts as a good ice-breaker for helping conversation flow! In no time, the newcomer and veteran siblings will be starting to form relationships.

A PHOTO-TAKING ADVENTURE

Go on a photo-taking adventure. This would include taking photos of the child's current family and residence. This type of photo-taking adventure is a great pre-placement visit activity for you, the children you already parent, and the child joining your family. Make sure the child has several pictures of the foster family and foster home, as well as the child's bedroom, school, favorite places in the neighborhood, pets, and anything else that seems important.

While you have the camera, take photos of the "new" family—parents and all of the children. Display several of the photos during pre-placement visits and send the new child a couple via regular mail or email. The brothers and sisters need to see the family as it will be, and the son- or daughter-to-be needs to see himself or herself as a member of your family. You can also use this visual to revisit discussions with the children you already parent regarding any pending role changes or changes in birth order. "When Jean moves in, you are going to be the big brother. Have you thought about what being a big brother means? Let's sit down and talk about your new responsibilities."

Jim and Andrea combined photo taking with a closure event:

Jim, Andrea, and their 12-year-old daughter Abbie were in the process of pre-placement visits with ten-year-old Grace. They felt it important that Grace be able to say goodbye to her classmates and her teacher. Andrea worked with Grace's teacher to plan a social event that was held in Grace's classroom. The social included snacks, games, and a brief presentation about adoption. Throughout the social, Andrea helped Grace collect phone numbers and email addresses. Jim spent his time taking lots of photos. Andrea had also purchased a new journal for Grace. Abbie invited each of Grace's classmates to write something they would miss about Grace in the journal and then sign their name. The principal and Grace's soccer coach were able to attend the gathering as well. Grace received the support of many peers and adults as she transitioned to her adoptive family. After moving to her adoptive home, the journal and the photos proved a source of comfort for Grace.

Overall, photos offer a means to get acquainted with the new son, daughter, brother, or sister, while simultaneously acknowledging that the child's past and current relationships are valued by the new family. We want to accept that the arriving child has a past while at the same time inviting the prospective adoptee to join the existing family. Moms, dads, brothers, and sisters make clear to the newcomer, "We know you have a past. We know that past is important to you. We will be helping you with that as you need us to. We also want to tell you about ourselves. We will be important in your life as well." The dual acknowledgment will allow the child to grieve her past and therefore she can accept your invitation to join your family!

Contact between visits

Time between visits or the lead-time prior to the start of visits can be maximized. This may be a particularly beneficial solution when the placement involves distance.

> Logan and Sophie parent two children by birth, Zack, age 11, and Paige, age nine. Seven-year-old Faith is soon to join the family. As Faith lives in a different state, two pre-placement visits were planned. On the first visit, Logan and Sophie would spend a period of four days getting to know Faith. The second visit would occur three weeks later and would include Zack and Paige. Between visits, via Skype™, the family was able to share with Faith their bedtime ritual in which each discussed the "best" and "worst" part of their day. Sometimes they did "bests" and "worsts" to learn about Faith's likes and dislikes and vice versa. What is the best and worst food for dinner? What is the best and worst rule? What is the best and worst chore? What is the best game? They learned that Faith's foster mom made chocolate chip pancakes on her birthday and that Faith just thought this was great. They also learned that Faith enjoyed playing the game *Trouble*, as did Paige. Faith was used to going to sporting events as she had two older foster brothers. Zack participated in athletics year-round. Faith's least favorite chore was cleaning her room. Her favorite dinner was macaroni and cheese and hot dogs. Her least favorite dinner was meatloaf. Paige agreed with the latter!

Learning likes and dislikes is a great way to begin to form relationships. Again, technology makes connecting with the child between visits or prior to the start of visits much easier than it was in years past.

Keep to your routine

When the adoptive family and their prospective child live in the same area, pre-placement visits do not always have to be an outing. In fact, sticking to your normal routine may be beneficial. It gives your adoptee the chance to truly see how the family operates. It allows the adoptee to view himself as a family member rather than as a guest. Outing after outing gives the child a false sense of the family. If Saturday morning is designated for chores, then assign the adoptee a chore. If Thursday evening is grocery shopping, take the child along. Errands offer the new child a chance to check out the neighborhood. Have your soon-to-be son or daughter help unload the car when you arrive home.

As you are completing your tasks, provide the child an overview of your expectations. For example, "When we go to the grocery store, I expect you to stay with me." Or: "We are going for videos. Today, it is Tommy's turn to select the movie. Your turn will be the next time you visit with us." Or: "When we all have our chores done, we'll play a game." Overall, incorporate as much "reality" about the family as is possible into your pre-placement period.

Keep in mind that your resident children will be watching to see how you will be treating their new sibling. They need to see you establishing boundaries while simultaneously welcoming the adoptee. They want assurance that they will not be forgotten, and they want to know that rules will apply to each child in the family.

Assign "getting to know us and you" activities

Typical siblings-to-be want to be helpful as the adoptee joins the family. Parents can assign specific tasks to help direct this caring energy in productive ways. Being in charge of an important undertaking also helps the children you already parent feel significant in the transition. For example, "When Johnny comes this weekend, I was hoping you could give him a tour of the house. Any time he needs anything this weekend, could you be in charge of helping him find it?" Or: "Sally is going to need to know the rules of the house. I thought we could all sit down and go over the rules. Would you like to lead the conversation? I think you could do such a good job. You could also let her know what kinds of consequences we use." Assignments could also be used to identify different family characteristics. For example, who tends to be grumpy in the morning, the ages of each child in the family, or which parent to go to for different types of needs (i.e. "Go to Mom when you want a snack. Go to Dad when you need help with math").

Let's look at one family's assignment:

Nicole was the eighth child to join their family. This is a lot of people to get to know! Claire, the mother, sat the children—young and older—around the kitchen table. Each child had tape, glue, and construction paper. Claire was ready with the scissors. In the middle of the table, Claire put a stack of old magazines. Each child was assigned the task of locating pictures that reflected his or her interests. By the time they were finished, each child had a collage of "All about Me." The collages were displayed on the kitchen bulletin board until Nicole became familiar with her new siblings and vice versa.

Brothers and sisters in all forms of adoption: Additional pre- and post-placement considerations

Sharing in the preparing

Once you have an idea of the age of the child or children who will be joining your family, there will be tasks to do such as shopping and setting up a bedroom. Include the children you already parent in these activities to the maximum degree possible. That is, do not carry out all of the preparations while they are at school. Brothers and sisters want to help. While shopping, let your resident children pick out a few items for their sibling-to-be. Help them sort through packed-away clothing and toys that they have outgrown and select items that will be useful for the new child. If old enough, let your children help assemble the crib or bed and other furniture.

Sharing bedrooms

THE PRIVACY FACTOR

If the addition of a new child to the family means that one of your resident children will have to share her bedroom, help her make a place just for herself. This should be a space that is off limits to the new sibling. It could be a foot locker for items of special importance or it could mean cleaning out a corner of the den. Assure the birth and/or previously adopted child that she will be able to maintain some of the privacy she is accustomed to.

The above recommendation is especially important if the new arrival is a school-age or older child. For example, the prospective adoptee who has resided in an orphanage setting long-term may have no idea about boundaries. The concept of asking permission prior to using or taking things belonging to others is likely a concept with which the older institutionalized child is unfamiliar.

SEXUAL SAFETY

As noted previously, some children will enter the family after the trauma of sexual abuse. Until the behaviors of a new arrival become clear, parents may want to consider the following measures to ensure the safety of all of the children in their home:

- A home with adequate bedroom space is preferable. If resident children and adopted children must share a room, then it is essential that the typically developing children be old enough to comprehend what would be considered a sexual touch. Brothers and sisters need to understand clearly that sexual advances should be immediately reported to the parent.

- Door alarms offer the ability to offset opportunities for sexual acting-out. An alarm on each child's bedroom door ensures that everyone is in their own bedroom. The child who has experienced trauma often feels a sense of safety as a result of a door alarm. He knows that no one has access to him. Thus, he can sleep soundly without fear of revictimization.

- Periodically, ask your children if sexual advances have been made. Children are more likely to tell when adults make clear that they are open to such disclosures. Include in this discussion what will happen if the child does report sexual advances. Children worry that they or their sibling will "get in trouble." They are frequently fearful of repercussions from the perpetrating child if sexual interactions are occurring.

- Explain the types of touch that are acceptable in your family (i.e. hugs, bedtime kisses, snuggling on the couch while watching a movie). Clarify rules regarding privacy.

- If you do discover sexual activity, attempt to react as calmly as possible. Make clear your expectations that the behavior you witnessed or were informed of needs to cease permanently. Be clear and direct and use anatomically correct language.

- Provide supervision for as long as necessary.

- Develop a working knowledge of sexual development. This will help discern "normal" sexual behaviors from those that are problematic.

- Establish "family sexual policies." This is a written list (use drawings or books with very young children) of sexual behaviors that are considered inappropriate in the family. For example, this might include:

  - I understand that if I want to enter another person's bedroom, I must get permission first.

  - I understand that when visiting another person's bedroom, the door must be open. I understand that if someone is visiting my bedroom, the door must be open.

  - I understand that undressing is allowed only in my bedroom and in the bathroom with the door closed.

  - I understand that everyone sleeps in their own bed.

  - I understand that there will be no sexual play and sexual touching, and that includes playing doctor, nurse, or things like that.

  - I understand there is to be no public masturbation.

  - I understand there is to be no sexual contact or sexual touching between children in this family. The only individuals who have sex together in this home are mom and dad and always with the door closed.

- I understand that there is to be only one person in the bathroom at one time.

- I will tell an adult if anyone sexually touches me.

- I will obey these rules of privacy—for example, no touching of another's private parts, purses, notebooks, private notes, diaries, no opening another's mail

(Deuhn 1999)

The advantage of a family policy is that no one child is singled out. Each child has the same rules regarding sexual behaviors. This list is reviewed as a family. Some families opt to have each member of the family sign this policy statement.

- Offer *all* your children sexual education—starting as early as need be. The child with a history of sexual abuse needs "normal" sexual information, as do typical children.

- Teach all of your children your values about the relationship in which sexual acts should occur. Often—once initiated— parents do a wonderful job teaching children about sex. Yet moms and dads need to be aware that the sexually abused child knows about sex. These children are naive about relationships. They must be encouraged to develop human connections in which sex is a beautiful part of that couple's display of love and commitment to one another. Start early as well with regards to this aspect of sexuality. Forming relationships—as many veteran adoptive moms and dads can attest to—can be a lifelong process for the adoptee who arrived after a history of sexual trauma.

- Joint parental participation—in two-parent families—is essential.

- Be vigilant! Do not allow yourself to believe that sexual interactions cannot happen in your home.

Being proactive about sex and sexuality may not come easily to some parents, and it also means talking to the typical kids about sex and sexuality at much younger ages than parents had anticipated.

However, proactivity ensures the sanctity of the home environment desired by all parents.

Sharing toys/electronics

Keep in mind the school-age sibling-to-be may not have the social skills to engage with toys and games designed for his actual age. Parents may want to keep purchases in this area to a minimum until the social and emotional age of the son- or daughter-to-be can be determined. Age-appropriate brothers and sisters may want to hold back the sharing of toys of special importance or electronic items that, if broken, would be expensive to replace.

Post a large calendar in a conspicuous place in the house

The addition of a child to the home creates an array of new appointments. Shortly after coming home, there will be your medical clinic visits and there will be your social worker arriving for post-placement visits. There may be speech, occupational, or physical therapy. The list will probably grow very quickly. Resident brothers and sisters need to know when you will be available and when they may need to find rides. They need to know when you will be home and when they will be arriving to an empty house. Or they need to be informed of when to go to a friend's house until you come and pick them up. Everyone will benefit from hearing this information and seeing it posted on the calendar. All children function better when they know what to expect.

Parent attachment first, then sibling attachment: 100 ways to be helpful!

Readers will be aware at this point that attachment is an emphasis of this book. Without a doubt, strong family connections are gratifying. It is important to point out that attachment first develops between child and parent. Subsequently, children grow into relationships with siblings, extended family, and the rest of the world. This is not to imply that siblings cannot interact with their new brother or sister. However, this is to say that parents need to carry out all primary caregiving over the first six to 12 months of the post-placement period—no matter the age of the child joining the family. Parents need to feed the child or provide the food; parents need to change the baby, bathe the newest family member, or teach appropriate hygiene. They need to be the ones there when the child awakens and when the child goes to sleep. Parents need to provide comfort. Parents need to rock the child or teach the child about giving and receiving affection. If the new member of the family is an infant, parents need to be the ones holding the baby most of the time. In fact, a sling is strongly recommended for young children. *Wearing* your newcomer is a great way to enhance attachment. It will certainly be tempting to let your older children assume many caregiving tasks; however, this would delay the attachment between you and your adoptee, thus delaying the transfer of the attachment to the rest of the family.

ADOPTEES TALK

How can an adoptive family help a new child settle into their home?

- Spend time with the child.
- Love and care for him.
- Make her feel welcome and comfortable.
- Give him treats.
- Give her reassurance and support.
- Decorate his room with him.
- Show her around everywhere she needs to know.
- Provide for the child's needs.
- Understand his child's feelings.
- Give her personal space.

Adolescents, especially females, often rush to carry out the caregiving. Parents must find ways to curtail this eagerness. This can be accomplished through a discussion of attachment and how it forms. After that conversation, you can sit with your appropriately developing sons and daughters and list ways that they can be helpful while not interfering with your caregiving of the new child. Your resident children can heat up bottles, get diapers, carry the diaper bag, change the sheets on the toddler bed, sing lullabies or nursery rhymes along with you, and so on. The children you already parent may be especially helpful with the language development of the new child and reinforcing rules. In fact, there are most likely a hundred ways they could help you without directly providing the care to the new child. It could be fun to make a list of these things! We certainly want to encourage strong sibling relationships; however, there are times when we must direct the manner in which the siblings interact with the adoptee.

Love at first sight?

Parents and brothers and sisters enjoy reciprocal affection. Hugs and kisses at bedtime, snuggling on the couch during family movie night, pats on the back, holding hands on outings all confirm the love that exists in the family relationships. Typical children believe that the infant, toddler, or older child entering the family will enjoy these demonstrative displays as well. Given that 90 percent of internationally adopted children arrive in America under five years of age[2], it makes sense to think that such young children would relish the opportunity to receive the loving caresses that they have lacked in their lives to date.

Yet the young child perceives with her senses. She is able to *sense* the loss of a voice, a touch, a sound. When you meet her, her impressions are:

"You don't look like anyone I know."

"You don't smell like my orphanage or my foster mom."

"You talk differently. You don't sound like any of the people I know."

"Your clothes feel different." "Your body is shaped differently from my caregivers."

"This bottle isn't the same." "What am I eating?"

---

2   Evan B. Donaldson Adoption Institute. "International Adoption Facts." www.adoptioninstitute.org/FactOverview/international.html.

"Why are you smiling?"

"What is going on?"

Realistically, infants and toddlers will grieve the loss of their homeland or foster family (Bowlby 1980). The young child's grief reaction may include distress and despair. Anticipate that the new son or daughter may react strongly to both parents and siblings. Many families describe loud and rageful crying, rocking, shaking the crib, head banging, arching of the back, pulling or pushing away from the new family members, and so on. Other parents describe a new child as listless, sleeping a majority of the time and appearing unaware of what is going on around him.

Parents and the resident kids feel rejected. Of course it is painful to feel that you have been pushed away by a child you have worked so very hard to bring home! Siblings take this rejection hard too. But rather than viewing these behaviors as a personal rejection, try to see them as reflective of the youngster's capacity to *sense* that a major change is taking place. The child is not rejecting his new parents, brothers, or sisters. The child is expressing his grief.

You may need to build an attachment. Again, a secure attachment between a parent and an infant develops over the first 12 months of life. Responsive and consistent caregiving are the two ingredients essential for the making of a secure attachment. Such a scenario has not occurred for the child in residence in an institutional setting or the child who experienced abuse. The trauma of pre-natal drug and/or alcohol exposure impairs the brain's ability to carry out the social processes necessary for attachment to occur. Thus, a negative behavioral reaction on the new son or daughter's part is because he or she hasn't yet learned how to engage in mutually satisfying reciprocal interactions.

Prepare yourself and the sons and daughters you already parent for the fact that "love at first sight" may be a one-sided endeavor for a time post-arrival of the newest family member. Talk with your typical kids before the arriving sibling disembarks the plane or moves from her foster home. Facts can offset many hurt feelings!

Pre-arrival of the new member of the family, there is much that parents and their existing children can do to ease the transition for themselves and the newcomer. Many of the ideas are practical tips that will contribute to helping the family remain ordered as it expands in size. Many lend to initiating that so-desired bonding—those close intimate ties that enrich the lives of mothers, fathers, sisters, and brothers. Forming connections between you, your typically developing kids, and your adoptive son or daughter starts the moment the match is made or the referral received!

Chapter summary

- Pre-placement is the time to begin navigating endearing relations among all members of the adoptive family. The birth and/or previously adopted children are more invested in the arrival of the brother or sister when they are involved each step of the way.

- The child with a history of abuse and neglect may join the family with unexpected sexual or aggressive behaviors. Parents are advised to utilize caution and the safety tips offered in this chapter. It is always "better safe than sorry."

- Attachment forms between child and parent first. Subsequently, children grow into relationships with siblings, extended family, and the rest of the world. The infant, toddler, or older child may not have the abilities to move in and attach. Mothers and fathers will provide for the needs of the new child immediately post-placement, while offering the brothers and sisters a multitude of ways to be helpful. Gradually, the sibling relationships will come to flourish.

- "Love at first sight" may actually take time to occur. Prepare for this in advance. Talk with your children about how attachment forms. Information can offset much heartache for each member of the adoption-built family.

- Children function best when they know what to expect—when there is a routine. Work toward developing a schedule as quickly as possible after the newcomer's arrival. Post the family's roster in a conspicuous place. Don't forget to include special time with each of your children on your agenda. All kids need quality and quantity time with their mom and dad.

6

"After He Came, Everything Changed!"

COMMON POST-PLACEMENT CHALLENGES

The chapter title comes from a sentiment expressed by a typical six-year-old brother regarding his younger adopted brother. He stated, "When he came to our house, everything changed. He screamed, he copied me, he pinched me, and he broke my toys." Indeed, the arrival of a child with a traumatic past can disturb the equilibrium of the family for quite some time to come. This chapter overviews the most frequent areas of life that change for the birth and/or previously adopted children when the family expands via adoption of the traumatized child.

Don't become discouraged while reading this chapter. Adoptive families do learn to cope with these common challenges. The resident children and the adoptee can grow up to be well adjusted. Solutions follow in the subsequent chapters!

Support systems shrink
"We don't see our extended family as much"
Lena, typically developing, was adopted as an infant. In her late adolescence, her parents adopted a sibling group of two sisters, ages one and a half and five. These arrivals had suffered complex trauma prior to their removal from their birth family. Each sister presented various difficulties. Lena recalls a therapy session:

"We had a therapy session where my extended family—aunts, uncles, grandma, grandpa—came. We talked about how our family couldn't handle it all the time and that we needed help from them. They were like, 'Yeah, you guys need help. We'll call and take the kids out to lunch.'

"But then a couple of my family members said, 'Why don't you just give the kids back? You shouldn't even have them because they're horrible for your family. We don't want you to live with this.' It made me feel like, 'I'm adopted. Do you want to give me back?' I think that every child should have a chance to be with a family. It hurt—'just give them back.' There was no thought of them at all.

"The conclusion of this experience was that my extended family never does anything. They don't call unless we call them. They don't want to come to holidays. Basically, when they call, all they talk about is, 'Are you going to give the kids back?'"

Lena was left questioning, "Why aren't my relatives more helpful? I spent so much time with them growing up. What happened? I am adopted. If I had problems, what would they have told my parents? Did they really ever accept me?"

"What I did not realize going into the adoption process was what a profound effect my soon-to-be sister would have on my extended family. We are able to visit with my aunts, uncles, and grandparents far less than we used to because of my sister. She is just so destructive that it is hard to take her anyplace. She breaks things, spills her drinks, drops her food, and so much more! We are afraid of the damage she could do to our relatives' homes."

Lena and her family are one example of the way in which extended family relationships fracture post-placement. Other families report a constant stream of advice flowing from their relatives. Many of these suggestions imply parenting flaws, and this scenario creates tension. Parents make the decision to avoid family get-togethers. Travel with a formerly traumatized child may present safety issues:

Norma and Elwin adopted three-and-a-half-year-old Eugene from Belarus. Already present in their family was their son, Elwin Jr., age nine, also adopted. Riding in the car with Eugene was a hazard. He kicked the back of the seat, refused to wear a seatbelt and threw anything he could get his hands on at the driver. Driving to visit out-of-state family members came to a halt once Eugene arrived in the family.

The loss of contact with aunts, uncles, cousins, and grandparents is not something that is easily, if ever, overcome.

"I feel left out of my own family!"

Family members may become isolated from one another:

Leslie was adopted at age seven. Now age 11, she is thriving. She has friends, she makes good grades, and she has many interests. She openly lets people know how happy she is to have been adopted. She is quite clear that her birth parents "couldn't get themselves together and that was their problem." Three other adopted siblings in her family, on the other hand, go to therapy, a psychiatrist, speech therapy, and occupational therapy. These services take a lot of time. Frequently, Leslie must stay with her aunt while her parents and siblings participate in their therapies. Recently, Leslie asked her mom, "Can I go to therapy so I can spend more time with you?" Leslie's mom was stunned.

The addition of a child with a traumatic past puts a family already crunched for time in the red! The typical siblings' time with their mom and dad shrinks. Without concerted effort, friendly, in-depth interactions between mothers, fathers, and their resident sons and daughters can become few and far between.

"It's hard to have friends over"

Rick is 13 years old. His home had always been the favorite place to hang out. The basement was complete with a pool table and up-to-date video game equipment. Rick's mom always kept an ample array of snacks on hand. Rick's friends came over after school and on weekends.

Rick's parents adopted Lydia internationally, seven years ago, and everything changed. Lydia is currently age nine. Rick says, "Lydia is great and I do love her. But around my friends it has been really hard. She wouldn't leave them alone. She tried to sit on their laps. She hugged them and sometimes she tried to kiss them. It was so embarrassing! My friends didn't know what to do around her or what to say to her. On their own, some of my friends stopped coming over. But, others, I stopped inviting. I started making excuses about having things to do. I can't go to their houses because I watch Lydia until Mom or Dad gets home from work."

In Lena's case, her peer relationships became a struggle too, for a dissimilar reason to Rick's:

"Out in public, sometimes they act fine. Sometimes they'll be disruptive. But it's not a major-scale disruption like at home where they'll throw a complete tantrum. I would be talking to my friends and they would ask, 'How are your sisters doing?' I would try to explain the behaviors but they never caught on. They would say, 'They can't be that bad. They're only children.' I would be like, 'No, these are worse problems than what normal children cause.' My friends thought I should look at things differently and that I was exaggerating. They thought I was the one who needed to change my views and to understand that these are children and this is what children do."

Children with residual trauma effects often display far more negative behavior in the home than in the community. So their needs are "invisible" to those outside the family. Attempts to explain what life is like with the newcomer falls on deaf ears.

"When we have friends over, he likes to show off to them. Our friends think it's funny. But they don't know what it feels like to have him all the time."

Post-adoption, the resident kids experience turmoil in their peer relationships. Friends, a prime means of support, can't relate to what is happening. Or the adoptee's behaviors are off-putting.

Family fun diminishes

Certainly, how kids play makes for enjoyable family interactions and long-lasting friendships. The newly arrived brother or sister often lacks the social skills to play in accord with his or her age. The child's pre-adoptive experiences shattered her social developmental domain as presented earlier in this book.

The child with a history of trauma views himself as "bad." Commonly, boys and girls blame themselves for their abuse, neglect, and/or abandonment. They think, "I don't deserve to have so much fun." Thus, some may enjoy the company of their family during outings. Yet look out afterwards! The adopted son or daughter plummets into a particularly poor behavioral period! In clinical practice, it is routine to hear the children already in the family at the time of the adoption or the parents exclaim, "We don't go out as a family very often anymore. There is such a 'pay back' the next day. It isn't worth the 'bad' behavior we'll get."

"We used to eat out Friday nights and Sunday after church. This has ceased since my brother arrived. He often threw food on those dining around us. When his meal arrived, he would scream—loudly—that it was 'yucky.' He would push it aside and pout while everyone else ate."

Family fun may trigger the lack of any good memories with the birth family or the few good recollections of the birth family or orphanage mates:

Peter, adopted at nine months old, wrecked every family holiday. One Thanksgiving, he threw the turkey out of his bedroom window. His parents and his three siblings—birth children—searched frantically for the 25-pound bird! "Where could it have gone?" asked Peter's mom repeatedly. "I know I put it in the refrigerator!" she stated. With 22 relatives on the way for

Thanksgiving dinner, the missing turkey was creating quite a predicament! Fortunately, Peter's dad located an open supermarket to which he rushed and purchased a new turkey. Later, the turkey appeared in the trash can. Eventually, Peter admitted his foul act.

Peter stated in a therapy session, "Every holiday and birthday, I can't stop thinking about what my birth family is doing. And I wonder what I would be doing if I were with them. I just want to be with them." Peter, like many traumatized adoptees, uses his behavior to try to show what he is thinking and feeling. Obviously, the ramifications of such behavior impacts the entire family's festivities.

Fun with the family, playing by himself, making and keeping friends—all facets of social interaction—will be compromised. It will be difficult to be the parents of the child no one in the neighborhood wants to play with—not even his own brothers and sisters! It will be a great disappointment to resident brothers and sisters that their sibling just "can't play like other kids." Really, enjoying "family game night," outings to the zoo, vacations, cheerful holiday gatherings, participation in Cub Scouts, baseball, basketball, soccer, ballet recitals, karate tournaments, school plays, band concerts, and so much more is the stuff of family life. Parents and kids alike want to have fun—lots of fun!

Post-adoption diminished teasing, fooling around, joking, kidding, playing, and plain old family fun is likely the area of family life that changes the most. Later in this book there is lots of information devoted to restoring the level of recreation in the adoption-built family.

Questions, comments, stares, and more...
Transcultural adoption: "Why does everyone have to stare?"

Parents and their same-race resident children will be impacted by a transcultural adoption. Certainly, there is rich learning when the family embraces the culture of the child's homeland and/or race. On the other hand, adoptive family members will find themselves the brunt of comments, questions, and criticisms, as well as being spotlighted by the gawks of curious strangers:

Tanner was excited with the arrival of his younger sibling from Kazakhstan. Over time, he noticed that everywhere his transcultural family went strangers stared. Some even asked questions such as, "Where did you get that one?" "How much did she cost?" "Where's Kazakhstan?" "What happened to her real parents?" Friends frequently asked, "Why does your sister look different to the rest of your family?"

Or, consider this scenario:

Rick was 15 years old and a sophomore in high school. He was adopted as an infant. He is bicultural: his birth mother is Caucasian and his birth father is of Middle Eastern decent. He has dark brown, almost black, hair and dark brown eyes. His skin is olive. He has resided with his adoptive parents in the same community his whole life. His appearance, in comparison to his Caucasian parents, has caused some issues over time. Strangers do look when the family is out. Kids have asked him why his skin tone is different from his parents'. However, overall, Rick has had little difficulty.

Rick's life changed when our country declared war on Iraq. An American soldier from his home town died in Iraq. Classmates he had known his whole life began implying that the death was due to "people like him." Rick was stunned. He had no idea how to respond to these remarks. It seemed the less he replied, the more the comments flowed. Rick's two Caucasian brothers, ages 12 and 13, attend the same school as Rick. They overheard these prejudiced statements. In their efforts to aid their brother, a fist fight broke out. Shortly thereafter, the parents were called to meet with the principal. The end result of the meeting was a school assembly designed to raise awareness of the value of cultural differences. At home, Rick and his parents and siblings began a series of discussions regarding how each family member could more effectively handle prejudice and discrimination in the future.

Sooner, rather than later, the kids already in the family at the time of the adoption need to be familiar with prejudice and discrimination.

Or as a final example:

Carrie arrived at 14 months old from China. By age three, she recognized the cultural difference between herself and her Caucasian parents and siblings. Each time Carrie saw an Asian woman, she asked, "Are you my mom?" This created much confusion for all!

Birth and adopted children develop cultural awareness at very young ages. Adoptees comprehend the loss of the birth mother far earlier than most adoptive family members anticipate. The adoptee's quest for cultural identity and desire to comprehend her birth circumstances has a ripple effect on parents and the brothers and sisters already in the family at the time of the adoption.

"How come your family adopted?"

Adoption, in and of itself, seems to peak the curiosity of kids and adults alike. Typical sons and daughters find themselves attempting to answer such queries as:

"Is he your real brother?"

"How come your family adopted?"

"Where's he from?" "Why did your parents go there to get a kid?"

"What happened to her family?"

"Why didn't her real mom want her?"

"What is adoption?"

"Could I be adopted if something happened to my mom and dad?"

"Do you know his real family?"

Recently, a nine-year-old typical sister stated, "I feel like I am invisible. Everyone asks about my adopted sister. It's all about where she came from, what happened to her birth family, how my parents got to China, and all that stuff. No one asks me how I am or how I'm doing at school or whether or not my soccer team is winning—nothing! I feel like I'm just not important anymore."

Often the limelight that surrounds the adoptee detracts from the other children. Resident brothers and sisters begin to feel disregarded.

In addition, intrusive remarks and inquiries—being in the public eye, so to speak—is fatiguing.

I want readers to know that rather than write a solution chapter for this common challenge, I am going to offer resources instead. I have laid the foundation for the necessity of arming children with the cultural education and ways to respond to the queries sure to come along when the family expands through adoption. I am directing parents to the writing of others more expert in this area of adoptive family life. There exists a preponderance of books, articles, magazines, websites, blogs, and movies devoted to these aspects of families built by adoption. Please review the resource section of this book to learn about all of this wonderful information.

The home's emotional climate has more storms

"My parents fight a lot more now!"

Clinical experience with appropriately developing kids makes clear that they do not view their parents as a happy couple post-adoption. The couple's sentiments below validate the resident sons' and daughters' opinions:

> "Our marriage has been deeply affected by our adoption. The havoc our adopted son's behavior has caused in our home has caused our relationship to be filled with tension and fighting, causing everyone lots of stress. Having a young child scream at you, smear his peanut butter across your walls, kick and hit you at various times has caused each of us a great deal of anguish."

The example of Derrick below summarizes the desires of the brothers and sisters with whom I have had in-depth contact:

> Derrick's parents, Ellen and Roger, adopted their two nieces, Jill and Joyce, when Derrick was 11 years old. Jill and Joyce were 12 and 14 respectively.
>
> Jill, Ellen, and Roger engaged in conflict from the day Jill arrived. Derrick stated, "Family meals have always been important to my parents. No matter what, we sit down to dinner as a family. Then along came Jill. Mom gets on her about eating with her mouth open and not using a fork. Dad yells at Mom to stop picking on her. The next thing, Mom and Dad are having a huge

fight! Mom feels Dad doesn't support her. Eventually, I take my plate to my room and turn on my television. I'm not even sure they notice that I have gone to my room. I just wish they would stop fighting."

Parents and the boys and girls living in the family pre-adoption all voice concern that marital strife arrives with the troubled adoptee. The expression "If mama ain't happy, ain't nobody happy" is particularly fitting in families that expand by adoption. Only, like the family, it expands to "When Mom and Dad ain't happy, neither are their kids."

Developing "value" competency

"HIS BEHAVIOR IS SO BIZARRE!"

Clear now should be that traumatized children exhibit behavior that certainly is out of the ordinary. Throwing a turkey out a window, storing bologna under the bed, consuming an entire pie in one sitting, and much more!

Actually, many of these children's behaviors were developed to survive the abuse and neglect they experienced. So the child who suffered trauma believes that his behaviors kept him alive. Giving up the behaviors is thus perceived as giving up the very things that saved his life and perhaps the lives of his siblings.

Mike resided with his birth mother and his three older birth brothers. Their birth mother would leave the children alone, sometimes for several days. The children became adept at rummaging through garbage cans in order to eat. The garbage also contained broken toys and tattered clothing. These items were treasures to these four children. Mike, adopted by age three and a half, continued to pick through the trash. On the neighborhood's assigned garbage pick-up day, he would delight in going from home to home digging through each trash can. He would excitedly arrive back at his own home with pictures, small pieces of furniture, toys, clothes, cardboard boxes, and so on. He thought these items were valuable contributions to his adoptive household.

Mike continued to believe that he needed to provide for the family. He felt his "value" was in what he could bring to the family.

International adoptees—even very young arrivals—are notorious for collecting bits of string, paper, and pencils. Food issues abound with the formerly institutionalized child:

> Vikki, adopted from Russia as an infant, has had food issues since her homecoming. As a baby, she would scream for her bottle. She'd grab it and guzzle it dry. As she passed through pre-school and grade school, no amount of sugar satisfied her cravings. She consumed her own and her three siblings' Halloween candy in one sitting! She rummaged through cupboards in the wee hours of the morning consuming dry hot chocolate, baker's chocolate, etc.
>
> At a family meeting, her older sister, Darlene, said, "She takes all my candy no matter where I try to hide it—even if I try to put it way in the very back of my closet! What is wrong with her? Is she ever going to be better? Is our family always going to be like this?"
>
> Vikki's value is on food, rather than the people who provide the food. She learned this value in the orphanage setting in which infants hold their own bottle and feed themselves—manage their own sustenance—before they are even six months old.

It is fairly easy to appreciate the development of various behaviors when we connect the behavior to its origin. Yet to hear the other kids in the family express poignant concerns about the state of the family is heartbreaking. Living day-to-day with behavior that is absolutely strange is a major challenge. Arguments ensue daily. Changing the behavior will take time—a long time. It is no easier for children to change their habitual negative behavior than it is for adults. We have all had the experience of making New Year's resolutions. We pledge to diet, to exercise, to eat healthier, to spend more time with family and friends, or to develop a hobby. February arrives and the resolution has already gone by the wayside!

Parents and siblings must learn "value competency." This is the ability to live—long-term—with children who, due to their traumatic histories, have developed values and ways of acting that are at dissonance with those of the adoptive family. Otherwise, the home front will be teeming with anger, anxiety, sadness, despair, frustration, and exasperation on a regular basis.

Privilege wars!

It is a struggle to dole out privileges in families with close-in-age children in which the adoptee is "younger" than her chronological age. She wants the privileges that go along with her actual age, as she sees her appropriately developing brothers and sisters receiving. Experience with the "little" adoptee gives parents caution. "If we give her a Nintendo DS®, she'll break it or lose it. Why spend that money?" On the other hand, "If we don't give it to her, she'll take her sister's Nintendo DS®." There is a high probability that the latter will occur.

Going to parties, sleepovers, or a visit to a friend's or cousin's house will be a quandary. "Can he be trusted?" "Can he ride his bike to the park like his brother?" "Should I let him go in the store alone?" Should he have a Facebook™ account, a cell phone, or drive the car? As kids grow up, so do the risks inherent in the privilege.

Typical sons and daughters earn trust and privileges. The newcomer with a traumatic past will lack the initiative to work for a reward or special item. Again, her values and morals are different to those of the family. Her ability to postpone gratification may be delayed too.

The green-eyed monster—jealousy—really rears its ugly head in this area. The envious arrival can wreak havoc with her parents and her brothers and sisters when she is denied what she feels she should have. Siblings' possessions turn up missing. Tampering with a resident child's stuff is an option. For example, Luke was enraged that his one-year-younger brother was the first to receive a cell phone. He took every opportunity possible to delete all of his brother's contacts, or send hurtful text messages to his sibling's friends. Luke accused his mom and dad, "You love him more because he is your birth child!" Such behavior has obvious ramifications for this brother–brother relationship and the home climate.

Reading, writing, and arithmetic: Going to school with my new sibling

"I am so embarrassed at school!"

Kids spend a lot of time at school. When the child who joined the family via adoption displays poor behavior in the academic setting, it is embarrassing.

> Abigail entered the family at age five. She and her typically developing sibling, John, attended the same school. One day, Abigail was found eating food off the lavatory floor. The food had apparently been dropped by a preceding student. The news of this behavior passed through the school quickly. At recess, numerous fellow classmates asked John, "What is wrong with your sister?"

> Randy's family adopted Sean when he was four years old. Randy was three years older than Sean, and so the two boys spent several years together at the same grade school. Each day, Sean had temper tantrums when he became frustrated with his in-class assignments. The school's response was to have Randy come to Sean's class to assist in calming him down. This interrupted Randy's education as well as causing his classmates to wonder what was going on. "Where was Randy going every day?" "What is the problem with his brother?" It wasn't long before classmates posed questions to Randy about his brother's "weird" behavior.

In other cases I have worked, school behavior has included suicidal threats requiring 911 to transport the child to the psychiatric hospital, running away, spray painting profanity on school property, stealing snacks out of other kids' lunches, stealing money from teachers' purses, entering the locker room and stealing other students' clothing, being aggressive toward classmates, hiding under furniture and refusing to come out when asked, getting up and walking about the classroom, "flopping" on the classroom floor, "barking" like a dog during class, masturbating during class, chattering while instruction was going on, hacking into the school computer system, passing pornography to fellow students, feigning serious illness, and visiting the nurse daily with one contrived symptom after another.

Kids will need help to determine how to deal with the queries of peers. Kids will also need outlets to manage the strong feelings that come along with the adoptee that displays "weird" behavior publically.

Homework battles

Parents want their children to reap the benefits of a good education. Typical kids who reflect their parent's value system mirror their parent's wishes in this area. They, too, want to do well in school. They understand that their future will be brighter due to academic achievements. These appropriately developing kids arrive home from school, have a snack, chat a bit about their day, and go about the business of tackling the evening's homework.

Helping the troubled adoptee with the three "Rs" may prove to be a different story. The child with a history of abuse, abandonment, and/or neglect simply lacks the motivation, compliance, attention, or skills to finish calculations or projects in a timely manner. Working with the child with a history of trauma to complete homework becomes a battle. Even if the assignments are finished, there is no guarantee the adopted child will turn his homework in to the teacher. It is not uncommon that worksheets are tossed out the school bus window or jammed in the bottom of the locker.

Homework battles cause the typical kids to flee to friends' homes or lock themselves in their rooms—they won't be seen until breakfast! Many enjoyable evenings are as lost as the homework that is cast along the highway.

Safety and security are compromised

For the majority, thoughts of home conjure up words like "safe," "secure," "peaceful," "loving," "happy." So, family life becomes particularly surreal when the adoptee arrives with aggressive or sexual behavior. When this behavior continues, home becomes a battle ground or a place in which a high level of supervision prevails. These scenarios are totally contrary to our notion of home. Cathy was nine years old, when her family adopted her one-year-older brother. She stated:

"We sometimes would have to go out of the house because he would pick up a bat and start hitting my bed, his bed, or the couch. When it was really bad, we'd be out of the house for at least four days out of the whole month. We'd have to go stay at Grandma's house. Any plans we had didn't happen. It was just terrible!"

This troubled sibling entered therapy. It was a two-year endeavor to cease his angry outbursts. He stated:

"My tantrums lasted forever, it seemed. I'd tantrum four or five hours at a time. I'd scream, swear, and call people names. I hit stuff and sometimes hit people. I wanted them to pay attention to me. Finally, after therapy, I got it. I got that I could control my temper."

Violence can arrive with any age child. It is common at the Attachment and Bonding Center of Ohio where I work to counsel very young children exhibiting aggression. Many are international adoptees. Again, the child deprived of affection and attention may not know how to show love.

Brothers and sisters will resent the child that moves into the home and harms them and their parents. Understandable is their total ire for the chaos that reigns as a result of these behaviors. Guilt may crop up as well.

Kyle, born to his family, was age eight when he witnessed his sister hitting and kicking his mother. Suddenly, Mom shrieked with pain. Abigail had broken his Mom's thumb! He asked himself, "Why did I just stand there watching? Why didn't I do more to help Mom?"

Youngsters immobilized by fear or those kids too young to help Mom carry these images of family violence for a long time to come, as well as their shame for "letting it happen." Reiterating a point made earlier in this chapter, children blame themselves for "bad" things.

The feelings express

The culmination of changes post-adoption creates strong feelings for the resident brothers and sisters. The common challenges create a multitude of losses for the children already in the family at the time of the adoption. Loss results in emotional responses. Summarizing the losses we have explored thus far, these include loss of parental time and attention, privacy, family resources, a peaceful family, space, a safe environment, happy parents/happy emotional home climate, family as it existed, changes in relationships with peer and extended family, birth order, learning about the "world" in a developmentally appropriate way, the brother or sister expected.

The feelings associated with these losses can be triggered by everyday ordinary situations. For example:

> George, a typically developing 11-year-old, was waiting at the baseball field. His mother was late again! Ever since the family adopted Grace, his mother was always late. George became angry. "Why did my parents adopt her? She is nothing but trouble. I want my 'old' family back."
>
> When his mother did arrive, George got in the car and slammed the door. He sat in the back seat with his arms folded and his head down. He didn't utter a word the entire drive home. His mother wondered, "Why is he so mad? I am only a few minutes late." While driving home she admonished George, "There is no reason to slam the car door, young man! You only had to wait ten minutes! When I was your age, we walked or rode our bikes. You need to learn to appreciate the ride!"

In reality, George's mother being late reminds George of the changes that have occurred in the family since Grace moved in. His anger is for the loss of the calm, peaceful, and punctual family that existed before Grace.

Chapters 8–13 will point out ways to keep kids like George and his parents on the same page with regard to what is going on in the heads and hearts of the children already in the family at the time of the adoption. Mothers and fathers will learn ways to facilitate the expression of the intense feelings that rise up and brim over, further dampening the home atmosphere.

Ambivalence: "What were my parents thinking?"

Typically, the early days, weeks, or months after the new arrival arrives is the "honeymoon" (Pinderhughes and Rosenburg 1990). This is usually a good period in which everyone is happy with the special addition. However, if the adoptee's problems don't fade, there is anxiety about the long-term state of the family. The culmination of the "common challenges" is ambivalence. While it is a "normal" part of the post-adoption process for parents, brothers, sisters, and the adoptee, it is tumultuous time. Parents ask themselves, "What have we done to our family?" "We can't handle this!" "This isn't fair to our other children." "Why didn't anybody tell us it was going to be like this? What are we going to do?"

A shrinking support system, bizarre behaviors, diminishing family fun, questions galore, parents at conflict, and more challenges cause the brothers and sisters to think:

- "Well, my life sucks now. On the other hand, I have certainly had it better than my sister."

- "I would never get away with the things she does. Why are my parents letting her act like that?"

- "They spend more time with her. Do they love her more?"

- "This kid is a lot of trouble. Maybe we shouldn't keep him."

- "I don't like to see my parents fighting. Are they going to get a divorce?"

- "She treats my family poorly. She should appreciate my family more. Why doesn't she?"

- "I don't like my new sister much anymore. I feel guilty for not liking my sister."

- "Did Mom and Dad make a mistake?"

- "What were Mom and Dad thinking when they decided to adopt?"

The birth and/or previously adopted children are no longer certain about their parents' abilities, their feelings for the newcomer, or their own place in their parents' lives. These are scary issues for a kid! Parents, grappling with their own anxiety, often overlook the ambivalence of their sons and daughters. Each member of the family begins to cope as best as he or she can. Yet the coping styles may not be preferable.

"I'm coping the best I can"

It shouldn't be surprising that the birth and/or previously adopted children struggle to cope with the adoptee and the changes that arrived with him or her. Parents report great challenges dealing with children with traumatic histories. One adoptive dad wrote:

> "Nothing works! We've tried it all! He won't sit in time-out. He won't stay in his room. He doesn't miss his electronics or anything else for that matter. He earns a reward but two days later he lies again. Right before he earns the reward, he blows the whole system. We've told him a thousand times to brush his teeth, get his backpack, and turn in his homework. Every day we tell him the same things over and over. I tell him, again and again, 'You won't have friends until you stop being so bossy.' Five minutes later he's back outside demanding that the other kids play what he wants to play."

Stymied as time passes and the hurt child continues to exhibit the same patterns of behaviors, parents run out of steam. Brothers and sisters do too! The kids had less ability to cope going into the adoption than did the adults. For pre-school and school-age children in particular, they haven't matured to an age at which they have formed solid ways of coping. Thus, they run out of ideas long before their parents. They settle into several coping styles that are ineffective and unhealthy. Mothers and fathers are encouraged to discern these manners of coping. They are signs that your resident sons and daughters need your help.

The withdrawn child

Certainly all children enjoy spending time in their bedrooms, being with their friends, or participating in extracurricular activities. Subsequent to an adoption, the family's birth and/or previously adopted children may increase the time spent away from the family.

They begin eating dinner separately, requesting to go to friends' homes weekend after weekend, and joining activities they never before expressed any interest in.

"I would try to help out as much as I could. But I also got involved in a lot of activities so that I wouldn't have to be around the disruption. I got involved in so many things. I got involved in volleyball and I had never played volleyball before in my entire life. I got involved in the dance team and student government. I worked 20 hours per week. When I wasn't working, I went out places so that I didn't have to go home, even though I wanted to go home because I felt guilty not being involved with home life as much as I should. I would think, 'Well, my parents have to deal with it.' I wanted to help, but I didn't want to have to be around the conflict."

This situation may be a reflection of the sadness felt regarding the changes in the family. This may be an effort to escape the growing level of conflict. Whatever the reason, though, the child's withdrawal often generates guilt. The resident child feels at fault for not making more effort to help the parents heal the hurting child.

The self-sacrificing child

This child carries out all parental requests, completes extra chores, makes wonderful grades, and may be very involved in and excel at sports, student government, and church activities. Parents may find themselves making such comments as "She never gives us any problems" or "He does so much to help out. We never have to ask him to do his chores." As parents are so grateful to have this cooperation, the self-sacrificing coping pattern often goes unrecognized. This child is attempting to "make up" for the difficulties caused by the child who joined the family via adoption. This child perceives the parents as being under so much stress that she does not want to add additional strain.

The acting-out child

Pent-up anger and resentment may be expressed through negative behaviors. The typically developing child becomes disrespectful, violates rules, begins to demonstrate poor academic performance, and/or changes her peer group. He may believe that the way to obtain parental attention is to replicate the negative behaviors displayed by his traumatized brother or sister.

> Jeremy is six years old. His brother, Karl, was adopted four years ago. Karl is now eight years old. Jeremy stated, "When Mom and Dad tell Karl that he can't have something, look out! There will be big fight! Karl will throw things and call my mom names." Jeremy could be talking about himself as well since he mimics Karl's behavior. He is quite clear that Mom and Dad "have to pay more attention when me or Karl acts bad."

The regressed child

This coping style is common among toddlers, pre-school-age children, and children in grade school. Younger children who are under stress frequently regress to earlier developmental stages. For example, behaviors such as temper tantrums, thumb-sucking, or bed-wetting re-appear in otherwise healthy children when a troubled child joins the family.

The "I'll cover for you" child

Resident children may conceal or cover up the negative behavior of their adopted brother or sister. Parents kept in the dark in this manner lack understanding of the depth of the adoptee's problems, so precious time is lost before obtaining services. This can revictimize the child with a traumatic past. While brothers and sisters may be attempting to decrease the anger level in the family, the new child is likely to be confused about the difference between *sympathy* and *empathy*. The resident child may "feel sorry" for her adopted sibling: "My life was so much better than yours. I'll keep quiet. I don't want you to have any more problems." The more helpful, empathic response would be "I'm so sad you destroyed my CD player. I will be telling Mom and Dad. I do hope you learn to make better choices."

Helen, a 15-year-old, resides in her family of origin with her adopted brother and sister—Willie, age 12, and April, age ten. Helen and April get along well. April loves it when Helen helps her with her homework or teaches her how to sew. Willie, on the other hand, is quite difficult. He waits for the girls at the top of the steps and then jumps out and punches them in the stomach. At night, he enters April's room. He stands at the side of her bed. She is often startled awake by his presence. April and Helen are afraid of Willie.

April and Helen also feel sorry for Willie. He has no friends and he is often "in trouble" with Mom and Dad. Mom and Dad are so stressed the girls don't want to add another layer to their burdens. So they have kept Willie's aggression and night-time escapades a secret since they started several years ago. Willie's parents and his therapist have no idea that Willie exhibits these inappropriate behaviors. His therapeutic goals revolve around an increase in responsibility, such as completing chores and homework. Certainly, violence and scaring his sister are matters that should take precedence over whether Willie takes the garbage out on Tuesday mornings.

The victim child

This coping style results because the adoptee is abusing one or more of the appropriately developing children—emotionally, physically, or sexually. While some children are very quick to bring abuse to their parents' attention, other children, like April and Helen, keep the abuse a secret due to fear of the perpetrator or fear of the parents' reaction. These resident children are at risk of developing a victim mentality. Victims tend to see the control and responsibility for their situations as someone else's fault. Victims blame others for their circumstances. Victims accept little responsibility for their actions. Their sense of self is diminished or destroyed. They expect things will go wrong, thinking, "Bad things always happen to me." Victims develop a sense of entitlement—"The world owes me." They become disappointed and/or angry when they are not treated in a manner that supports their belief system. Immediate treatment is suggested for any family that learns about child-to-child abuse.

In conclusion, common challenges crop up post-adoption when the child with a traumatic past doesn't integrate into the existing family system as expected. Ambivalence, a "normal" stage in adoptive families, will result and prevail. This can be a time of turbulence. Parents question their decision to adopt and their parenting abilities— as do the resident children. Coping with the changes adoption has brought to the family proves challenging. Parents, brothers, and sisters run out of the energy needed to keep on a steady course. It is important to know that there are solutions to this particularly uneven, jarring time. There are ways to make the journey smoother. The remaining chapters offer the route to navigating relationships when new kids join the family.

Chapter summary

- Support shrinks post-placement. Extended family and friends can't relate well to the experiences of the family expanded by adoption. Intra-family relationships may suffer as well, as the new arrival begins to dominate the family time. Brothers and sisters often lack access to traditional types of help such as therapy and support groups. Mothers and fathers must hone their skills to parent their combination of traumatized and typical kids in a balanced manner.

- Giggles and chortles may be replaced by their negative counterparts—gloom, blues, and melancholy. Trauma fractured the adoptee's social skills and her ability and desire to engage in family fun. Brothers and sisters who hoped for a fun playmate are soon discouraged. The sibling that arrived is not the sibling expected.

- Transcultural adoption or the fact that the family composition now includes an adopted child casts the family in the public eye. Resident kids are bombarded with questions. They will need assistance to respond to the array of queries, questions, and glares that come at them from classmates, teachers, neighbors, and strangers.

- Fierce sibling rivalry, intensified parent conflict, bizarre behaviors, and more alter the emotional climate of the home.

School may no longer be a safe haven. Families that enjoyed peaceful camaraderie prior to the arrival of the newcomer may struggle to attain this level of happiness post-adoption.

• Safety and security may be jeopardized when the traumatized transplant brings with him sexual or aggressive behaviors. In these families, the level of vigilance needed to secure the well-being of each child in the family drains the family's energy tank dry. The typical kids—who wouldn't dream of hitting their parent or being sexual with a brother or sister— experience total shock at the happenings in the family. Guilt becomes a companion as well when these appropriately developing children believe they "should" be doing more to help Mom and Dad keep themselves safe and manage the adopted sibling.

• Thoughts of "What has happened to my family?" or "What were Mom and Dad thinking?" and "Is my sister ever going to learn to behave?" permeate the birth and/or previously adopted kids. Their anxiety about their new brother or sister and the changes in the family lend to coping styles that are ineffective—at home and in the world.

• "Common challenges" can be lessened or overcome. Mothers, fathers, sons, and daughters and the adoptee can navigate smoother, peaceful interactions.

7

"My Brother or Sister Won't be Living with Us Anymore"

DISRUPTION, DISSOLUTION, DISPLACEMENT, AND OTHER LEAVINGS

Most chapters in this book present families successfully navigating their adoptions in spite of an array of challenges. Tragically, this will not be the case with all adoptions.

Some children will leave the home in which they have been placed in expectation of adoption and go to another pre-adoptive or foster home prior to the finalization of the intended adoption. This is referred to as *disruption*.

Some children may require a treatment option that means living outside of the family temporarily—*a displacement*. There are instances in which displacement becomes a permanent living arrangement. The child may reside in residential treatment until the age of emancipation. In these cases, the family retains legal parental rights and responsibilities—the child still has a family.

In other instances, adoptive parents will legally terminate their already finalized adoption and forfeit all parental rights and responsibilities. This is the *dissolution* of an adoption. The custody of the child transfers to a public agency for purposes of finding another placement, or a new family may be privately located for the child. Others may abruptly leave the family after reaching the age of adulthood. These adoptees, unable to form an attachment to their adoptive parents and siblings, may return to their birth family, take up residence with a boyfriend or girlfriend, or go on to live with another family.

These types of leavings are emotionally charged situations for all involved. The child with a history of trauma may once again be without a place to call home. The adoptive parents and brothers and sisters have their dreams shattered and experience a loss akin to the death of a child and sibling. Those left behind also feel a sense of failure.

Sometimes there is anger and outrage toward the family from their own friends and family, from some other adoptive families, and even from some adoption professionals. Parents, sons, and daughters experience a lack of support at a challenging time.

This chapter explores the various ways the adoptee may leave the family. Content will offer ideas about helping the brothers and sisters cope when their sibling won't be living in the family anymore or while receiving treatment.

When parents make the decision for an adoptee to leave the family

Most parents make the decision for their son or daughter to leave the family after a continuum of efforts and services have been exhausted. These families have worked hard to locate and participate in various therapies. They have made vast efforts to alleviate the adoptee's trauma residue, his fears about intimate relationships and/or fantasies of returning to his birth family.

> Joan and her sister Faith were adopted by Margo and Jay at ages four and one and a half, respectively. By age eight, Faith was developing well. Joan, on the other hand, by age 11, had been aggressive since her arrival in the family. Joan had suffered two and a half years of physical abuse at the hands of her birth father. When she arrived in foster care, she was bruised from head to toe, and there was evidence that she had sustained at least one broken bone. This seemed to instill in Joan a pattern of violent behavior that has been irreversible to date.

She has always pushed and shoved to try to get her way. She punched kids time and time again. She broke a boy's glasses. She hit another child with a stick, and he had to go to the hospital for stitches. She often tried to trip Faith as she came down the stairs.

Over her years with Margo and Jay, Joan participated in individual therapy, family therapy, special education services, psychiatric services, occupational therapy, speech therapy, and two psychiatric hospitalizations. She was moved from a small classroom for children with behavioral problems to a day treatment program. Margo and Jay implemented every type of behavior modification suggested by all professionals with whom they consulted. Ultimately, exhausted and concerned for the safety of Faith and other children, they agreed that placing Joan in a treatment facility was necessary.

Joan, at age 14 and a half, entered the Christian Youth Home. This displacement has now lasted two years. Margo, Jay, and Faith visit Joan frequently. They continue to participate in therapy. They supply clothes and special personal items. Overall, they remain her family, yet it is debatable whether Joan will ever return home. She continues her pattern of assaultive behavior.

Certainly, Joan's parents accepted a commitment and continue to maintain their parental obligations to Joan. I have provided services to many families like Margo and Jay who only as a *very last resort* displace, disrupt, or dissolve their adoption of a physically or sexually abusive child. They do so with their hearts wrenched. Yet they also do so knowing that "home" needs to be a place of safety and security for everyone who lives there. Regardless of Joan's past trauma, abuse of family members is unacceptable. Just as an abusive spouse needs to leave the home, so do abusive children.

Yet there are other cases in which the option to terminate the placement is implemented quickly and with little or no professional assistance:

Rosie spent birth through age five in Eastern European orphanages. She was then adopted by an American couple, who had several young adult birth children. Within nine months, this family opted to dissolve their adoption of Rosie. The rationale was due to aggressive behavior, defiance, and an inability to play nicely with peers. They located a family and privately completed the legal transfer of parental rights. This phenomenon is currently being referred to as "re-homing" or "re-placement." In her new family, Rosie has a mom, a dad, and a typically developing brother, Eban, age seven. Eban was adopted as an infant.

Rosie herself writes of her experiences:

"When I was in the orphanage, I felt sad because the other kids got adopted and I didn't. I thought it was because something was wrong with me.

"When I got adopted, I thought it was going to be fun because in the orphanage it was not fun. When I got adopted, I was afraid of them getting rid of me. I was kind of afraid of learning a new language because I thought people would make fun of me.

"When I met my new parents, I was happy and scared because I was wondering if they would keep me and be nice to me.

"You might be wondering if it [living with my family] was fun. Well, sometimes it was fun. The bad part was that sometimes you will never find out who your birth mom is. The good part was if you found her. My brother Eban found his birth mom. We visit her once every year.

"The hardest part of being a new family member is getting used to all the rules and getting to know people. The other hard part is loving them, because you don't know if they will get rid of you.

"When I found out I was moving to another family—a second family—it just broke my heart. I felt sad because I had faith in my first parents. When I met my new family—Jill and Peter—I felt happy. My biggest challenges in my new home was showing love and giving love.

"I was afraid of this new family because it was really hard letting go of the other family—the first family—because you thought they loved and cared about you but they didn't. If your child is threatening to do bad stuff, don't call the police, just have them talk about their feelings or take them to a therapist. My second mom and dad took me to Arleta's. I did not like her at first, but if you do what is right, you can fix the problem."

At present, Rosie is doing extremely well. She has come to accept her first family as the conduit to ending her bleak orphanage life and as the means to finding her "forever" family. Yet, certainly, her struggles could have been lessened had her first adoption been successful.

Prior to a disruption, dissolution, or displacement, parents are encouraged to do some serious soul searching. Questions such as the following need to be explored:

- If my birth child was acting this way, would I move her? Why do I view the adoptee differently?

- Have we truly given this child enough time to adequately adjust and integrate into our family?

- Are we certain that this isn't a temporary crisis?

- Are we moving the child because he isn't meeting *our* needs?

- Have we fully examined (with an objective adoption professional) our original and current expectations? Were they and are they realistic?

- Have we truly attempted to attach to this child, even if the child is rejecting?

- Have we sought every possible avenue of formal (therapeutic) and informal (peer) support?

- Have we made efforts to educate ourselves?

- Have we worked to implement a variety of parenting techniques?

- Would altering our lifestyle (e.g. moving to a smaller, less expensive home to lower our mortgage and thus provide money for therapeutic services or provide a stay-at-home parent) help our child?

- Are we blaming an agency for our troubled adoption, or are we accepting our role in our current situation?

- Have we given consideration to the aftermath? What will happen with each of us after the child leaves? How will the other children in our home be affected?

The adoptee leaves the home: The impact on brothers and sisters

Just as the decision to adopt a child and that child's arrival and presence impacted each member of the adoptive family, so will the adoptee's leaving affect parents, brothers and sisters, and the adoptee.

Consider this: the adoptee must deal with being abandoned again. The pain of another rejection stings and reopens the old wounds of previous losses of birth family and possibly other caregivers. He must move on to another family, or he must return to a foster home or a placement in a facility. He gets very little time to mourn before he is expected to form new relationships, go to school, and participate in extracurricular activities.

Parents must grieve a child. There are now four places at the dinner table instead of five. A birthday passes with no celebration. A bedroom is empty. Months later, a toy found in the back of a closet is a reminder of the child who once called the parents "Mom and Dad." Anger, sorrow, frustration, guilt, despair, confusion, and many other emotions plague these families, often for years after the adoption ends.

Brothers and sisters must cope with the loss of their sibling. Following is an overview of several pertinent issues to keep in mind when a brother or sister experiences the dissolution, displacement, or disruption of a sibling.

"Where is my sibling going?"

This first question requires that someone explain to the children remaining in the family where the adopted sibling will be living.

WHEN THE SIBLING IS GOING TO A TREATMENT FACILITY

Residential treatment, a group home, a specialized boarding school, a specialized adoption-competent ranch—these are living arrangements unfamiliar to most typically developing children.

Consistent with earlier advice, clear and honest explanations need to be offered. If some type of residential treatment is the option, information about the facility can be printed from the Internet and shared with the birth and/or previously adopted children. Parents can explain their view on what the treatment center has to offer and why they feel it may be helpful for the sibling to live there. Once the troubled adoptee is settled, it is likely that a tour can be arranged. Older children often benefit from meeting the staff. Adolescents can sit in on treatment team meetings or an occasional therapy session.

Recently, in setting up a meeting for a 12-year-old currently residing in a treatment facility due to running away and fire-setting, her 17-year-old sibling asked to participate. During the meeting, she listened attentively and asked numerous questions. She provided insight about her sister. After the meeting she stated:

> "It was hard to hear all of the things that are wrong with my sister. I mean, I know that they are true. It is still hard to hear. But I am happy I got to be a part of the meeting. I know there are a lot of nice people really trying to help her. I feel better about this whole situation now."

The same open exchange of information is recommended when discharge of the adoptee is planned. If the adoptee had been unsafe or abusive, the resident kids especially need to know that a safety plan has been developed and what it entails. The typically developing children also need help recognizing that their traumatized sibling is not likely "fixed." These kids ask, "Is she going to be all better?" Progress may have been made. However, the adoptee, brothers, sisters, and parents still have much ground to cover to become a family. Certainly, there are cases in which the troubled adoptee returns home only to resume her previous harmful ways. Subsequently, this child may again depart to a treatment facility or the parents may then decide to terminate the adoption.

When the adopted sibling is
MOVING TO A NEW FAMILY

If the move is to be permanent, parents should expect immediate queries from siblings such as "Who is this new family?" or "How do we know they are safe?"

Regarding "Who is this new family?" often the two families meet. This openness quells many fears the children remaining in the family have about their sibling's new family.

Ben was adopted at age two from Guatemala. After years of various therapies, evaluations, special education services, medication, an array of parenting strategies, and much discussion and prayer, Tanner and Erica opted to dissolve the adoption when Ben was nine years old.

Ben's sexual behaviors had become more than they could deal with. He masturbated incessantly. This sexual stimulation had been present upon his arrival on American soil. As time passed, he attempted to lie on top of other neighborhood children. He talked about wanting to "rape" these kids and his cousins. Many children feared Ben. He could only go outside if an adult was present. He wandered the house at night. Tanner and Erica's birth son, Matt, age 12, often awoke to find Ben standing next to his bed. Door alarms had to be installed to curtail this behavior. Matt often stated that he felt as if he "lived in a jail."

Ben's new family had two sons, whom they had also adopted through adoption dissolutions. The two families opted for a first pre-placement visit at a restaurant. Lunch went well. The new couple brought many photos of their family. Their home was lovely, and they had a large yard. They loved going to the beach. They had two Irish Setters. The best part for Matt was when the new mom said, "Our other sons had brothers and sisters too. They still email and call once in a while. In the summer, we arrange a long weekend visit. We'll all talk about this and see what works out for you."

At present, Matt remains in contact with Ben. He is comforted knowing that Ben is safe and is doing okay. Ben is happy that his "old family" hasn't forgotten him and that they "aren't mad at me."

Most children benefit from knowing where their sibling is going. Many children fare better from ongoing contact. Contact with brothers and sisters can occur on a continuum. Many children are satisfied with just knowing how the former sibling is doing. This information can be obtained by the parents and passed on to the resident brothers and sisters. Others want letters, email, current photos, phone calls, an occasional Facebook™ post, or a face-to-face visit.

There are cases in which this continuing interaction creates stress. The adopted brother or sister may still not be placed in a "forever" family. He or she may be incarcerated. These types of living arrangements cause grief because the implication is "My sibling isn't doing well" or "My sibling doesn't have a family." This is especially true when the family adopted a sibling group, and the child that left the home is a birth sibling to others kids remaining in the adoptive family. There are also instances in which the sibling was sexually or physically abusive. In these cases, mothers and fathers need to weigh the benefits of contact versus the emotional strain and determine which is best. Overall, moms and dads can decide the level of contact based on what is safe and what makes sense.

Responding to questions from others

Expect that the sons and daughters remaining at home will be asked many questions as fellow school students, Sunday school classmates, youth group members, the next-door neighbor, the bus driver, the lady at the convenience store, and so on realize that they haven't recently seen the adopted sibling.

Parents, brothers, and sisters will likely be asked a myriad of questions when a dissolution, displacement, or disruption occurs. Parents will need to settle on a way to tell friends and relatives about their decision to move the adoptee out of the family. The birth and/ or previously adopted children will also need some help responding to the queries posed by kids and adults. They will need a "cover story."

> When Matt's adopted brother was "re-homed," his parents were so grief-stricken that they didn't even think about Matt's school friends inquiring about what had happened to Ben.
>
> Matt, a very resourceful young man, said, "I just tell them we had to 'unadopt' him because he wasn't working out. He needed a different family and 'we found him a good one.'"
>
> According to Matt, his classmates seemed to accept his answer. Quickly, the discussion turned to baseball or the upcoming math test.

In another case, the family's neighborhood was comprised of many homes lined along blocks. The kids, from streets away, all knew each other. Several youngsters had already noticed that Diana's brother hadn't been out to play in weeks. He was also absent from school. Diana's parents sought professional assistance. This mental health guide had experience with adoption dissolution. She was able to help them think clearly.

They first sorted out who was already aware of their decision to dissolve their adoption and who wasn't. Then they listed those people they would see regularly, and who, as such, would notice and require an explanation. It is helpful to think about how many people may ask questions and in what situations. Parents and kids are better able to respond when they are prepared for what may be coming when they arrive at church, their favorite restaurant, school, a sporting event, the community pool, and so on.

The actual explanation was compiled by sifting through what was "private" and what could be shared. Ultimately, the family prepared the following response:

> "Sadly, Vic had behaviors that were not safe for Diana. After much advice from professionals, it was uncertain that his problems could be alleviated. As such, we felt it necessary to ensure Diana's safety. It was a profoundly difficult decision. However, we are at peace with the decision. We have no hard feelings toward Vic. His past was just too great for him to overcome. We will always miss him and continue to pray for him. He is living with another family at this time."

This statement was mailed or verbally stated to those it was necessary to inform or to those who asked. From this, Diana opted to extract her own statement:

> "My brother had a lot of serious problems. So he went to live with another family who can take care of him. I miss him a lot, but this is safer for our family."

Diana was also offered the choice of simply saying, "I would prefer you ask my mom and dad. It's too hard for me to talk about." This deferring to the parents is always an option for the children who remain in the home.

It must be kept in mind that brothers and sisters' responses—cover stories—will most likely be met with shock or with silence. Few of their peers will be able to relate to losing a sibling in this manner. In such instances, parents and professionals could consider connecting these brothers and sisters to other children whose families have experienced a displacement, disruption, or dissolution. In Diana's case, she continued on in therapy and she was introduced to another youngster who had experienced a sister leaving the home. The two find each other comforting.

All too frequently, families such as Matt's or Diana's are left alone to deal with the aftermath of a child leaving home. Busy professionals move on to other cases. The case worker may feel guilty and thus withdraw from their previous relationship with the family. Adversarial relationships cause a "You made the decision so you'll have to deal with it" reaction from some professionals, family members, and friends. Or well-meaning friends and family members stifle grief with comments such as "Well, it was for the best," "Now you can move on," or "She was never right for your family."

Actually, it takes little time and effort to extend some empathy to these parents and children. We need to offer some guidance about managing and coping with the aftermath.

Bobbie and Amber, currently ages 11 and 14 respectively, were the brother and sister to nine-year-old Sam. Sam arrived at age five after spending five years in an Eastern European orphanage. He very recently left the family to join a new adoptive family (dissolution).

Amber writes, "I wanted a girl and expected it to be more like it was with my biological brother. I wanted her to admire me like Bobbie did for a while and help her grow when she became a teenager like I am now. I learned he was a brother when my parents emailed a picture from their hotel abroad.

"Instead, we lost our typical routine and normal lifestyle. We had a decrease in fun activities and *definitely* lost time with our parents.

"We had no preparation. We knew some of the children available had a disability (medical or physical) but we didn't know anything about the problems Sam had. He painted my bedspread, took food in his closet which grew mold, tried to have sex with my brother, made sexual comments to friends and cousins—which made it difficult to have friends over—stole change, and broke whatever was important to me.

"Our parents divorced after he came. It was so hard to go to visits at my dad's house because Sam would demand all the attention. The visits were ruined. I stopped going. Eventually, he moved to my dad's house until a new family was found for him.

"I am feeling mad, sad, frustrated, confused, and guilty. I also wonder if I will ever see him [Sam] again."

Bobbie says, "I also expected another sister—the perfect little sister who would look up to me.

"No, no, no—I got no preparation. I have a list of losses—friends, family, stuff, privacy, time with parents, feeling safe, peace, fun, and on and on.

"I tried to cope by talking to people I trust and when I really needed a break I tuned the world out with music whether it was playing it, listening to it, or writing lyrics. I also wrote in a journal in a poem format because poems help me express my feelings.

"I have a lot of feelings! I feared saying much as I thought he [Sam] would harm me if he knew I was talking about him. I am most disappointed about the fact that I couldn't help my brother to become better than he is or help him learn. I reached out to him over and over. He didn't respond."

Would Mom and Dad give me away?

Nearly all children ages three to five years old have fears about being abandoned, getting lost, or no longer being loved by their parents. Loss of a sibling makes these fears seem all too real for children born to the family. Appropriately developing adopted children, already all too familiar with abandonment, are now watching their parents move a son or daughter out of the family. These children wonder, "Would Mom and Dad give me away?" "What would I have to do to be forced to leave the family?"

Parents may notice that these healthy kids regress or exhibit more fears after an adopted sibling moves. They may also engage in negative behaviors with increased frequency. Sometimes they begin repeating the exact behaviors of the child who is gone. This may especially occur if the siblings are related by birth.

At times, the birth sibling bond is stronger than the parent and child connection. Adopted birth siblings, then, will strive to be reunited. The rationale may be any of the following:

- *Loyalty*: "She is my birth sister. I belong with her."

- *A desire to contribute to the healing process*: "I have to help her. She is my 'real' sister."

- *Fear*: "We have never been separated. I am scared to be without her."

- The two (or more) siblings are connected by a *trauma bond*. The victim child is linked to the exploitive dynamics of the abusive child.

Thus, the adopted birth sibling still at home will begin to spiral out of control. Irrationally, this child believes that his destructive actions will cause him to go live with his traumatized birth brother or sister. The behavior of the adopted child who appeared healthy now plummets. His trauma has been triggered by the separation from his birth brother or birth sister.

It is important that parents be alert to any changes in their typical children. More so, it is critical that parents assure them of their place in the family—repeatedly! Adults must be clear in their explanations: "Vic left the family because he wasn't safe." "Joan left the family because she kept hurting people." "You are staying in the family because you are safe." "You don't hurt people." "In a family, everyone needs to be safe." Seek professional help if necessary. *This may be needed immediately in the case of separations involving birth siblings.*

In addition to the points above, typically developing children may need parental and/or professional help to resolve the immense feelings that accompany the leaving of a sibling. The subsequent solution chapters (beginning with Chapter 8) offer ways to help youngsters express feelings for all types of changes that occur in families built by adoption.

"I'm 18!" When the adoptee makes the decision to leave the family

Passing from childhood to adulthood brings with it the expected tasks of leaving home and becoming a productive and independent member of society. Gaining independence includes such social markers as attending college, trade or technical school, service in the armed forces, or getting a job—developing a career or skill. Then there is moving to an apartment and working toward home ownership. Dating, marriage, and having children—preferably in this order—are other adult goals to be accomplished. Perhaps there is also a desire to fulfill an element of social responsibility through community involvement in one's neighborhood or society at large.

In healthy families, parents and children look forward to retaining close, intimate ties throughout adulthood. Whether children settle near their parents or far away, parents and siblings want contact via phone, email, social media, visits on special occasions, or simply to be with one another. Family members hope to receive support, assistance, encouragement, praise, motivation, congratulations, and so on from one another. The family is to be a buttress during bad times and the spot to celebrate joyous events.

The young adult with a history of trauma may struggle at age 18 and beyond. His launching—the process in which youths move into adulthood and exit their family—without cutting off ties completely or fleeing the family totally may not be smooth or happen along a contrived timeline. A successful launch into adulthood will be contingent upon the adoptees':

- level of attachment between himself and his parents, brothers, and sisters

- resolution and/or management of the early trauma—abandonment, neglect, and/or abuse

- possible substance abuse issues

- capacity to seek and maintain a job

- ability to access and utilize resources (life skills programs, mental health services, drug rehabilitation programs, Vo-Tech programs, etc.).

The manner in which she transitions into adulthood can impact her as well as her brothers, sisters, and parents. Unfortunately, many adoptees with traumatic pasts do leave the family in chaotic and destructive ways. Their potentially bright future was snuffed out early in life, prior to joining the adoptive family:

> Joel, adopted at age four, is now 24. He had various behavioral difficulties through the age of 21 which culminated with selling and using cocaine. Sitting in a jail cell at 19, he realized that his life was "going nowhere." Fortunately, he was court-ordered to drug rehab. He also received community service and probation. At age 23, he entered college. He successfully completed his freshman year and is looking forward to being a sophomore. He frequently reflects back on the person he "used to be" and appreciates that he "got it" and that his parents remain supportive and available.

> Margo, adopted at a young age, became a teen mother at 16. She had an on-and-off-again relationship with Curt, the baby's father, over the next two years. At 18, she decided that she wanted to "make a go of it" with Curt and so the two got a place of their own.

> Curt is a rather unsavory character in Margo's parents' eyes. He goes from dead-end job to dead-end job. Margo often calls home for help to care for her toddler son. Frequently, Margo and Curt fight and Margo returns home. Then Curt apologizes and she goes back to him. This cycle has been occurring for four years.

> Her parents and siblings encourage Margo to think more of herself; to believe that she can do better than Curt. At this time, Margo continues to reside with Curt.

> April had been a pleasant child from age two through age 14. Her adoption brought her parents great joy. April and her older sister got along famously. Georgia, April's senior by one year, and April were inseparable. They did everything together.

> At 14, April began to deteriorate. Her bright smile faded. She withdrew from the band and athletic endeavors. She no longer enjoyed going to the mall with Georgia on the weekends.

Then April became interested in boys. Boys called the house at all hours of the evening and early morning. April sneaked out her bedroom window. Sometimes she was gone the entire weekend. When she did arrive back home, she refused to discuss her whereabouts. She stomped to her room and slammed the door.

Eventually, at age 17, she began going steady with Darrell. Abruptly, she left the family to move in with Darrell. She has remained in his home, with his family, for several years now. She has refused to talk to her adoptive family or to visit.[1]

Steven, a difficult adoptee, exited the family at age 20, after a huge fight with his father. Refusing to comply with curfew for the "umpteenth" time, his father said, "If you don't like it here, you can move." With that, Steven did. He has opted to have little contact with the family.

Harry was adopted from foster care at age five. He had many memories of the domestic violence that occurred between his birth mom and her paramours. He carried with him a strong desire to return to her, to help and protect her. At 19, he fulfilled this desire. He found her and he spent the next few years working and supporting her. He tried and tried to get her to seek help—to no avail.

He realized that he couldn't continue in this lifestyle. He kept hearing his adoptive parents' voices: "You can choose to live your life however you want." "You are very bright. You can be whatever you want." "Our door will always be open for you." Tentatively, he called home. After some discussion and meetings with his parents, he moved back home. Harry will graduate from technical school next year. He now enjoys close relations with his mom, dad, and brother.

---

1   April is known in the adoption therapy community as a *sleeper*. This is a child whose adoption and/or abuse issues are not obvious or go undetected for years. Because the child often functions so well in early childhood and grade school, it is assumed that the child is resilient and her past has had no impact—it is but water off a duck's back. No one sees the need to discuss it or to create a lifebook when there are no "obvious" issues. But then the adolescent task of identity development triggers the trauma and abandonment. Overwhelmed, the child deteriorates. When this occurs, it is most commonly around the age of 13 or 14, but can also happen in later adolescent years.

These scenarios demonstrate that the adoption journey doesn't always culminate in the manner expected or desired, or as established by arbitrary societal standards, when the child experienced early trauma. Overall, relationships with such young adult adoptees may fall along a continuum from close to severed or be of an on-again-off-again nature.

Younger and older resident siblings will be full of questions when the now adult adoptee unexpectedly leaves the family: "Doesn't he like us anymore?" "Why is he living with another family? Did we do something wrong?" "Will he go to jail?" "How long will he be in jail?" "Is he safe?" "Will he come back?" "Is he even going to visit us?" "Why didn't he even say goodbye?" "What should I say to my friends?" "Why does he want to live with his birth family? I thought we were his family." Many of these queries may not have immediate answers for mothers, fathers, brothers, or sisters.

There will be emotional devastation when the adoptee walks away from the family, barely looking back or not keeping in touch at all. The same feelings of guilt, sadness, failure, anger, and frustration occur as when parents make the choice to move their adopted child on. Either way, the dreams of "happily ever after" are crushed. Brothers, sisters, and parents experience the loss of a son, daughter, or sibling. Here is a sentiment expressed by Craig, a typically developing brother, currently age 15, in a family expanded by the adoption of older kin children:

> "My parents adopted my cousins, Sam and Kyle, when they were nine and 11. They are now 21 and 23. At first, I was excited—I would have two more brothers! I already had two so now there would be five of us. Sometimes it was fun. Boy, other times the fights were huge!
>
> "This year, Sam just moved out one day. He didn't tell anybody. He did it when we weren't home. He hardly calls. He almost never returns my calls. Right now, I hate him. I absolutely hate him. We took him in and gave him all kinds of things. Things he would never have had with his own parents. Then he just turns around and screws us!"

Dreams of grandchildren, nieces, and nephews fade. Recently Daryl, a 21-year-old young adult adoptee, appropriately developed, stated:

"I watch my parents with their brothers and sisters at Christmas, Thanksgiving, and summer barbecues. They laugh and joke. They hug. I love spending time with my cousins. They are among my best friends. I know that I'm not going to have this kind of adult interaction with my sister and brother, and that my children probably aren't going to have fun and relationships with their cousins. It is so disappointing. I was so excited when my parents adopted them. But I'm coming to realize that they're never going to be normal."

At this time, he is correct. His sister, at 23, has abruptly left the family and his brother, at 17, is already fighting a drug addiction.

Some parents, brothers, and sisters find that they can adjust their values and the yardstick by which they measure success in order to sustain long-term connections with a troubled adoptee. For example, in the case of Margo described earlier, her parents were not happy with her untimely pregnancy or her choice of partner. However, they have come to recognize that Margo is an attentive mother. She nurtures her son, and she reaches out for help to make sure that he has what he needs. She far more closely mirrors her adoptive mom and dad as a parent than she does her birth mother. Her parents also want to look out for her son—their grandchild and the nephew to their resident children. So they have opted to continue to model positive relationships. They help, yet they don't enable. For example, assistance is offered in the form of diapers or food, or they may pay a bill directly. Assistance is never in the form of cash that Curt may blow on things for himself. This family has found a way to support their daughter/sister and grandson/nephew, and enjoy the positive aspects of her personality and lifestyle.

Overall, adoptive mothers and fathers will have to establish boundaries regarding the types of support they are willing to offer their adult son or daughter. Moms and dads will need to help the brothers and sisters in this area. It is quite common for the departed adoptee to contact the adolescents still at home. The purpose of such calls is to ask for money, belongings, the phone number of a friend on whose couch they can sleep, and so on. Family members may need to ask themselves:

- What are parents', brothers', and sisters' obligations and responsibilities to adult siblings? How long do family members carry out efforts on behalf of the adoptee? On behalf of any child, brother, or sister?

- Can family members draw boundaries between support and enabling as necessary? Support contributes to gains in development and responsibility. Enabling stymies growth.

- Incarceration, drug addiction, untimely pregnancy, and so on—what is the impact on the typical kids left behind? Parents worry, "How do we prevent our other children from following the example of the adoptee?" Again, in the case of Margo, her parents are still raising Margo's three younger siblings—their birth daughters. Margo's lifestyle has caused them to increase their communication about birth control and sexuality, managing finances, and other essential life skills. If the resident children are younger, parents must make extra efforts to encourage them to follow a different path to that of their older, troubled brother or sister. Provided that parents have maintained strong attachments to these children throughout the adoption experience, they will see the consequences of such actions and younger and older children alike will move along a more traditional route. Keep in mind that sons and daughters with healthy connections to their mothers and fathers mirror their parents' values.

Chapter summary

- Unfortunately, a small percentage of adoptions will end in disruption, displacement, or dissolution. The aftermath will include a backwash of grief for all members of the adoptive family.

- The typical brothers and sisters will emerge from the loss of a sibling, via disruption, dissolution, or displacement, better when provided honest and accurate information about where their sibling will be residing upon departing the family. The children remaining in the family need a "cover story" to best respond to the queries that will be posed as peers and adults realize that a child has left the family.

- Siblings—especially those connected by birth—are prone to strong attachments to each other. Frequently, when a sibling leaves the adoptive home, there is a desire to reunite with this brother or sister. Parents must be on the alert for this situation. Take note of the emotional state and the behavior of the remaining siblings carefully. Seek professional assistance quickly if there are negative changes in the functioning of the children you continue to parent.

- Young children and/or those children previously adopted by the family may experience anxiety post-disruption, dissolution, or displacement. They question, "Will Mom and Dad keep me?" "What would I have to do to make Mom and Dad give me away?" Mothers and fathers are encouraged to provide ample reassurance to these vulnerable kids regarding their permanent status in the family.

- The after-effects of the chaotic or unanticipated leaving of the now 18-year-old adoptee are similar to the reverberations caused when parents choose for a child to leave the family. Questions abound and grief flows. The additional issue is that of setting boundaries. Mothers and fathers must decide how to help their trauma-affected young adult. Adoptive parents must assist siblings in learning the difference between supporting and enabling as well.

- Throughout the adoption process, parents must care for their attachments to their healthy sons and daughters. Moms and dads want to strive for open communication that stresses the family values pertaining to substance abuse, marriage, sexual relationships, and other valuable life matters. Talking and keeping close parent–child connections will help the appropriately developing children follow the path to successful adulthood—no matter the behavior displayed by the adoptee. As previously pointed out, the attached child mirrors his or her parents. Reflect what you want to see your children imitate at all stages of their lives.

8

"Help Me Cope, Please"

STRIKING A BALANCE POST-ADOPTION

We have now reached content that offers ways for the adoption-formed family to "strike a balance"—meet the needs of each of their unique children. The ideas that follow—in this chapter and subsequent chapters—help resolve the challenges that commonly crop up post-adoption. These trials tend to tip the family's equilibrium in the direction of the adoptee. After the arrival of the traumatized child, time and resources are consumed healing this hurt child. Life revolves around the premise that once the adoptee with a history of trauma is "better," "fixed," or "healed," we will be a happy, peaceful family again. Adoptive family life goes on hold like planes circling an airport. Rather, families can move forward steadily—each son or daughter can flourish and thrive!

"I need support!" Parents as a primary means of support

Post-adoption support systems often shrink. Examples of this phenomenon were offered in previous chapters. Friends and extended family members drift away because they don't understand the issues faced by mothers, fathers, brothers, and sisters. The adoptee's chaotic ways interfere with the capacity to attend a party, a holiday gathering, and so on. The time involved in caring for the traumatized sibling separates the brothers and sisters from their parents. Soon after the adoption finalization, each family member is moving in different directions. Relational fractures occur among parents and their typical children.

Adoptive moms and dads need ways to guarantee that their resident children receive the care and nurture essential to maintain the strong attachments enjoyed pre-adoption. Healthy emotional connections ensure that each son and daughter can blossom. This chapter addresses the common challenge of making sure that brothers and sisters are supported amidst the post-adoption adjustment. Ideas are offered to keep parent–child bonds intimate.

Parents caring for themselves: Put your oxygen mask on first

I always think about adoptive parents when I'm on a plane. As the flight attendant states that adults should put their oxygen masks on first in the event of an emergency, I am reminded that parents truly help their kids survive and grow! Parents provide the primary means of support for all of their children.

Yet each mother or father has only so much energy. Energy is comparable to a tank of gas. There is a continuum from full to empty. Parents who top off their tanks frequently are better able to handle the day-to-day challenges of balancing their responsibilities than are parents who wait until the "almost empty" light comes on to tank up.

Keeping up energy requires that parents keep their tanks full— especially in the whirlwind of activity that everyday life seems to have become! There are no benefits to any sons and daughters when parents are worn out, exhausted, frustrated, overworked, stressed out, rushing from one place to the next, distraught, nervous, and in general just run down.

Some veteran parents are going to help us out with ideas as to how they have been able to "fill up" for themselves and their children.

CAROL, A PARENT OF FOUR—THREE BY BIRTH AND ONE BY ADOPTION

"This past Christmas I asked my family—my siblings, my parents, my aunts, and cousins—to pool all of the money they would have spent buying gifts for myself, my husband, and my children.

Instead of buying the traditional clothes, movies, or jewelry as gifts, I asked for a cleaning service. A few of my own siblings thought this was a bit different. But I really don't care. It's what I needed. I would do the same for them if they asked me. It totaled enough to have the house cleaned, from top to bottom, eight times!"

Carol is a great example of someone who can *ask for what she needs.* You don't have to do everything by yourself! Actually, you most likely can't without exhausting yourself. In passing this suggestion on to other families, another mom asked her family for gift certificates to restaurants, especially those with a delivery service—no traffic and no waiting in line. She now spends less time in the kitchen. No, she doesn't use the extra time to get something done. She relaxes!

HEATHER AND RAY PARENT FOUR CHILDREN— THREE BY BIRTH AND ONE BY ADOPTION

Heather says, "I used to organize some events at school like the spelling bee, bake sales, etc. Then, when Sam joined the family I thought I needed that time to be with him. Now I realize there is a compromise. Instead of organizing the event, I volunteer. It is a lot less time but still fulfilling."

Notice the word *compromise.* Too often, parents just stop doing pleasurable activities totally. Heather found the middle ground. Can you?

DENISE AND HER HUSBAND PARENT FIVE CHILDREN— TWO BIRTH/STEP-CHILDREN AND THREE ADOPTED KIDS

"The transportation to and from appointments, errands, and extracurricular activities was just a nightmare. I finally decided to ask two of my neighbors for help. They are retired. They were delighted to help out. I have free time now. I have returned to cooking some homemade meals. I have always enjoyed preparing food from scratch. My parents live out of town, so the neighbors are also like having another set of grandparents. I make sure to give them a gas gift card here and there. The kids help them shovel their walk and driveway in the winter—these things go along with riding in their car, and it saves these neighbors the money of paying someone to do it. I wish I had asked sooner."

Transportation is a time-consuming task. It is as if life is all conducted in the van these days. Time in the car does allow for conversation, and many kids seem to get their homework done while en route. However, there is the unproductive flip side of using the smart phone, popping a movie in the DVD player, and of course playing hand-held electronic games. Think about your car time. Is interaction occurring, or are you all together but each is actually doing his or her own thing? How can you change this?

TOM, AN ADOPTIVE FATHER OF THREE CHILDREN—ONE TYPICAL AND TWO IN THE PROCESS OF HEALING FROM TRAUMA

"Before the kids, I used to go to the gym every day. I enjoyed this immensely and felt good about myself. Once the kids came, this went by the wayside. I began getting depressed. I decided I needed to exercise, but I couldn't work out getting to the gym. So I bought a treadmill. In the long run, it is cheaper than paying the annual gym fees. I feel good again. When I get angry with the kids, it's a great way to release my frustration."

BOB, A FATHER OF FIVE—THREE CHILDREN BY ADOPTION AND TWO BY BIRTH

"We lived in a house with a large yard and a lot of landscaping needing lots of maintenance. We moved. We now have a large detached condo. I enjoy sitting on the deck watching the landscapers mow the yard and trim the shrubs. My wife and kids enjoy the clubhouse. The pool is open year round."

Over time, I have known many families who have made the decision to move. Some of the moves occurred due to the cultural composition of their family or to locate to a better school district. But other moves have occurred for reasons such as Bob described. Still other families have moved to lessen their mortgage payments. This means that Dad can stop working a 60-hour week and spend more time caring for himself and his children.

NINA, A PARENT OF TWO ADOPTED CHILDREN—
ONE BY BIRTH AND ONE ADOPTED

"Fortunately, my daughter by adoption doesn't mind going to her room. So, in the evening, she goes to her room 30 minutes earlier than my appropriately developing daughter. She doesn't have to go to sleep. She just needs to play in her room. This is my special time each day to be with my 'healthy' daughter. Sometimes we play a game, sometimes we talk, and sometimes we just watch a television show. Twice a month, they both go to their rooms an hour early. I use this time for me!"

ROBERT, A STAY-AT-HOME DAD, AND PARENT OF
TWO CHILDREN BY BIRTH AND ONE BY ADOPTION

"I use the Crock Pot™ a lot more. It is quick. It has definitely cut down on how much fast food we eat. Two nights per week, we use paper plates—no dishes and no arguments about who's going to do the dishes! Lessening the housework frees up time!"

LORRAINE AND PETER, THE PARENTS OF SEVEN
ADOPTED CHILDREN, ALL OF WHOM HAVE
VARYING DEGREES OF LEARNING DIFFICULTIES

Lorraine and Peter use a *divide and conquer* approach. She handles three of the children's academic needs while he handles the other four.

"The teachers are informed which parent is assigned to which child. We do their IEP meetings via telephone. The nice thing about cell phones is the speaker phone option. Our district also has Skype capacity. We can participate in a meeting from anywhere. We go once each year, for each child, in person, so the teachers can meet us and we can meet the teachers. After that, everything is by phone or Skype™. This saves a lot of travel and a lot of time off from work. We also limit the calls from the school to those involving actual emergencies. If we see their number on the caller ID, we know it is important and we need to answer. Otherwise, a note home will do. We also require that all permission slips, requests for cupcakes, anything the kids need to bring in for a project, etc. be mailed directly to us. That way, we don't find something in a backpack that requires we change our routine or plans at the last minute. The level of cooperation we receive from our school saves an immense amount of time!"

From early bedtime, to moving, to gift cards, to modern technology, there are ways to free up time. Planning, creativity, asking for help, setting limits, compromising, and establishing priorities are essential in gaining and maintaining the well-being that moms and dads will need to balance the combination of typical and traumatized sons and daughters.

Parents caring for their typical kids
START A HABIT: DATE BOOK REQUIRED

"It was a crazy time. I don't too much remember tenth grade pretty much. It just was. We used to go to school. I don't remember what we used to do there. I don't know what classes we took. I used to play basketball. That's what I would do. We all lost a big chunk of time."

Most frequently, the word "habit" is associated with something we want to break! However, I want you to start a habit! The habit is spending regular time with the children who were already in the family prior to the adoptee's arrival. I have rarely encountered a typically developing child—of any age—who does not mourn the loss of the parental time and attention that has been diverted to promote the healing of the adopted addition to the family. Resident children are often sacrificed as parents think, "We can make up the time once John is better" or: "The other children are more capable. They can do without as much time." These thoughts are misperceptions. For example, Roger, the adoptive father of two boys, one by birth and one by adoption, stated:

> "Initially when we brought Ray home (at eight months of age), I had a tendency to protect and nurture him more than my biological child, Vince (18 months old). I had deeply rooted feelings that he had been 'wronged' by his birth parents, through no fault of his own. I was determined to make up for this by giving him special attention. As time passed, I found that this caused jealousy with Vince. I honestly thought that Vince would understand why his adopted brother needed extra attention. I now see this was an impossible concept to expect Vince, currently age eight years old, to understand."

All children need time—in quality and quantity. Schedule "appointments" with your birth and/or previously adopted children. This is one habit I hope you never break!

"Our time with our parents was taken. My brother and my dad used to go golfing and every Sunday I used to go shopping or out to eat with my mom. We can't do this anymore because they take up so much time."

TONY AND MAUDE, PARENTS OF THREE CHILDREN— TWO BY BIRTH AND ONE BY ADOPTION

> "We live close to our jobs and our kids' school. We often surprise the kids by showing up to take them out to lunch. Sometimes, we spontaneously take them out of school for an afternoon to go do something special. While we value education, we value our time alone with our kids too. Our adopted child has many needs and this makes it difficult for us to go out as a family, or to go out without him, on weekends or evenings. Given the choice between social studies or time with the children, we choose time with the kids."

Acknowledge accomplishments

A mom once said to me:

> "My older healthy daughter has won numerous awards for
> academic excellence, athletic achievements, and community
> service. They sit on my desk collecting dust. I just can't seem to
> find the time to hang them up."

Shortly after this conversation, she was helped to find respite
services for her two adoptees, both of whom struggled due to the
institutionalization experienced in their early years of life. This gave
her the opportunity to spend time with her daughter framing her
awards. A celebratory dinner topped off this mother-and-daughter
day.

Parental recognition bolsters warm, pleasant feelings on the
child's part. Attending award ceremonies, sporting events, school
plays, choir performances, dance recitals, and so on are important
ways to show sons and daughters your pride and interest in them.

Children with histories of trauma don't always function well
on outings. Many adoptive mothers and fathers report needing to
alternate their attendance at special events. Now, parents have the
technological means to upload the winning touchdown or solo voice
performance to their co-parent at home. Again, the family expanded
by adoption must hone their ingenuity to strike a balance.

Simple requests: "All I want from my parents is…"

All kids have needs. As parents well know, all sons and daughters have
wants! Many of the "wants"—post-arrival of a troubled sibling—are
quite simple and far less expensive than the latest electronic gadget!
When asked, "What do you want to make life more enjoyable or
satisfying?" the appropriately-developing kids commonly respond, "I
want to be on time for basketball practice." "I want a birthday party
without my adopted brother home. He wrecks stuff like that." "I want
privacy." "I want some time alone." "I want a place to store important
things—something my sister can't get into. She steals my stuff. I just
hate it."

DIANE AND DAVE PARENT SIX CHILDREN—FOUR BY BIRTH AND TWO BY ADOPTION

> Dave said, "The two adoptees steal and they have no boundaries. We got each child a foot locker. Anything important gets locked in the foot locker. We also had a small room we used as a junk room. We got rid of the junk, gave it a fresh coat of paint and some furniture. This is now a space for anyone who wants to spend some time alone."

Certainly, parents won't be able to give their sons and daughters everything, but many of their requests can be fulfilled. By asking, parents convey that they know the family has changed in ways that lead to daily trials and tribulations. This acknowledgment helps brothers and sisters understand that mom and dad are paying attention, and they do care.

KEEP KIDS IN THE LOOP: INFORMATION IS A KEY SUPPORT

Libby, a healthy 14-year-old sister to several adoptees, says:

> "Keep communication open with your parents. Along through the adoption, kids should continue to talk to their parents and tell them how they are feeling, because a lot of times kids won't say anything—then the parents don't know. The parents don't focus on them because they are so focused on the disruptive child, and so kids need to let their parents know at all times what's going on, and if they have any questions, they always need to talk to their parents about it."

Cole and Becky, parents to three typical adopted daughters and one adoptee still in the process of healing from past traumatic experiences, carry out Libby's advice to "keep communication open":

> "Before Gabe's adoption we had been told that he had been a 'failure to thrive' baby. However, when we got to Guatemala there was much, much more involved than this failure to thrive. Little did we know that it was a lot of mental health issues that were lying ahead, and that he wasn't going to assume the same role as the other kids did in the family—he wasn't going to blend and adjust as quickly or maybe not at all.

"As we have identified his needs, we've had many family meetings about why he eats up so much of our time. Jennifer, Jessica, and Mary are well informed about his mental health diagnoses. We really believe in sitting the kids down and sharing information. We keep telling them that our goal is win-win, and that you're part of this too because you are in the family."

Cole and Becky conduct regular family meetings on the last Wednesday of the month. Gabe goes to his grandmother's for dinner while the rest of the family reviews the month over pizza. Topics include feelings, ongoing problems, potential solutions, facts about Gabe's special needs, and so on.

In a different scenario, a healthy brother once emotionally blurted out to his mother, "I have tried so hard to help him, but he just isn't getting better. I just don't know what else I should be doing. I feel like such a bad brother." Shocked, his parents quickly obtained professional assistance to help educate this young man about his brother's issues. Education and lots of conversations corrected this youngster's misperceptions.

Frank and Penney parent their resident son, Scott, adopted as an infant, as well as two siblings with a pre-adoptive history of sexual and physical abuse:

"We had a very short honeymoon period. Scott was having a hard time understanding why their behaviors were just so off the wall. We reviewed everything we knew about Marcus and Celeste. Scott is responsible, and we knew having information would help him in the long run, and it has—he has really benefited from these talks. We explained the types of abuse—physical and sexual—the children had experienced. We helped him understand why this abuse caused them to act so differently. It was a lot for a kid to handle. However, we kept working on it.

"Eventually, Scott figured out that Marcus often tries to agitate him to get his attention because he hasn't learned how to ask for what he needs or wants. The lying and their control issues are about their need to protect themselves. Marcus and Celeste don't trust us yet, so they don't believe we can take care of them and keep them safe. Scott has learned to ignore a lot of their behavior. Or we hear him say to Marcus, 'You don't have to throw things at me to get my attention. You could just ask me if I have time to play with you.'"

Scott has been able to understand why his new brother and sister act the way they do. He has learned effective ways to cope with his siblings-by-adoption.

When we keep kids in the information loop, we support them in their efforts to cope with the changes adoption has brought to their family. Information joins the family. As stated by Becky above, "We're all in this together." Uniting to move the family forward forges attachments in the family built by adoption.

A last point that needs to be made regarding education is the issue of privacy. Sharing the adoptee's history with the birth and/ or previously adopted children requires helping these resident siblings realize that the information is private—it should stay in the family. This is not because there should be embarrassment about what happened to the adoptee who experienced trauma, and it is not because there is something "wrong" with or "bad" about the adoptee because of his or her pre-adoptive experiences. It is because the adoptee's history is a private family matter.

Create new supports

Typical sons and daughters can also benefit from interaction with other children and adolescents residing in adoptive families. Talking with friends joined by adoption offers:

- the opportunity to be understood by others in similar situations and with similar concerns

- a means to gain information about the issues of their adopted siblings

- an avenue to enhance skills in the areas of problem solving, stress management, communication, expressing feelings, and handling sibling rivalry

- a place to obtain answers to adoption-related questions asked by curious strangers or classmates

- a location to explore the facets of life in a transcultural adoptive family

- a way to make friends to call on in difficult times in adoptive family life.

Currently, as their needs become recognized, there are groups cropping up for the birth and/or previously adopted kids. Check with adoption agencies in your area to see if such a service exists.

Network with veteran families yourself. Perusing the parent group database of the North American Council on Adoptable Children reveals that over 900 local parent support groups are available. Wherever there are parents, there are school-age boys and girls, tween, and teens. Once connected, kids start tweeting, texting, and friending on Facebook™. Play dates and sleepovers happen as well.

At our Attachment and Bonding Center of Ohio annual pot-luck picnic, we see parents, adoptees, and typically developing children grouping up. The relationships formed at this informal social outing last long after the picnic is over! If your agency sponsors social events, be sure to attend. You and all of your children will make friends that "get it"!

"There was absolutely nothing that could have been done to assist me prior to adoption. You can never truly be prepared for what is ahead without actually living it. Anyone who has never experienced it can't tell you anything. Although perhaps first-hand experiences would help, sort of like a window into what's to come. Kids could get into groups and share stories. I think having people like yourself to talk to and interact with before and after an adoption is essential in successfully coping with your new home situation."

Novel approaches to child care

It is easier to preserve attachments between parents and resident sons and daughters when the family has access to child care. Going out as spouses and pursuing adult hobbies are made simpler too when mothers and fathers know that all of the children are safe and sound.

Yet barriers do exist regarding accessing and utilizing child care when one or more adoptees exhibit behavioral difficulties.

Typical siblings as child care providers

Older brothers and sisters are very often a main source of child care in families. However, in families whose composition includes one or more traumatized members:

- The typically developing children in an adoption-expanded family may not feel capable of supervising their sibling.

- Typically, oldest children assume caretaking duties of younger children. Adoptive families may find that this does not work if the older children are the adopted children. The adoptee's social and emotional delays may render him immature and lacking a full sense of responsibility.

- Parents often feel that the brothers and sisters are already making enough sacrifices. Asking them to look after a troubled sibling so that the parents may pursue a pleasurable activity seems too great to request.

Extended family, friends, and professional respite resources

Grandpa, Grandma, aunts, uncles, or family friends—depending on health, geographic location, level of support—are the traditional and best source of family babysitters. Adopted children have often already been cared for or moved in with "strangers"—some multiple times. Before we seek professional respite services—unfamiliar to the adopted son or daughter—let's be certain this is necessary. Mothers and fathers are encouraged to explore their support system thoroughly. Perhaps a friend, neighbor, or relative has been overlooked. Perhaps there is a new face from a support group.

For some families, a child care facility or a respite family may be the only option. A respite family is a home in which the parents are familiar with the special needs of adoptive children. They may be foster or adoptive parents. A respite provider could be a retired school teacher or a social worker who has become a stay-at-home mom.

Barriers in this area may include:

- Some behavioral difficulties are unwelcome in child care settings, in respite families, or in the homes of extended family members and friends.

- The child's older age makes finding child care difficult. Respite families, relatives, friends, and professional day care facilities question why a child age 13, 14, or older needs a babysitter.

- Parents are concerned that the level of supervision will be inadequate.

> Lynette is eight years old. Her parents, Doris and Sam, just picked her up from an overnight stay with her respite provider, Dawn. Dawn is a professional child care provider who works for an agency, which has a grant to fund this service. Adoptive parents call the agency to schedule services with Dawn.
>
> Dawn is quite experienced. She has raised two adopted children to adulthood, and she has fostered many children.
>
> Lynette reported that staying at Dawn's was great. She had "lots of fun" and she got to "eat whatever I wanted."
>
> Doris was quite upset by this. When the family arrived home, Doris called Dawn. It turned out that Lynette didn't exactly get to eat "whatever" she "wanted," but, by many parents' standards, Dawn does have lax rules about food. It is one battle she prefers not to take on.
>
> Doris decided that Lynette would never respite at Dawn's house again.

Now let's back up and look at this situation more closely. Lynette has some sexual behaviors. She often masturbates, and she runs up to total strangers in an effort to "hump" their legs. Dawn may have less than ideal standards about food, but Dawn understands supervision. Doris needs to know that Dawn can ensure Lynette's safety. In this instance, Dawn kept Lynette close by all weekend so that Lynette had no opportunity to behave sexually with anyone.

Safety is a main criterion in utilizing respite as a support. In the scheme of things, does it really matter if your child stays up a bit past bedtime, watches a little more television than you would like, or has a few too many snacks for a day or two as long as she is kept safe?

Other difficulties may include the following:

- Parents are also concerned that the child with a traumatic past may steal, break knick-knacks, overeat, and so on. Well, what if he does? What is the worst thing that can happen? He certainly won't be the first child to shatter a glass or plate. Stealing carries a natural and logical consequence. She'll have to return the item and apologize.

- Children with mental health issues often act nicely for relatives or respite families. Parents are upset when their child's behaviors are better for their sister or neighbor than for them. This scenario makes adoptive parents feel as if their son or daughter's problems are the result of their parenting. This actually occurs because the child isn't trying to build the intimate relationship with an aunt or a cousin that she is working on with her parents. The level of closeness of the relationship is the trigger for the challenging behaviors.

- The child often acts poorly upon returning from child care. Parents determine that it is easier to keep plugging away than deal with another bout of negative behavior. Many children do exhibit more negative behaviors upon returning to the family. Of course, they do! They have no idea how to reconnect. Remember, we are talking about children with poor relationship skills.

Overall, periodic rest stops let everyone stretch their legs, get some fresh air, and get back on the road ready to proceed on with the trip. Barriers can be overcome! On the following pages are some examples of the types of child care created and utilized by other families. If I haven't convinced you yet to go sign up for a support group, think about how many ideas in this book have come from adoptive families! Veteran parents are a wealth of resources and creative ideas.

MAGGIE AND BRENT PARENT ONE CHILD BY ADOPTION

Boy, have they gone through babysitters! Clarissa, age nine, is a very anxious child. She becomes fearful when her parents go out. She thinks they won't come back. Her anxiety leads to quite the behavior. Her first child care provider couldn't believe that Clarissa was flushing the cat down the toilet! Another caregiver was locked out of the house as she ran out to retrieve the cell phone she had accidentally left in her car. She used the phone to call Maggie and Brent to come home! She had had enough of Clarissa.

A tenacious couple, they kept at it. They were determined to go out to dinner or a movie once in a while. One day, while raking leaves, Maggie noticed 17-year-old Mya, a neighbor girl going into her house. Mya had a twin, Ali.

Later, she went over to their house and inquired about the twins' availability to watch Clarissa. She explained some of Clarissa's issues and felt that together perhaps they could manage Clarissa. She had decided to try the *strength in numbers* approach.

The girls, eager to earn some extra money, came over one Friday evening. After Maggie and Brent left, Mya and Ali braced themselves and held on to the cat. Within a few minutes, Clarissa threw herself on the floor and started having a major meltdown. Mya pulled out her phone and said, "Why don't you call your parents and see what they're having for dinner? Here, I'll dial the number."

Brent, expecting the worst, answered the phone. (Maggie was ready to get a to-go box.) A crying Clarissa said, "Are you coming home?"

Brent replied, "Of course we're coming back, and I'll bring you a dessert. Here, let me tell you the choices."

The conversation calmed Clarissa down. She sat with Mya and Ali and watched part of a movie. She happily awaited her cherry cheesecake.

Now, calling Mom and Dad while they are out is a ritual. It provides the reassurance Clarissa needs to stay at home with Mya or Ali. That's right—Clarissa no longer needs two babysitters.

Many children with anxiety do well when they have a family photo, a special item given to them by a parent to hold on to, or if allowed to make a quick call to Mom and Dad. It is a "visible" way to keep their parents with them while parents enjoy a date.

LORRAINE AND PETER PARENT SEVEN ADOPTED
CHILDREN ALL WITH VARYING MENTAL HEALTH ISSUES

"Five of our children have special learning needs. This makes homework time-consuming. Arrival home from school means homework, dinner, more homework, and then baths and bed. There is little time to simply be a family.

"We reside in a state that has a program through which adoptive families can receive respite monies. We find a provider and the state provides the dollars.

"In looking at the regulations, there was no mention of 'where' the service needed to take place. We completed an application, clearly explaining our plan. The application was approved.

"The next day, our neighbor, Helen, a retired school teacher, came over as the school bus was unloading. Helen took the youngest three and worked with them on homework while Lorraine handled the remaining four. Homework was done in half the time!

"This *in-home respite* allowed time for games, a movie, or some extra snuggles. This is exactly what we wanted—more time to respite *with* our kids!"

JOSH IS A SINGLE ADOPTIVE DAD OF
TWO OLDER ADOLESCENTS

"I am a history teacher. But I am also establishing a martial arts studio. In order to boost the number of students, I started offering 'demonstration nights.' For a five-dollar fee, parents could drop off their children, who would be kept busy watching various accomplished instructors demonstrate their skills. Parents would have three hours all to themselves.

"I circulated a flyer to all the local adoption agencies and support groups. Soon, my classes were full. I continue to provide these respite demonstration evenings. As an adoptive parent, I know how hard it can be to get a break."

ANNETTE AND WAYNE PARENT FIVE CHILDREN, TWO BY BIRTH AND THREE THROUGH ADOPTION

"We are very involved in our church. We identified two families in the church we trust and who we feel mirror many of our thoughts on raising children.

"In times of crisis, our birth children go to spend time with these families. This leaves us free to deal with our troubled adopted children. The typically developing kids get a nice break. The adopted children with problems get the extra attention they need in their times of adoption-related crisis.

"We have named this *reverse respite*. It sends a nice message: 'In our family, everyone takes breaks, not just the adoptees.'"

DARLENE PARENTS HER TWO BIRTH DAUGHTERS, GLORIA AND MICHELLE, AND THEIR ADOPTED SIBLINGS, JUSTIN AND JUDY

"I am now a single parent, since my husband moved out. My youngest adoptee, Judy, age seven, is prone to very aggressive outbursts. Gloria was going off to college soon and I was unsure that I could manage Judy alone.

"I have a strong faith. I called my clergy. I explained my situation. He agreed to give me some time at the next service to address the congregation.

"I stood in front of my fellow parishioners and let them know how valuable their generosity had been to many members of the church congregation. They had provided rides to doctor's appointments, casseroles to the ailing, light home repair and yard work to the elderly church attendees, and so on.

"I was now soliciting their assistance. I didn't have a medical problem, I explained. I had a child with a mental health issue. I needed some assistance with child care.

"Well, within short order, I had child care. I also had soup, baked goods, and a few young adults mowing the lawn!"

In closing this segment on child care, we'll hear from Jill and Mitchell, parents to three adopted children, two typical daughters and a son working to heal from his past hurts. Jill says:

> "The best way to cope when dealing with difficult children is to take breaks. Make sure that they are part of your weekly schedule. After three years of living with our son who has mental health issues, we've only recently started scheduling respite. It's made a huge difference. I put my son in day care one day a week. I have the entire day to be by myself without the stress of his crazy antics all day. We can also schedule on Saturday, which gives us time to be with our healthy kids. It's something I really look forward to.
>
> "We had been hoping that our son would improve, but he is not progressing very quickly. For the past three summers, we've put our lives on hold. We were hoping and waiting for him to catch up, because the thought of doing family things without him seems so cruel. Only recently have we faced the fact that he may never be able to do these things.
>
> "With the help of our therapists we've come to realize that the family needs to go on. They made it sound so simple; why didn't we think of it before? If you have a child who is blind, the entire family doesn't stop going to movies. They make arrangements so everyone can be happy. We need to do the things that families do, like going to the amusement park for the day, something the girls will enjoy. Our son could never handle this right now. That means we'll find a place for him to stay, somewhere safe where he's enjoying the things he can. This is what's best for everyone."

Chapter summary

- Parents are the main support for their sons and daughters, whether these boys and girls are typical or traumatized. The best way for mothers and fathers to carry out this care is to first oversee their own needs. Mom and dads who develop the means to keep their energy tanks full ensure that they have the supply of emotional stamina needed to balance their family responsibilities.

- All children need quality and quantity time with their moms and dads! Brothers and sisters in adoption can't go on hold until the adoptee is "better." Start a habit to have regular dates with them today. Make it a habit to keep throughout your adoption journey.

- Parental recognition of their kids' accomplishments goes a long way to bolstering their self-pride. Children beam when parents exclaim, "Good job!" The chaotic life of the family that includes a traumatized adoptee lends to overlook day-to-day achievements and successes. Do your best to catch your kids' good deeds and triumphs. Your acknowledgment verifies for your resident children that you still do notice them in spite of the challenges occurring in the family.

- Parenting doesn't require mystic qualities like mind reading. You can simply ask your sons and daughters what they need to feel supported. There is often simplicity to their requests that makes fulfilling them easy.

- Information is the key to sustaining brother and sisters post-adoption. Talking, surfing the Internet, including them in therapy appointments, and so on keeps them in the loop! It helps them comprehend why the newcomer presents challenges, and what efforts are being made to help the ailing sibling and the family—as a whole—move forward. The typical kids' need for information parallels that of the parents.

- Supporting brothers and sisters may also mean forming connections with other adoptive families. Look for opportunities to network with adoptive parents. Wherever there are mothers and fathers, there are kids!

- Safe child care makes it easier for parents to spend time with youngsters, tweens, and teens. Parents can also spend time together as a couple or pursuing individual activities of interest. Obtaining child care may require creativity. It may also require adjusting expectations. Some traumatized adoptees, until they become healthier, aren't capable of pursuing the types of outings that their brothers and sisters would enjoy. Yet arrangements can be made so that the adopted son or daughter engages in the activities he or she can enjoy, while the rest of the family partakes in what is gratifying for them. This is a facet of the balance that must happen post-adoption so that each unique child has his or her needs met.

9

Triggers, Losses, and Feelings

FACILITATING YOUR SONS' AND DAUGHTERS' GRIEF

Grief is not a popular topic. Yet grief is a part of the journey when the family expands by adding a child with a history of trauma. Brothers' and sisters' grief issues have been pointed out throughout this book.

"This is not the brother or sister I expected!"

The culmination of the losses post-adoption is that of the expected brother or sister. This loss is amplified for those adoptive families which include one or more children whose trauma results in mental health diagnoses, such as Posttraumatic Stress Disorder, Attention Deficit/Hyperactivity Disorder, Reactive Attachment Disorder, Bipolar Disorder, Obsessive-Compulsive Disorder, and so on. This is not to minimize the experience of any adoptive family. It is to state that central to all the losses is that of the person that the adoptee could have become. Complex trauma, for some children, robs them of the opportunity to participate fully in all aspects of life. Thus, the fun playmate, the sibling who would value the teachings of an older resident brother or sister, or another family member with whom to reciprocally exchange affection—the expected newcomer—is not the child who arrived. Parents and siblings must mourn the loss of the person that the child may never become because of the traumatic experiences suffered prior to the adoption. There is no difference between parents and siblings in their level of grief in such instances (Miller *et al.* 1990).

"I think there are a couple of losses. I think the kids lose their innocence, like my adopted brothers; he lost his innocence but way before he came to our house, so he had already learned to rob and steal and lie to get by. So when you come to a good home, all you know is how to protect yourself. You don't know how to operate in a family unit. But, as far as I'm concerned, if I want to be selfish about it, I lost time. You lose trust in people. One bad experience and my brother (birth) will never adopt kids because of this experience. When you adopt kids, you don't know what you are going to get. You lose everything, man. The whole way you're used to living, you lose. You gotta rebuild and start over and patch everything up when everything was just peaches and cream before."

Sibling rivalry: The grief beneath is triggered

Grief-related thoughts and feelings often underlie sibling rivalry in adoption-built families. Anytime there is more than one child in the family, sibling conflict is unavoidable. The positive side is that it can be a valuable experience. It teaches negotiating, compromising, and listening to another's point of view. Sibling disagreements better prepare children for relationships outside of the family—with peers, co-workers, college roommates, boyfriends and girlfriends, and so on.

In complex adoptive families, sibling rivalry will share some elements in common with families built by birth, such as, "Mom, she's using my makeup again" or "Dad, make him come inside. I want to play basketball with my friends." Yet siblings propelled by unresolved grief collide with fierce intensity—giving the words "sibling rivalry" a deeply forceful meaning!

Day-to-day situations trigger feelings—anger, frustration, resentment, sadness, embarrassment, despair, rage, jealousy, guilt, fear—about the losses experienced due to integrating the adoptee into the family system. Everyone has triggers. Some triggers bring up happy feelings. For example, a song on the radio conjures up a memory of a first, special love. Other triggers raise unpleasant or unhappy emotions. You stop at a bakery. The smell of fresh-baked chocolate chip cookies permeates the air. Fond memories of your deceased grandmother come to mind and you feel sad.

Sibling rivalry is intensified because the grief due to the now altered family is unleashed *plus* the emotions about the situation at hand. For example, recently, a 12-year-old birth daughter stated, "I wish he had never come into the family. We can't go bowling anymore. I miss it!" The brother to whom she was referring cannot tolerate the noise of a bowling alley due to a Sensory Integration Dysfunction. Loud shouts of people making strikes, bright lights, and the racket of the pin-setting machines and the ball return cause him to emotionally dysregulate. Before long, he is having a meltdown. At eight years old his outbursts resemble those of a child age two; the public display of screaming, kicking, and crying is embarrassing and so the family stopped going bowling. Bowling is about much more than lost fun. Bowling signifies the loss of the family as it was and the loss of the brother this young girl had eagerly awaited.

Or another example:

Paulette, a nine-year-old adoptee, her brother, and her dad went shopping for the perfect Mother's Day gift. The three had a great time at the mall. On Mother's Day, however, Paulette wouldn't get out of bed. This made the family late for church. After the service, she became angry because she didn't like the chosen restaurant. She spilled her pop and "accidentally" dropped her hamburger and fries on the floor. The intended happy day quickly eroded into a "bad day." Paulette's father was quite confounded: "She was so happy shopping for the gift. She seemed to be looking forward to Mother's Day." Paulette's mom felt rejected: "She doesn't want me for a mother." Paulette's brother angrily stated to Paulette, "Why do you have to ruin every holiday!"

Mother's Day triggered Paulette to think about her birth mother. After the trip to the mall, she couldn't stop thinking about why her birth mother "gave me away." All of her feelings about her abandonment flooded her. She expressed her emotions on Mother's Day with her negative behavior. In turn, her brother's anger surfaced for the loss of the pleasant family gatherings he was accustomed to prior to Paulette's arrival in the family.

Table 9.1 depicts thinking that contributes to sibling conflicts. The statements each contain losses and feelings. As examples:

- "You're adopted and I'm not." Anger motivates a typical sibling to shout this at her adopted brother. The anger could be rooted in the changes that have occurred in the family. Or the resident child may be angry that her adopted brother was in her room for the hundredth time! The negative behavior is a reminder that "I had more privacy before you came." The feelings of being invaded are compounded by the loss of the family as it was.

- "Can you really want me as a brother or sister?" Just as the adoptee wonders how his adoptive parents can want him when his own birth parents didn't, he perceives he is unlovable to his new brothers and sisters. Insecure about his current relationships, he utilizes negative behaviors to sabotage the potential intimate ties. He thinks, "It is easier to push people away before they decide to leave."

- "They are so lucky to live together." The adoptee's grief for the birth siblings living elsewhere is triggered by observing brothers and sisters in the adoptive family.

- "I asked for a brother or sister." It is my fault that Mom and Dad aren't as happy as they used to be.

- "You look different. You're not even from America. I look at you and 'see' that our family is different. I long for the old family. I am tired of people looking at us when we are out in public. I hate it when people ask me, 'Is that your sister?'"

TABLE 9.1 FREQUENT THOUGHTS CONTRIBUTING
TO SIBLING CONFLICTS IN ADOPTIVE FAMILIES

Typically developing siblings	Adoptee
I want to "unadopt" him. He is so hard to play with. I wanted to teach her things. I'm the one that wanted a brother or sister. You're adopted and I'm not. You look different. You're not even from America. If I'm not good, will I have to move? I hate being told that I have to set the example. I am tired of babysitting. Why wasn't I enough for Mom and Dad? I would never get away with the things he does. Do Mom and Dad love him more?	Can you really want me as a brother or sister? I wish my brothers and sisters would play with me the way they play with each other. My brothers and sisters are so lucky to live together. I want to live with my birth siblings. I look different from everybody in my family. They are having friends over again. They are going out with their friends again. They act so "perfect." Mom and Dad love them more because they were born to them. My brothers and sisters get more, and get to do more, than I do.

The interplay of triggers, feelings, and behaviors cause conflict to erupt with greater frequency and intensity in the adoptive family. Resolving the grief beneath brothers' and sisters' disagreements lends to a more peaceful household.

So, a first step in reducing sibling rivalry is to identify the losses and the feelings felt by both the already resident children and the adoptee. Then, using the ways of helping grief flow described later in this chapter, facilitate the verbal expression of the thoughts and emotions kids develop due to their life changes. In the meantime, here are some other points to keep in mind when helping resident and new kids form relationships:

- Stress increases sibling rivalry. Monitor the amount of stress each child is experiencing in all areas of his or her life. Reduce stress whenever and wherever possible.

- Parents influence their children's sibling relationships by the general emotional climate created within the family. Generally, family conflict breeds sibling conflict.

- Families who don't have enjoyable times will have more conflict. One adoptive mom recently stated, "On a really bad day when we're all on each other's nerves, I order pizza and pick out a movie. A good mood arrives along with the pizza!"

"We lost shopping time. It seems like we are always worried about money. It seems like we can never get anything done. As soon as something is finished, it seems like there is a problem with Gabe and we all have to stop and wait for that to end."

The way parents resolve their own conflicts sets a strong example for kids. How do you resolve conflict? Is it the way in which you want your children to resolve conflict?

Sibling rivalry conjures up—triggers—parents' own memories of their relationships with their siblings. Here again, parents need to gain awareness of how past experiences contribute to their reactions to their children's individual actions as well as to sibling interactions.

General knowledge about children and grief

A first step in helping the children already in the home at the time of the adoption to express emotions is having some general knowledge about children and grief. On the following pages, we'll briefly explore the developmental nature of grief, the potential negative issues that result when kids are unable to share their feelings, factors that affect the capacity to grieve, and the stages of grief. This information will help parents recognize that their son or daughter is grief-stricken, and it will clarify the types of grief-related thoughts and feelings that correspond with the particular age of a child, tween, or teen.

Grief is developmental

Everything with kids is developmental—crawling to walking, to skipping, jumping, hopping, and on to dancing or athletics. There is also babbling, to saying a first word, stringing words together into sentences, making conversation, and joining the debate team. Every aspect of a child's life is about establishing a platform from which more complex skills grow. Grief is another area of sons' and daughters' lives that becomes more intricate—with thoughts and feelings—as the child matures.

Grief in infants and toddlers

Infants and toddlers recognize significant changes in their environment as well as the loss of a loved one they were used to being with. They will communicate their grief via crying, changes in eating and sleeping, and body language. They are visibly distressed. They may be difficult to console. A change in primary caregiver or the amount of time spent with a parent can cause grief for these young children.

Grief in three- to five-year-olds

Children age three to 5 have fears about being abandoned, getting lost, or no longer being loved by their parents. They notice that parents do not have control of everything that happens to them. This threatens their sense of security. Children of this age blame themselves for the loss. They feel that a loss occurred as a result of something they did or because they are inherently "bad." The appropriately developing child may feel grief as a result of these fears as well, thinking, "I wasn't enough for Mom and Dad. They had to adopt another child." "Mom and Dad spend more time with my new brother. They must not love me anymore." "Mom and Dad can't make Jimmy stop hitting us." "Jimmy is bad because of me."

Grief in six- to ten-year-olds

Children age six to ten begin to comprehend that loss is permanent. This can bring about a multitude of feelings at the time of other significant changes in a child's life. For example, this is the time children enter school. So, as they are mastering new tasks, they are struggling to come to terms with the post-placement family changes. Boys and girls gain awareness of family relations—"Aunt Joan is

Mom's sister, and Grandma is their mother." Thus, the adoptee's status in the family is understood with more depth. That is, the abandonment of the adoptee causes the typical sons and daughters to recognize that not all children stay with the parents to whom they are born. There is a firmer understanding of biological versus adopted. The implications of what it means to be an adopted member of a family or a birth child sink in more deeply. Concerns about being abandoned or left without parents intensify. Brothers and sisters also begin to realize the full extent of the trauma experienced by their adopted sibling.

Issues that may crop up in this school age group include: "What would happen to me if something happened to Mom and Dad?" "Would Mom and Dad ever give me away?" "Why don't some parents 'keep' their children?" "Why do people have kids if they aren't going to keep them?" "Could I ever be sexually abused?" "Where are my brother's birth parents?"

The other children in the family also gain in their understanding of the impact of the adoption on their lives: "Janet's sister is so nice. Why didn't I get a sister like that?" "I love going to Janet's house. Her family is so happy. Why couldn't our family be like that?"

Peers' curiosity blossoms at this age as well. Increased questions are put toward the birth/previously adopted and newly adopted children about the cultural composition of their family and adoption in general.

Grief in pre-adolescents

Pre-adolescents, ages 11 to 13, are faced with puberty and increased academic and peer pressures. When loss is added, they become more vulnerable and insecure. A capacity to think abstractly occurs at this time. They begin to explore the spiritual and socio-political aspects of their life and the lives of others. Adoptees, brothers, and sisters will explore various questions: "Why does God let bad things happen?" "Why did my sister get abused?" "Why has my life been so good?" "Why did her parents give her away?" "Why can't we stop drug use?"

Children come to discover that life is not fair. There are harsh realities in life. Typically developing siblings may develop a survivor's guilt: "How do I live a 'normal' life when my sibling suffers so much?"

Grief in adolescence

Adolescents, ages 13 to 18, have an adult understanding of loss. However, they have not had as many experiences of loss as have most adults, so they lack the coping skills to deal with grief. Developmental issues of independence and separation from parents can interfere with the ability to receive support from adults. This situation also causes a need to hide feelings of grief. Otherwise, they appear as if they are not in control of themselves. This contradicts the image of autonomy they desire in adolescence.

Adolescents also rely more heavily on peers for support with everything in their lives. Typically developing teens, who may have lost friendships throughout the adoption process or whose friends cannot understand their losses, lose this developmentally appropriate manner of coping with their grief.

Earlier in this book we touched upon the fact that the identity process for adopted adolescents is complicated. The identity process for brothers and sisters in adoptive families in which a sibling has mental health issues is also difficult. The crisis of identity is intensified when one's environment includes both sibling and family distress (Balk 1990; Hogan and Greenfield 1991). Siblings serve as points of reference for each other in the development of identity (Bank and Kahn 1997). Siblings look at themselves in relation to their brothers and sisters to determine who they are. Yet now the task of determining a personal identity must occur in the context of a distressed and sometimes even deteriorating reference point—a brother or sister with mental health diagnoses (Judge 1994).

It is clear that children—adoptees, brothers, and sisters— experience loss and grief at all ages and at each developmental stage. Myths along the lines of "children are too young to understand what happened" and "children will get over loss quickly" are falsehoods that need to be discarded. Our discussion of the developmental nature of grief and loss also clarifies that loss occurs as a result of experiences. So myths related to "shielding children from loss and grief" are also unfounded. Further, we do children a great disservice when we think, "It would hurt her too much to talk about it." Children who are not provided opportunities to grieve are at risk for:

- decreased social, emotional, and cognitive developmental growth

- regression to earlier stages of development for an extended period of time

- inability to concentrate—impaired academic progress

- physical difficulties—fatigue, stomach aches, appetite changes, headaches, tightness in chest, shortness of breath, low energy, difficulty sleeping

- depression

- anxiety

- risk-taking behaviors

- withdrawal from friends or extracurricular activities.

Factors that affect the capacity to grieve

Factors that affect the capacity of the individual to move through the grieving process include the nature of the loss. A sudden, unexpected loss is believed more difficult to grieve. The level of significance of the loss is also important. The loss of a child or parent is considered among the hardest losses to grieve. Other factors are the willingness to experience the feelings associated with the loss and the quality of support systems. Children are more able to cope with grief when there is at least one available adult.

These elements are present in the adoption-built family post-arrival of the traumatized sibling. Thus, moving through the grieving process can be a complicated process for adoptive mothers, fathers, brothers, sisters, and the adoptee. Yet available to your typical children are you—the parents! When mothers and fathers take the helm, children can navigate the thoughts and feelings that come along with the common challenges.

Stages of grief

Grief includes five stages—shock/denial, bargaining, anger, depression, and ultimately acceptance (Kübler-Ross 1969; Kübler-

Ross and Kessler 2005). Children (and adults) fluctuate between these stages rather than pass through them in an orderly progression:

- *Shock/denial*: The individual can't believe or refuses to believe what is happening. "I can't believe that my sibling acts this way!" "I would never steal anything!" "My parents really aren't going to keep this kid!" "He isn't like us at all!"

- *Bargaining*: This stage is an attempt to make a promise or bargain in order to achieve an improved situation. "God, if you help our family, I'll make sure to live a good life. I'll do my homework and pick up my room just like my parents want." "If I was a better brother, my adopted sister would act okay." Children often manifest this stage of grief behaviorally. Parents feel as though they are always making a deal to get compliance. "Honey, will you take the trash out?" "Yes, if I can have a cookie."

- *Anger*: "I get so mad when he swears at Mom!" "Why didn't the social worker tell us adoption would be like this!" "How could his birth parents abuse him!" "I resent the time he takes up!" "I would never get away with the things he does!" "I hate the way he treats my family!"

"I used to just walk away and stuff and pretend like it never happened or I used to get real mad or I used to watch TV or do my homework. Now, I just get tired of it and pretend like I can't hear it and stuff."

- *Depression*: This is a period of great sadness. "I miss my 'old' family." "We just used to sit around and have fun." "Mom and Dad are always so stressed." "I stay in my room a lot. I can shut everything out there." There may be decreased interest or pleasure in activities or hobbies. There can be a loss of energy or feeling tired. Many experience a change in appetite, with significant weight gain or weight loss. Sleep patterns may be interrupted—sleeping too much or too little. Making decisions or concentrating is difficult. Feelings of hopelessness, guilt, and worthlessness prevail, as does irritability—a main symptom of depressed children.

- *Acceptance:* This stage may also be referred to as integration or reorganization. There may not be total happiness in this stage, yet there is peace, movement forward, understanding of what has happened, and coming to terms with what may not change. Anger and depression dissipate. Periods of accepting the loss last longer than the periods of sorrow and rage. For example, a 16-year-old resident brother, who has moved into acceptance, stated:

> "Obviously, there have been difficulties. My parents have to devote much more time and effort into caring for my sister and, consequently, there is less time to spend with my brothers and me. The household hasn't been peaceful in years, but you get used to it. Clearly, my sister's behavioral issues do not permit us to participate in many activities in public, but, once again, you tend to forget what life was like before your sibling and learn to accept the way things must be. All of these changes are entirely understandable and do not detract from the quality of my life or the relationships between members of my family. Betty has forced me to become far more patient and compassionate than I ever would have been without her. Her struggles make witnessing her triumphs even more rewarding than those of a typical child. It is encouraging to think of where my sister would be if we had not adopted her."

Facilitating your sons' and daughters' grief: Letting feelings flow

A sentiment from a now nine-year-old resident sister:

> "My younger adopted sister has made me feel very angry with all the tattling. She liked to make me and my sisters look bad, so that she could feel better about herself. She makes me feel like I am always going to get in trouble and it is very overwhelming. I wish that I had known to talk about my feelings and not just stuff

them until I explode. If you talk about your feelings with your parents, you will not only feel better, but you will have caused less drama."

The birth and/or previously adopted children will "feel better" when they can talk about their feelings. Certainly the home's climate is enhanced when no one is "exploding"! Offered next are several components that will help children convey verbally how they feel about the common challenges that arrived along with the sibling with a history of trauma.

"Normalize" feelings

Brothers and sisters experience a range of emotions along a continuum of intensity. Many typical children believe that they shouldn't have "bad" emotions for a family member, especially one whose early years were riddled with unpleasant experiences. The resident children also "don't want to dump on Mom and Dad." They view their parents as stressed enough caring for the hurt arrival.

"Along through the adoption process, keep talking! Know that we (i.e. typical children) won't always say anything. We think you are too stressed with the 'new' kid. Let us know it's okay to talk to you, and that you want to talk with us."

Foremost, the appropriately developing children need help "normalizing" their feelings. They need parental permission to understand that anger, fury, irritation, resentment, fear, distress, trepidation, melancholy, despair, cheerlessness, envy, bitterness, and so on are feelings that correspond to the circumstances. They also need to know that, even if stressed, their mothers and fathers *want* to be "dumped on." Parents certainly want their sons and daughters to be happy.

The ripple effect: Talking about "it"

The *ripple effect* is often the tool to rid the barriers that prevent the flow of feelings. For example, earlier we wrote about George. He becomes angry each time his mother is late picking him up from baseball practice. The next time George's frustration surfaces, his Mom could say:

> "George, I've noticed that you become so angry when I am late. I'm thinking that I am late a lot since Vikki came to live with us. This didn't used to happen. Is it hard for you since Vikki came?"

George's mom puts forth a ripple. This is an idea of what the problem might be. She identified a possible reason for the furious feeling and she labeled the emotion. Children, even healthy sons and daughters, often need assistance pinpointing the source of grief and naming the feeling.

Initially, the child may deny the information or simply not want to talk about it. But a ripple has been created. George now knows that "Vikki" is a safe topic. His mom is open to talking about his thoughts and feelings about Vikki. He has learned that having negative feelings is acceptable. Enough ripples usually lead to waves—of conversation and grief. Eventually, kids will respond to the safety net the parent has offered. There will be an outpouring of sad, mad, fear, jealousy, and so on.

Validate feelings: No stifling!

Many readers remember laughing at the old sitcom *All in the Family* as Archie told Edith to "stifle herself." Once you have feelings flowing, don't follow Archie's advice. That is, comments that shut grief off: "Your brother didn't have life as good as you! You need to be more patient with him." "Your dad and I are doing the best we can. He (adopted brother) needs more than you (typical child) do."

Rather, validation of feelings is the more effective method. Validation is affirming the emotions being expressed: "Yes. It is so sad that the family can't spontaneously go bowling anymore. I miss those times too." "Yes. I would be mad too if my brother spilled paint on my bed. You are right. You have lost a lot of privacy." "I was embarrassed when he wet his pants at the store too. It is so hard to go out now."

A time to grieve

The grief process can't occur at all if it isn't given time, and, today, time is hard to come by. The busy pace of life most families keep inhibits the flow of feelings. The family keeps attending the next volleyball game, school concert, karate class, birthday party, and so on. Coping with grief is put off for another day. However, parents are encouraged to set aside their own time to grieve and time to make it possible for children to express their feelings.

Feelings flow over and over

The developmental nature of grief means that emotions resolved once may need to be explored and given a new perspective from pre-school to entering college. So expect to repeat, repeat, and repeat some more! Children learn best by repetition. Grief is resolved in a similar manner. We must periodically, and over time, explore with brothers and sisters the lost expectations associated with the sibling they thought was arriving and the changes that adoption has brought to the family. In this manner we ensure the flow of grief needed for sons and daughters to retain their emotional well-being throughout their growing-up years.

Chapter summary

- Even though grief isn't a preferred topic, it becomes a part of post-adoption life. The sibling that arrives with a history of trauma affects all facets of family life—privacy, peace and quiet, birth order, time and attention, safety (possibly), and so on. Children learn about the atrocities that occur in society at earlier ages than parents would prefer. In some families, there will be the need to grieve the loss of the brother or sister so eagerly awaited and desired. Some adoptees experience complex trauma that robs them of their capacity to perform "normally" within the family and society at large.

- Sibling rivalry has its positive aspects. From it emerges an array of valuable life skills—cooperation, collaboration, solving problems, accepting other's opinions. Sibling rivalry will have these qualities in adoptive families. Yet sibling rivalry will also have grief as its underpinning. The collision of grieving brothers and sisters gives rise to intense sibling rivalry. Parents and their children must delve beneath the day-to-day skirmishes and ferret out the root of the sibling rivalry. The emotional well-being of each son and daughter and the home's climate will then improve.

- Armed with a general knowledge of grief, parents can assist their sons and daughters in resolving the grief that arrived with the adoptee with a history of trauma. Children are able to let their feelings flow when a caring parent is available.

- Grief is developmental. Mothers and fathers can expect to review feelings that arise from the common challenges a number of times as their children mature.

- Facilitating emotions is critical. Children who are not offered the opportunity to grieve experience arrested development, lose interest in activities and friends, and are prone to physical illnesses, as well as mental health issues such as depression and anxiety.

- The successful resolution of grief leads to acceptance. The typical children put into context the turbulence experienced. Sons and daughters emerge with a balanced—and often more positive—outlook about their sibling with complex trauma and about adoption in general.

10

"You Know Your Birth Mother and I Don't"

BLENDING CHILDREN WITH DIVERSE BIRTH HISTORIES—AN EMERGING COMMON CHALLENGE

Today, the culture of adoption is shifting. Openness—varying levels of ongoing connections between adoptive families and their children's families of origin—is becoming more the norm (Evan B. Donaldson Institute 2012).

Social media—Facebook™, for example—contributes to the openness trend as well. Adoptees and birth parents find and "friend" each other. Today's adoptive parents are also encouraged to share details of each of their children's birth histories as well. It is true that children need this information in order to carry out identity development. Adoptees need to integrate their past and present experiences to answer the question "Who am I?"

Thus, in adoptive families in which reside a combination of adopted children who may be typical and/or traumatized, parents must tackle the matter of helping each son or daughter accept his or her particular set of birth history circumstances.

This chapter piggybacks off the preceding chapter. This emerging common challenge has the capacity for adoptees to receive the benefits of openness and information, yet also grief and sibling rivalry may result as well:

Lizzy and William, both internationally adopted, bicker chronically! There is rarely a minute of peace and quiet in this adoptive family! Lizzy's birth mother opted to care for her for six months before placing her in the orphanage. William's birth mother abandoned him at the hospital—he went directly to an institutional setting. William stated, "When I am around Lizzy, all I think about is my birth mother. Why didn't she even try to keep me? I am so angry that I didn't get to live with my birth mother at all! Lizzy got to live with her birth mother!"

Eli, Lisa, and Noah are the adopted children in a family that also includes four older birth children. Eli, Lisa and Noah were all adopted from foster care due to their birth parents' substance abuse issues. Noah's birth mother has since rehabilitated herself and she and Noah have been able to resume a relationship. This has certainly rattled Eli and Lisa. They ask, "Why doesn't my birth mom get better so I can meet her?" "The older kids got to live with you their whole lives. Why did I have to get adopted?" "Why can't we go find my birth mother?" "Do you think my birth mom is okay?"

Anthony, adopted as an infant, has enjoyed an open adoption with his birth mother his entire life. Samantha, arrived at age five, from China. She has sparse statements describing her abandonment. To say that she is jealous of Anthony is an understatement! Each time Anthony's birth mom calls, mails a package, or attends his Taekwondo tournaments, there is fallout! Samantha is sure to break his toys, call him names, rip up his completed homework assignments, and more! She states, "Why does he get to know his birth mother and I don't?" "Why did he get a good family as a baby, and I had to live in the orphanage?" "Why didn't you adopt me sooner?"

Overall, there is no shortage of examples that could be offered when it comes to the unique stories with which adoptees enter the adoptive home. There is also no scarcity of feelings, behaviors, and questions that occur when we blend youngsters from diverse backgrounds. Thus, the purpose of this chapter is to offer ways to help children cope with the specific circumstances that led to the need to be adopted. This is a process that will heal past wounds. The adoptee can form an attachment to his adoptive mother, father, sister, and brother. As grief subsides, sibling interactions can calm too.

Preparing yourself as a parent

Previous content under the heading "Dealing openly with the adoptee's past" in Chapter 4 asked parents to self-assess in terms of providing information to their children that is likely to generate grief reactions—for them and you. It is suggested that mothers and fathers review this content. Give thought to the questions that were posed and the points that were made, if you haven't already done so.

Parents also have the option of seeking professional assistance. Adoption/trauma-competent professionals converse with kids about their pre-adoptive experiences on a daily basis. Of course, this is also another area in which veteran adoptive parents make for a good sounding board. Adoptive moms and dads are also fortunate that with a click of their mouse they can access books and articles that provide sensible advice regarding talking to kids about what I call the "tough stuff"—abandonment, abuse, neglect, substance abuse, emotional abuse, and more.

Facilitating healing of individual children using the life book

The purpose and benefits of a life book

The life book is the most valuable tool that exists when talking to kids about their past. Parents are strongly encouraged to make a life book for each of their adopted children. The life book contains the child's "story"—a truthful, chronological account of the events that led up to his adoption. The *story* is also referred to as a *narrative*. The life book helps children organize themselves across past, present, and future. This provides a continuity and a coherence as to who they are as individuals (Siegel 2001). Identity development is one benefit of the life books. Other positives derived from the life book are:

- Self-image improves. Faulty thinking transforms. Young children, tweens, and teens learn that they were not the cause of their trauma.

- Behavioral change occurs. No longer plagued by thoughts of being "bad" or "defective," and no longer fearing reabandonment by the adoptive family, children internalize the values and morals of their new-found moms and dads.

- Grieving occurs, and thus children experience cognitive, social, emotional, and physical growth.

- Fact is separated from fantasy. Facts allow the child to heal. Via this type of healing, the child sheds her psychological connection to her birth family. She moves forward to attach to her adoptive family.

Organizing the content of the life book
Frequently, I have children draw their own life book pictures.

I am mad because I had to eat oatmeal avry day.

I am mad because I didnt get to Play.

I am sad because I had to live in the orphange

#2

I am sad because I am in my crib all day.

im thinking that she is prtty.

I am mad because I Want Angela not Mom and Dad.

Thier happy that thier geting a new child.!!
Mom and Dad came to get me

I am scared if they will be nice to me.

I am a little happy because they might keep me. :

here you go

The orphanage worker man brought me to My New Mom and Dad on the side of the road.

me, Mom and Dad going to the Hotel.

Me, Mom and Dad are flying from Russia to America.

We LEAVE FOR MONTANA. She RETURNS HOME WITHOUT ME.

MY NEW MOM & DAD GETTING ME.

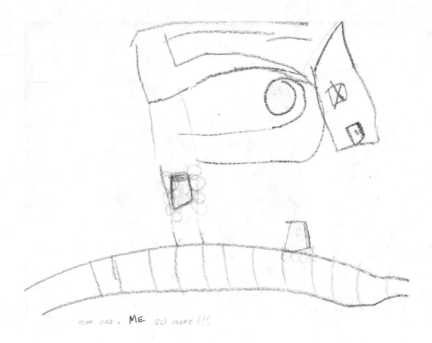

MOM. DAD . ME GO HOME !!!

If my mom and dad had me as a baby they would have rocked me in there arms Rock Rock

And they would have held me.

They also would of sang to me to.

Interspersed with the child's art are photos of their orphanage, homeland, orphanage mates, birth family members, foster families, adoption finalization day, and so on. The documents that describe their birth family, any summaries of the experiences that brought them into foster care or the orphanage, birth records, birth certificate, adoption decree—everything that relates to the child's life prior to the arrival in the adoptive family—is holed-punched and put into a three-ring binder.

The principles that guide life book formation include:

- Tell the child the truth. Children can, and must, grapple with the truth in order to heal. Say "I don't know" when necessary, rather than attempt to fill in the blanks with opinion, conjecture, or untruths.

- Place the photos, documents, drawings, and so on in chronological order—any story goes from the beginning to the end.

- Construct and deliver the story in a developmentally appropriate manner. Use vocabulary that your child can understand.

- The narrative is comprised of accurate, respectful adoption language—*birth mom, birth dad, birth family, birth siblings*. The adoptive family is *Mom* and *Dad*. If you are parenting the child, *you* are the mom and the dad!

- Repeat, repeat, and repeat some more! Children learn best by repetition. The adoptee needs to review the content *many times* before she can internalize the story and express her painful emotions for her losses.

- Be willing to initiate the life book. Kids think about their adoption a lot! Yet many keep their thoughts and feelings private. Young and older children fear that discussing the birth family will make Mom and Dad feel rejected.

- The life book is an ongoing process. As new information comes to light, it needs to be incorporated into the child's narrative.

Anticipate questions throughout life book and beyond

Take some time as you gather all of your child's history together to review it. Think about the questions that your son or daughter might ask as you make the life book. Give some thought to how you want to respond to these questions. Have confidence in yourself as a parent to talk honestly and openly with your adoptee about his early experiences.

Among common questions children ask are these:

- "Why did my birth parents use drugs?"

- "Do you think my birth mom thinks about me?"

- "What do you think my birth mom is doing now?"

- "Do you think she is in jail?"

- "Does she have any more children?"

- "If they get better, can I go live with them again?"

- "Are my birth parents sorry for what they did?"

- "Why did I move so much in foster care?"

- "Why didn't anyone in my country want me?"

- "Why didn't the orphanage ladies take me home?"

- "Do you think my orphanage friends got adopted?"

- "Are my birth parents alive?"

- "Are my siblings safe?"

- "Do you think my siblings think about me?"

- "How did you find me?"

- "Why did you pick me?"

- "What would you have done if I had been your baby?"

Facilitating healing among children using the life book

It is clear that the life book is a wonderful means of helping individual children heal, grow, and join their adoptive families.

I often conduct life book work—jointly—with all of the children who arrived in their family by adoption. We all sit around a large table, drawing and talking. Parents are always in these sessions. I prefer that parents provide comfort to any boy or girl who expresses grief during life book work. This promotes parent–child attachment, rather than therapist–child attachment. I also want to transfer my knowledge to mothers and fathers. The more effectively moms and dads can communicate about the "tough stuff" with their sons and daughters, the sooner everyone gets to stop coming to therapy! Time for family fun is increased!

Working with children together offers many rich opportunities. Examples follow.

Coping skills are developed and implemented

Returning to the vignettes that opened this chapter, via joint life book sessions Lizzy realized that William wasn't just a "mean" brother, always attempting to provoke her. In fact, she learned that William's ire actually had little to do with her at all. Lizzy was a trigger for William's mad feelings. Once unleashed, the resentment was displaced onto Lizzy. Equipped with this knowledge, Lizzy started reacting to William differently. She ignored his rude comments. Or she said, "Oh, I see you are thinking about your birth mom again. Why don't you go talk to Mom about her?"

Isolation diminishes

I have provided services to many families who adopted an individual child on multiple occasions, or who adopted a sibling group related by birth. I am always amazed at how little these siblings discuss adoption or their pre-adoptive histories with each other. Once, in working with a larger sibling group, the youngest brother was practically jumping up and down with joy that he could finally ask his oldest birth sister, "What did our birth mom look like?" This sister never talked about the birth mother. So her brother was afraid to inquire about the birth mother or the reasons the children were placed in institutional care. The isolation that is a part of feeling "different" due to the child's adoptive status can be greatly reduced by getting adoptees talking.

Continuing with this group of brothers and sisters, the two oldest worked together to draw a portrait of the birth mother. Each brother and sister old enough to have memories of the birth home pooled these recollections into a document which became the core of their life book. Each learned that they shared similar feelings and thoughts about their pre-adoptive circumstances. At times, there was surprise. There were exchanges of "You miss her (i.e. birth mother) too?" "I think about her on my birthday just like you!" "I, too, wonder how she is doing." "I also think about seeing her again someday."

Since these kids dialogue as questions or observations about their past crop up, their unity facilitates their ongoing healing.

Tolerance for unwelcome behaviors increases

Typical kids, whether birth or adopted, can comprehend that experiences determine how each child performs in the family, at school, and in the community at large. Such understanding increases siblings' tolerance for each other. Referring to Anthony and Samantha whom we met earlier in this chapter, Anthony was staggered by the fact that Samantha resided in an orphanage for the first five years of her life. He knew she came "from China," but he had never really given thought to what that actually meant. Currently age nine, he was able to recall lots of things she didn't get to do or learn. He said, "No wonder she acts the way she does. She knows a lot, but it isn't like the stuff I know. I guess I need to be more patient with her!"

Empathy is increased and displayed

Anthony was moved by the visible sadness that Samantha displayed for the loss of her birth mother. He realized that her jealousy was because, unlike him, she knew nothing about her birth family. She didn't know whom she resembled. She didn't know the origin of her athletic dexterity or her creative art skills.

Unbeknownst to Samantha and his parents, Anthony wrote his birth mom. His letter was really a request: "Could you become Samantha's 'step-birthmom'?" Although the birth mother was a bit taken aback, she agreed. Samantha has since had many conversations with her. Certainly, she recognizes that her birth mother may have placed her in the orphanage for very dissimilar reasons to those that led to Anthony's placement, yet Samantha is quite comforted by the fact that she can speak with a "live lady" that "gave away her baby."

Anthony's empathy—the understanding of another person's feelings by remembering or imagining being in a similar situation—is a touching example of how siblings-by-adoption can learn to relate to each other.

A wealth of healing occurs when we use the life book with children individually and as a group. Parents are encouraged to initiate conversations surrounding general adoption-related questions and concerns, as well as the "tough stuff" between all members of their family. Human connection requires knowing each other—intimately and deeply. As the examples in this chapter make clear, mothers, fathers, brothers, and sisters attach when given the forum to share their life stories. Thus, openness in adoption includes contact with the birth family and sharing the adoptee's background information with each adopted son or daughter. Openness can also be a joint effort.

Chapter summary

- Openness is the trend sweeping the adoption community. Adoptive families are "friending" birth family members in person and via social media. Parents are encouraged to provide children with as much information as possible regarding the circumstances that led to their need to be adopted. The healing benefits of this new culture of adoption are untold. Yet sibling conflict may arrive for families blending multiple adoptees, typical and/or traumatized.

- The life book is a wonderful tool to facilitate children's recovery from abandonment, abuse, multiple moves, orphanage residence, and more. Constructing sons' and daughters' life stories requires that parents prepare themselves to talk with their children about "tough stuff." Mothers and fathers need to examine their views about grief and truthful disclosures as a first step in the life book process.

- The core of the life book is the narrative—the youngster's story. The life book moves the child—chronologically—from his early beginnings to his final destination—his adoptive home. This journey enhances self-esteem, resolves grief, replaces fantasy with facts, and stills behaviors. The adoptee emerges with a full sense of identity and purpose.

- When carried out jointly, life book work helps children grow in their relations with their siblings. Brothers and sisters share experiences in an intimate manner that spawns tolerance, empathy, unity, and the capacity to cope and accept each other. Thus, openness in this manner leads to the types of relations parents, brothers, and sisters envisioned when they invited the adoptee to join their family.

11

"My New Sibling's Behaviors Are So Bizarre!"

LEARNING TO BE A PEACEFUL FAMILY AGAIN

We've learned that adding a child to the family via adoption can bring some bizarre behaviors to the family. A once peaceful home may transform into a battleground, teeming with conflict. This is certainly not the way family life is supposed to be. Well, help is on the way! In this chapter, we're going to review four main reasons for the unwelcome behaviors. Understanding lends to tolerance, which in and of itself calms the home's emotional climate. It is important to point out that the four areas covered are actually intricately intertwined. Breaking down the sources of unwelcome behavior is simply a means to clarify how various aspects of trauma residue play out in the home. I'll also offer strategies—16 in total—that offer a powerful plan to help restore the home environment to a more harmonious and tranquil place! Mothers, fathers, brothers, sisters, and the adoptee benefit when the home climate is calm and serene! In this chapter mothers and fathers set the tone for the suggested changes. The kids march along.

The behavior is so bizarre because...

Development is at discord with chronological age

Chapter 2 presented that the trauma experienced by the newcomer interrupted his cognitive, social, emotional, physical, and physiological development. The adoptee is "younger" than his chronological age. In particular, the steps that lend to moral development are frequently incomplete. Thus, the adopted arrival may be missing the skills pictorially represented in Figure 11.1. I believe that the lack of skills in this sequence contribute significantly to the family feuds that erupt post-adoption.

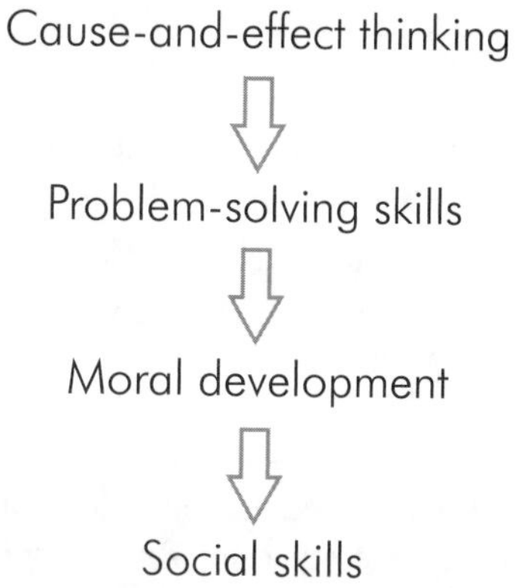

Cause-and-effect thinking

⇩

Problem-solving skills

⇩

Moral development

⇩

Social skills

FIGURE 11.1 DELAYED MORAL DEVELOPMENT

Mary Lou, adoptive mom to eight-year-old Margaret who arrived in the family at age four, makes clear the challenge of living with a child with underdeveloped cause-and-effect thinking:

"I feel beside myself repeating the same thing for three years. I guess I just can't understand how someone can continue to make the same mistakes, over and over, for so long despite discipline of every typical sort. I don't know if I'd call it anger or just frustration, but, either way, it does make me want to stand on the roof and scream sometimes!"

A lack of cause-and-effect thinking means that the traumatized child does not connect her actions to the consequences of her actions. Usually, she can repeat the words describing what will happen if she doesn't do her homework or take out the trash. Yet, in the moment, her disorganized brain processes prevent her from implementing the correct choice.

This faulty logic is what renders many "normal" parenting tools ineffective. Time-out, removal of privileges, sticker charts, grounding, threats, reminders, warnings, and so on requires the child to have the logic to act according to family rules.

Lags in problem-solving skills lend to what I call the "I make toast in the refrigerator" syndrome. The child with a history of neglect and/or abuse does not generate solutions. He has one way of solving a problem—lying, stealing, a temper tantrum, shouting, stomping off, manipulating. Until this child can learn to create and utilize solutions—"I can make toast in the toaster"—negative behaviors are perpetuated.

Moral development is the capacity to control one's own behavior internally. Developing this internalized set of guiding principles requires logical thinking. Thus, a child with delays in this area does not exhibit empathy or remorse. She can hit her sibling and feel totally justified in her actions!

"I mean, it wasn't like he was some wild maniac. He was just—it wasn't something that my family was used to, like lying and stealing. He was just the worst liar in the world. You could be like 'Is it night-time?' He would be like, 'No it's daytime. I swear it's daytime.'"

So, in part, altering negative behavior means that this "young" son or daughter must "grow up" developmentally.

Learning to be a peaceful family again: "Growing up the 'young' adoptee"
STRATEGY #1: GROWING CAUSE-AND-EFFECT THINKING

Different parenting tools must be acquired to facilitate the type of developmental gains that will allow the adopted son or daughter to truly grow up and act his or her age. Among these new tools is learning about and implementing *natural and logical consequences* (Cline and Fay 2006).

For example, the natural and logical consequence of purposefully breaking household items is that the child must replace the item. Payment can be money or chores, or the next time you are in the store you can be sad for the child as you say, "Well, I'd like to buy you that shirt. However, I'm putting that money toward the CD player you broke during your meltdown." Once home, count out the money before putting it in a safe place or the bank. He needs to "see" the exchange of money. Then be done—move on! Don't say, "See, how do *you* like it?" "How does that feel?" This is anger talking and anger renders the natural and logical consequence ineffective. Anyway, the point was made, and we are learning to have a calmer household. That's the beauty of natural and logical consequences. Something simply happens—no anger, frustration, or irritation needed!

STRATEGY #2: GROWING SOLUTIONS

This tip actually comes from a veteran adoptive family. Jean and Matt parent four children, two by birth and two by adoption. Jean said:

> "Talk about sibling rivalry! My kids fight a lot! And, I do mean fight—push, shove, punch. My adopted son's first reaction is to hit. I used to feel like I was a referee. Then I decided to take a different approach. I sat the fighting children at the table with some cookies and milk, when the fight was over a larger issue, and made them come up with solutions. I sat with them or listened while I cleaned the kitchen. I made suggestions as I felt necessary. I have a lot less fighting now and a lot more free time."

Jean's method could work in any family. The cookies and milk disarmed the children. Once calm, they were more open to resolving their dispute. Jean also decided which disagreements warranted her help and which didn't. She didn't involve herself if the matter was minor. All kids need to learn to generate solutions, especially the child whose development was shattered by abuse, neglect, or abandonment. Working together to "make toast in the toaster" promotes the type of unity needed to form connections among typical and traumatized siblings.

"Usually when I get mad, I go and do something else and come back later and start talking about it again. Go out and shoot hoops or take a jog or walk. And then I come back and talk with my parents about it."

STRATEGY #3: GROWING MORAL DEVELOPMENT

Natural and logical consequences promote some of the qualities needed to help the child who has experienced trauma move from the pre-conventional to the conventional and post-conventional stages of moral development (see Chapter 2). Negative behaviors dissipate when the child can think logically and make decisions based on a universal sense of right and wrong, rather than acting on what feels good in the moment.

Parents can also use restitution to help the child develop morals and values. Restitution has two parts. The first part is saying "I'm sorry." Notice the "I'm." Troubled adoptees tend to say "Sorry." The "I'm" is necessary because it means "I am taking responsibility for my action." The second part is "How can I make it up to you?" Now, don't get carried away with this second part. A very simple chore or a hug is more than enough to make the point to children of all ages. The important component is that the "make up" activity is connected to the unpleasant act.

Grace, age seven, came to live with her adoptive family when she was five years old. The family was comprised of her parents, Jenna and Stephanie, and her two older sisters, Ella and Zoe, ages ten and 12 respectively. Grace had the most annoying habit of taking sips from anyone's drink. If a can of pop was sitting on a coffee table, Grace would make a point to pick it up and drink from it. This just seemed disgusting to Grace's older sisters.

Jenna and Stephanie decided that this was a behavior they would like to see Grace give up. So, each time she drank from an open drink, she had to apologize and "make up" by buying a new beverage. She had some options as far as purchasing new beverages. She could have water when the family dined out. The purchase price of the beverage she would have ordered was deposited in her "beverage bank," which Jenna kept in her possession. Or she could carry out a simple chore to earn 50 cents—the fee she owed for a contaminated drink. Simple chores included carrying a laundry basket, helping to fold towels, helping to make a bed, helping to clear the table, etc. It didn't take Grace long to decide that contaminating other people's drinks wasn't worth the price.

STRATEGY #4: HANDLING "IT'S NOT FAIR!"

Ella and Zoe, the appropriately developing kids, appreciated the way in which their parents dealt with Grace's beverage behavior. Their harkened cries of "It's not fair" diminished when they were able to see that steps were being taken to curtail their youngest sibling's behavior. This will be true for most resident children. When they see that parents are working to alter the unwelcome conduct, there will be fewer cries of "It's not fair."

Humor may also diffuse complaints of "It's not fair!" Statements such as "My brother got a new truck" or "You would never let me get me away with what he does!" are responded to with "Okay, the next time Mom gets a new bra she'll get one for everyone." Immediately, the child replies, "I don't need a bra!" Kids draw the correct conclusions: everyone in the family gets what they need and sometimes they get what Mom and Dad feel like buying.

STRATEGY #5: SHERLOCK HOLMES, JESSICA FLETCHER, OR NANCY DREW YOU ARE NOT!

It does seem that today's parents often want to be fair. Parents move from child to child, striving to find the answer to the latest misdeed. The detective parent seeks to uncover the culprit—beyond a shadow of a doubt. If there is only one deceitful child or thieving child in the family, parents can bypass these time-consuming and frustrating interactions and go directly to that son or daughter. The usually truthful children resent such inquisitions. This process slowly erodes the quality of the attachment that existed with these typical children prior to the adoption. If, at some point, a child was wrongfully accused, the parent can right the wrong—apologize. What a valuable lesson for all of the children in the family!

"He would lie about anything for no reason—about something you wouldn't even get in trouble for, he would just lie. He would steal stuff and lie. He stole from the house. I got him a job. He stole from work. Why are we even having this conversation? You know he stole it! Why are you asking me where your ring is? Where do you think it is? He stole it. Anything that we can't find, he stole."

STRATEGY #6: PARENTING DIFFERENTLY

Parenting a combination of typical and traumatized children will require parenting each type of child *differently*—utilizing parenting tools designed to offset trauma residue. Family compositions that include a child with autism, learning disability, Down Syndrome, for example, do this every day! In the long run, parenting differently will lend to the overall healing of the adoptee, and the entire family will realize an improved atmosphere. So, actually, everybody will win in the long-term picture. The family meeting offers the forum to explain this to the healthy children. Most birth and/or previously adopted children do well with this concept as long as they are kept informed.

Colette and Greg parent three children, all by adoption:

> "We have three adopted children. Our daughter, now 12, despite being identified as a healthy infant, has been diagnosed with Fetal Alcohol Syndrome. She has many significant needs that will last her lifetime. Our third child, currently age eight, was identified by his caseworkers as 'only' having some speech delays. In reality he came to us very traumatized and with serious attachment issues. We identify our middle son, Blake, age 11, as our healthy child. In our family, he is the 'normal' one.
>
> "We do parent each child differently and we have very different expectations for each child. This isn't stressful to us. It would be very hard to parent them all the same. Placing the same expectations or rules on each of them would set them all up for failure. We have always parented them according to their individual needs, so this is what they expect and they don't complain about it."

"I fear attaching to all of you!"

The newcomer who arrives with an insecure style of attachment thinks two main thoughts:

- "I have to push you away before you decide to abandon me. It hurts too much when people leave me."

- "I am bad. That's why I got abused. That's why I got left by my birth family."

These thoughts drive an incredible array of negative behavior! Frequently, parents are correcting the adoptee with attachment issues all day. The end result is constant conflict! This chronic quarreling unintentionally validates the adoptee's irrational thoughts. He says, "See, I am bad. I am always in trouble." Or it meets the adoptee's unconscious need to create distance: "When you are angry with me, we aren't close. If we aren't close, then I won't be sad when I have to leave." He is protecting his heart from further emotional pain.

STRATEGY #7: PICKING AND CHOOSING
WHICH BEHAVIORS TO CEASE

Parents must prioritize a few negative behaviors at a time. This will mean living with various rule violations. To some degree, the adoptee will be "getting away" with behaviors for which the resident children would receive consequences. Yet working a smaller number of behaviors will result in more overall change. This is a difficult concept for parents, and for brothers and sisters, to accept. Again, communication and education can help the resident kids understand that what is "not fair" is actually going to contribute to healing their sibling. In the long run, everyone will benefit. It can be a challenge to select which behaviors to work toward ceasing, and which to let go (for now). Behaviors that jeopardize the safety of the adoptee, brothers and sisters, and parents are always selected first to extinguish. Behaviors that lend to long-term impaired functioning of the adoptee are second. Stealing, for example, may lead to incarceration. So stealing should be a priority. After the first two categories are covered, any behavior can be selected, keeping in mind that there are some battles you cannot win. You can most likely ask a child to go to her bedroom; you can't make her sleep. You can make a child do her homework; you cannot make her turn it in.

STRATEGY #8: ELIMINATE BATTLES WHEN POSSIBLE

Shannon, a single mom, provides an example:

> Shannon adopted Peggy when she was eight years old. Peggy is now 11. A few months ago, Shannon received a foster care placement, Justin and Joey, six and seven years old. Peggy was

instantly jealous of any time or attention Shannon provided the young boys. Arrival home from school was particularly challenging. Shannon would put out cupcakes and milk for the boys. Peggy usually got her own snack and a drink. However, loud, snarling complaints of "Why do you get them their snack?" and "I want what they're having" prompted Shannon to put out three plates of cupcakes and three glasses of milk. This fight was resolved.

Ignore, avoid, and eliminate lesser issues. The more you can overlook, the calmer your home.

STRATEGY #9: MAKE A NOTE

Many parents and the children already living in the home at the time of the adoption find it helpful to post a note in a spot where they will observe it several times each day: "I live with someone who rejects my hugs." "I am teaching Billy to be honest." "I live with someone who won't do his homework." "I live with a daughter who wets the bed." "I am teaching Sally to be more careful with her things." "I live with someone who smears his poop." Each day the note serves as a reminder to deal with the particular behavior more calmly or to let the behavior go totally.

STRATEGY #10: TAMING THE PORCUPINE: NURTURE IS A KEY

It will be helpful at this point to refer back to the cycle of needs in Chapter 2 which was described like this…

A baby cries. The baby's primary caregiver, Mom or Dad, attends to the baby—a bottle, a clean diaper, comfort, a binky, and so on. The baby calms. During this process of going from fussy to feeling safe and secure, there is eye contact. There is talking: "You are such a good baby." "What a beautiful girl you are!" And there is warmth—babies get warm when we hold or swaddle them. Feeding and fragrance are also a part of this very sensory cycle; perhaps we put lotion on the baby. Movement occurs—rocking or bouncing the baby on our knees. Touch is involved every step of the way!

So, when we talk about increasing nurture—forming secure attachments—we are really talking about ways to increase the components of the cycle of needs through the child's senses: eye contact, food, smells, movement, talking and touch (Keck and Kupecky 2002). The ideas in this strategy reflect these "key" ingredients. The end result is a recipe for a happier and healthier family!

Of course, nurturing a traumatized child is no small task. Adoptive parents are being asked to hug and caress children who are quite similar to porcupines! Their quills—behaviors—rise up, shoot out and penetrate—reject the parents and the siblings—frequently! Yet, nurture is an entitlement. The types of changes that parents want—and that the family needs to be happier—are likely not going to occur until the adoptee's void of hugs, kisses, caresses and tickles is filled! Remember, the child that experienced trauma was robbed of thousands of repetitions of the cycle of needs! Nurture can be as simple as a hand on the child's shoulder, a candy kiss placed in his mouth, a love note in a lunch box, "I love you" written with soap on a mirror, painting fingernails, styling hair, scratching a back, sprinkling chocolate chips on pancakes, rubbing lotion on sore shoulders, baking cookies, warming mittens in the dryer on a cold school day morning.

These are all *direct* and *indirect* ways to begin to increase nurture. Obviously, your typical sons and daughters would love you to nurture them in all these ways as well! The more affectionate attention they receive, the more they retain a secure attachment to you. Kids—securely attached—will act in accord with the parents' morals system. So, if as a mother or father you are worried about your birth and/or previously adopted children taking on the negative behaviors of a troubled adopted child, spread the nurture on thick to all the kids!

If you want about a hundred more nurture suggestions, then look in *Parenting the Hurt Child: Helping Adoptive Families Heal and Grow* by Gregory C. Keck and Regina Kupecky. This book provides list after list of ways to nurture children, and they are applicable to *all* children.

Theraplay®

The developers of this form of therapy define it as "a structured play therapy for children and their parents. Its goal is to enhance attachment, self-esteem, trust in others and joyful engagement.

Because of its focus on attachment and relationship development, Theraplay® has been used successfully for many years with adoptive families" (Jernberg and Booth 1999).

> Sean was 15 years old. He was adopted at age three by Wilma and Andy. He had presented various challenges for 12 years! He especially liked to dismantle things. Anything he could get his hands on was immediately taken apart, because he wanted to "see how it worked." Unfortunately, he lost pieces of items, and so many of his learning projects were ruined. He loved to take batteries. It was difficult to keep a flashlight, the remote control, the other kids' toys, and so on operational.
>
> He displayed symptoms of an ambivalent attachment. He hated it when Mom was out of the house or out of sight. He called her on her cell phone constantly. Even if she didn't answer, he kept calling and leaving messages. When she was home, he followed her everywhere. She had had a shadow for 12 years!
>
> Theraplay® was selected as one intervention because Sean so resembled a three-year-old socially and emotionally. He eagerly participated in the activities. He especially enjoyed a cookie game. He laid across his mom's lap and looked into her eyes. She held an animal cracker, and she provided directions. "I want you to bite off the back feet. Good! Now, bite off the head! Great, you are listening so well!" He giggled and giggled and asked for another cookie and another cookie and yet another cookie!

Children, little to big—sometimes very big—love Theraplay!® Give it a try. Make sure to stock up on the cookies—the other kids will want a turn!

"Music soothes the soul"

Isn't this heading true? There is simply nothing like music to connect people to one another or to raise a down mood. Who doesn't tap a beat on the steering wheel when driving a long distance? Or start singing along with the current top hit or a favorite oldie? Your wedding was accompanied by a special love song. You sing your child to sleep with a favorite lullaby. Even picking up toys is done to the Barney "Clean up" song. The iPod® rage is another indicator of the pleasure millions of people receive from music. Did you also know that:

- Music helps develop brain areas involved in language and reasoning.

- There is a link between music and spatial intelligence—the ability to visually and mentally picture things. This is a type of intelligence used in math and solving problems.

- Music provides a means of self-expression.

- Performing to an audience in a concert or chorus helps kids conquer fears. They learn that anxiety can be overcome.

- Information from the National Education Longitudinal Study showed that music students received more academic honors and awards than non-music students (Ingels 1992).

- Students with coursework or experience in music performance or music appreciation scored higher on the SAT (College Entrance Examination Board 2001).

- The musician must make decisions about tempo, tone, style, rhythm, and so on. This makes the brain become incredibly good at organizing and conducting numerous activities. This has a great payoff for lifelong attentional skills (Ratey 2001).

- Singing, chanting, and rhythmic play can increase your child's vocabulary, improve coordination, enhance self-esteem, contribute to emotional regulation, and reduce stress (Campbell 2000).

- Rhythm is essential. The brain's rhythm-keeping regions, when not functioning properly, are often causes of depression and other mental health disorders. These regions are also in charge of regulating sleep, and this is probably why sleep problems are seen in children with mental health issues. Regulating heart rate and the release of stress hormones require the brain to keep proper rhythm as well (Perry and Szalavitz 2006).

This list could go on to fill volumes!

In therapy, I connect my iPod® to a speaker. I find that even the most difficult children will settle down and gaze intently into their parents' eyes during songs about family and adoption. Some of my clients' favorites are from the CDs *Do You have a Little Love to Share*, *Adoption...The Songs You Love*, *The Spirit of Adoption*, and *Chosen: Songs of Hope Inspired by Adoption*. Let music bring your whole family closer together!

STRATEGY #11: ATTACHMENT STARTS AT HOME, AND THEN TRANSFERS TO THE LARGER WORLD

Attachment is a process initiated in infancy which then grows. Children connect to brothers and sisters, grandparents, aunts, and uncles. Subsequently, the security established by Mom and Dad and the pleasures derived from relationships span to the neighborhood, school, and the world at large.

Thus, as the traumatized adoptee heals, there will be a definite curbing of negative behaviors on the playground, at family outings, at church, and everywhere else! But, while the recovery process is occurring, a few thoughts about school are likely welcome. Again, I've called on some experienced moms and dads to offer some food for thought.

Valerie and Peter parent five children—three by birth and two by adoption:

> "Our one adopted son caused many problems at school. This was an embarrassment to our other children. Eventually, we made the decision to place him in a small private school. It means that we had to cut expenses in other areas. But it has been worth it! Our kids can go to school and not worry about what he will do and who will say something to them about what he did. It has cut down on the conflicts between our kids. Now we have time to talk about their day rather than talking to them about their brother's day at school and how they were affected by their brother's actions."

Michelle and Mark parent one child by birth and one child by adoption:

"We home-school both children. Our adopted son throws fits on and off all day, every day. The stress of his screaming affected me and my daughter. One day per week, he goes to a child care center. He is able to do well outside of the home in relationships that aren't as intimate. He enjoys going, and my daughter and I enjoy some nice time together. I am considering sending him to public school for a year. I think my daughter could use an extended break. It has been six years of these fits."

Louise and Ray parent three birth sons and one adopted daughter. Ray states:

"Our daughter had various negative behaviors at school. She threw things at teachers, stole school supplies, walked out of classes, etc. When the principal confronted her, she would often become highly argumentative with him. He would call me at work. Sometimes I had to leave work and go calm her down. Other times, they wanted me to take her home. In these instances, I would have to go to work early the next day or stay late to get my work done. I was losing a lot of time with my boys. Finally, Louise and I sat down with the school and explained that we couldn't do this anymore. Eventually, they moved our daughter to a special education classroom. This has improved our home life. I can make it to all the boys' games now."

Vivian and Frank are a family home-schooling a resident child and two newly adopted children. Vivian says:

"I provide instruction to my two sons. My adopted daughter gets her lessons online. Her control issues are too great for her to take directions from me. The whole day is calmer since we made this choice. We are able to have some enjoyable time during the day."

The transfer of feelings

To an extent, we all transfer emotions via behavior:

Pat, husband to Marian and parent to one typically developing adolescent and two adolescents with complex trauma issues, has been under stress at work. His company was sold and the new management is restructuring the manner in which Pat's department operates. Pat must attend meetings and learn new ways to conduct business. Many of his co-workers have sought new employment, so Pat must also learn to work with a new team of colleagues. He arrives home each evening grumpy. He complains about his job, the clutter of the home, the dinner selection, and so on and so forth. Shortly after his arrival home, each family member feels down in the dumps. Pat is transferring his feelings of anger about his work situation to his wife and children.

The traumatized newcomer transfers feelings with frequency and intensity. In essence, the adoptee enters the adoptive family with unresolved emotions from his traumatic experiences. The newcomer begins to transfer these feelings, by acting out behaviorally to the adoptive parents and siblings. The adoptee's unconscious overall goal with this behavior is to watch and see how the family members handle feelings. The manner in which his mom, dad, brothers, and sisters express their emotions becomes his template for resolving his own feelings. But the intensity of the adoptee's emotions can be overwhelming to family members. Thus, family members find themselves depressed, angry, anxious, and frustrated—daily! The stress level in the family rises.

The traumatized arrival communicates feelings through behaviors for a variety of reasons:

- Children who have been beaten, raped, abandoned, institutionalized, separated from siblings, and/or moved from foster home to foster home have internalized tremendous feelings as a result of these traumas. Inside, they feel rage, sorrow, hopelessness, helplessness, profound sadness, frustration, loneliness, and lost. Who wouldn't? Their traumas are so extensive that it is difficult for them to find words to describe their sufferings.

- Traumatic experiences often occur when they have little or no language development. A majority of trauma occurs between the pre-natal period and the pre-school years.

- Their world is riddled with cognitive dissonance. They look around and feel out of sync. For example, as the international adoptee matures, she realizes that her life in the orphanage was a different beginning from that of the other children in her neighborhood, her pre-school, kindergarten, and so on. Inadvertently, among the adults in the adoption community, the act of being adopted is frequently portrayed in a positive light. "Your birth mother was so poor, she couldn't keep you. She wanted you to be adopted because she loved you so much." The adoptee is put in a situation that is inconsistent with her thoughts and emotions. She feels sad and angry that she was given away, no matter what the circumstances. She feels the loss of the life that was supposed to be. Yet she is not sure how to convey these feelings, because those around her are not demonstrating that they understand her perspective, which seems to be so different from theirs.

- Children adopted from the child welfare system frequently lack the opportunity to convey their thoughts and feelings. They were uncertain as to how long they would be in residence with a particular family. They felt that there was no point starting a process of healing that they may not be able to finish. Therapies are interrupted because they must move. Services are not provided due to lengthy waiting lists. Or services are not initiated due to a philosophy that promotes that time and love will make the problems disappear.

- Certainly, much of the above holds true for the children of international adoption. Harried orphanage staff can't make time to respond to the emotions of a roomful of youngsters. Therapeutic intervention is a limited or non-existent commodity in foreign institutions.

STRATEGY #12: MIRROR, MIRROR ON THE WALL

Parents set the tone for the family. Typical children follow the lead of Mom and Dad. In fact, resident sons and daughters tend to be replicas of their mother and father. Adoptees arrive in the family mirroring many qualities in common with their birth parents or orphanage setting. They must learn to internalize and reflect the characteristics of their adoptive parents.

But when the child's mirror is that of parental anger that explodes, spewing out hurtful words, this is frequently how children begin or continue to act. Certainly, parents develop guilt for such actions. Self-confidence in one's parenting abilities crumbles. Mothers and fathers begin to ask themselves, "Why am I always yelling?" "Why did I get mad over that?" "Why can't I snap out of this?" "Did I make my adopted son the way he is?" "What have I done to my other children?" "What kind of parent am I?" Worries become consuming: "What is going to happen to our family if things don't change?" "How can we live like this?" "What if my son doesn't have a 'normal' life?"

When families enter therapy, statement like these are common: "I have never been so angry. I didn't even know that I could get this angry—especially at a child!" "I am now on anti-depressants." "I am taking medication for anxiety." "I have high blood pressure now." "At times, I have to walk away. Otherwise, I fear I would hurt my daughter. I feel crazy for having these thoughts. What kind of a parent feels like they could physically hurt their own child?" "He pushes my buttons! He knows the things that make me angry and he does them on purpose to make me mad! Why is he doing this to me?"

One mom parents seven children by birth and adoption; the two oldest girls (currently ages 16 and 17; arrival ages nine and ten) have histories of complex trauma. She writes:

> "I have uglier feelings from dealing with these children than I even thought I could possibly have. Then I feel guilty for my feelings. For example, I wonder if I had to do this all over again, would I? Then I feel badly for thinking how much easier my life could have been. I love the girls. They deserve a home, a good family, and unconditional love, just like everyone else. As hard as I've tried, they don't always reciprocate, which not only makes me feel unappreciated but also that I haven't done a good enough job—that I'm not a good enough mom."

Brothers and sisters report:

> "I don't think there was anything that could have prepared me or my family for Betty and her needs. It's the kind of thing that is very hard to understand until you see it, and the only way to really learn how to deal with my sister is to live with her day

in and day out. No speech or reading can prepare you for the rage, manipulation, and defiance these children put up as a guard, and the constant anxiety they experience dealing with everyday situations.

"Betty is a masterful irritator, and she demands to make her presence felt by interrupting whatever you are trying to do. The only way to cope with this is to escape; to read a book or watch TV in another room for a while. Her presence is always much more enjoyable after you haven't seen her for a while."

"He will go into my room. He will take stuff from my room. He hides it in his room and I won't find it for like three weeks. He just really frustrates me. He's just like uncontrollable pretty much."

"Whenever we're talking to each other it seems like we lose our tempers more easily. Because it's not like we're talking to each other just for fun anymore—it seems like we are always mad at each other."

Learning to bypass angry interactions takes a conscious effort on the part of parents and, in turn, the birth and/or previously adopted children. Parents who learn to mirror calm, nurturing, empathic exchanges reflect the emotional image needed to still the home waters. Thus, mothers and fathers need to identify ways to reduce the intensity of their interactions with their children. Anyway, prolonged anger isn't good for anyone! Chronic anger contributes to heart disease, heart attack, prolonged stress, diabetes, more frequent colds, and a host of other health problems.

"I'm the type of person if there is a problem I want to fix it 'cause then I don't have to worry about it anymore. You know in that case it wasn't my problem. I don't want to be, like, it's my parent's problem, but it really was my parent's problem. I didn't want to go to them and be, like, why do you have this demon living with me, because they probably already feel bad enough. So I didn't feel the need to come down on my folks for that and in coping with the problem I just left it alone. It wasn't my problem. I played video games, went swimming, and we have a lot of woods behind our house so I would go walking.

When you do stuff that you like to do you're not worried about what this idiot is over here doing. So it is easy to get away when you have stuff around you that you have had all of your life."

Parents may want to consider the following ways of avoiding stressful situations:

- *Take a time-out.* A large majority of issues don't have to be processed right this minute. Moms and dads have the option of removing themselves from situations that aren't jeopardizing the safety of any member of the family. This provides the opportunity to step back and ask, "Is this behavior worth tackling?" "Can I let it go?" "How can I challenge this situation calmly?" "Do I need to wait until later in the day when my son or daughter is calm?" "What is the outcome I really want?" Once you formulate your plan, return to the children and take your desired action.

- *Adjust your expectations.* When a son or daughter is not achieving the family's or society's definition of "normal," the family's expectations are unfulfilled. So, sentiments like these, need to shift: "He pushes my buttons! He knows the things that make me angry and he does them on purpose to make me mad!" "He is ruining the whole family!" "She should be more grateful!" This child did not asked to be abused, neglected, and discarded. He is hurt to the core and is acting in a manner designed to protect and shield himself from further pain.

  Expectations of your spouse, your support system, church members, and so on likely need to be reviewed and altered as well. For example, one mom stated:

  > "I will always be deeply hurt by the fact that my own sister often implies that I am the reason my boys struggle. However, she is my sister and I do love her. I don't want their adoptions to cut us off. So I compromise. On really difficult days, I call a friend I made at a support group. But I attend a book club with my sister. This works for

both of us. We spend time together, and we can talk
about something we both enjoy."

- *Apply skills from other environments.* At work, for example, we
all learn to tolerate habits of co-workers. We also learn to get
along with those whose political beliefs, work ethic, religious
preferences, and style, are diverse from our own. We learn to
co-exist with an array of philosophies without yelling and
screaming. This same "value competency" can come home
with us at the end of the day.

- *Seek professional help.* Many adult find that the services of a
therapist can be quite helpful for themselves, and their sons
and daughters. A professional who isn't in the trenches can
often see more clearly the types of interventions or solutions
that would benefit individual family members and the family
as a whole.

- *Keep reading!* The mantra for adoptive families is education,
education, education! As Dr. Seuss said, "The more that you
read, the more things you will know." The more you know,
the more you can help yourself and all of your children!

- *Review Chapter 3.* Refine the suggested strengths. All of them
lend to successful outcomes in the family built-by-adoption.

This adoptive father offers nice closure for this segment of content:

"Although obvious on the surface, it is incredibly important to
find out what works for each individual child. Both of my sons
exhibit behaviors that can be completely maddening! One of the
boys is softer spoken and is immediately responsive to even a
marginal rise in voice volume. The other is the child we had to
stop spanking when he was three because the only response we
would get was laughter. Anger seemed to make him happy. I
am learning, thanks to the wonderful perceptions and advice of
my wife, that we do much better if I lower my voice and speak
calmly rather than yelling and ranting like a madman. Sometimes
parenting is a moving target, so you need to be adaptable."

The role of emotional dysregulation: Parenting "deerly"

Brain development is contingent upon environment. A nurturing, sensorily stimulating environment best incubates and forms the brain. When this process is interrupted by neglect, physical abuse, sexual abuse, pre-natal drug and alcohol exposure, maternal stress, and so on, the brain may be unable to form the pathways and connections that lead to emotional regulation, development of social skills, or a secure attachment. Areas of the brain responsible for memory, learning, empathy, and remorse can also be impaired by these early traumas.

The stress of living in a chaotic and/or neglectful environment—an orphanage, a dysfunctional birth home—creates a brain—a human being—more vulnerable to real or perceived stress (Child Welfare Information Gateway 2001). The child, traumatized prior to adoption, arrives in the new family with an overactive stress response system. So he or she will enter the states of "flight" or "fight" easily and long after placement in the healthy family system.

Reiterating an earlier point, children with histories of trauma are like deer. Deer flee in an instant when frightened! One second they are calmly grazing in your front yard (if you live in deer country!) and the next they are darting in every direction, seeking safety. This happens when there is no real threat—a branch falling—or when there is a danger—a hunter. This latter, has caused deer to be on perpetual "red alert." Deer are always wary of their environment.

Traumatized adoptees are similar to deer. They quickly enter states of "freeze," "flight," or "fight"—even when there is no visible threat or demand. Thus, parenting "deerly" is another way to restore a peaceful home environment.

STRATEGY #13: CONSEQUENCES VS. REACTIONS

In order to "parent deerly," moms and dads need to adjust a mentality in which anger and consequences dominate. Everything doesn't need a consequence! Healing the traumatized newcomer is really about how parents and siblings react to the behavior. This is certainly more easily said than done! Yet conflict sends the child deeper into flight or fight, and more negative behaviors occur in these states. Calm, cool exchanges between the parent and child lend to less behavioral difficulties. Under these circumstances, the brain can begin to re-organize itself and the child heals! The family has a peaceful, emotional climate.

STRATEGY #14: APRON STRINGS, ANYONE?

Adopted children need *time-ins*—they need to be *with* their parents (Keck and Kupecky 2009). Before opting to send the child away from family members, stop and ask, "How can I bring him in closer to me right now? What can I do to help her calm down?" One great mom of several adopted children says "Apron strings" to an agitated child. This means "Come here and let me give you a hug. Let me help you calm yourself. Then we can talk about what has happened and how the problem can be solved."

This mom's approach is quite advantageous. She is assisting her sons and daughters in learning how to regulate emotionally. Mother Nature designed emotional development to transfer from parent to child. The "cycle of needs" makes this clear. A fussy infant is supposed to be held—until calm and happy—by a caring parent. The child who was in residence in an orphanage or neglectful birth home missed this essential sequence. This son or daughter arrives in the family unable to settle emotionally. Fortunately, with a little help from Mom and Dad, kids can learn this vital skill at later ages.

"From the moment my twin sisters arrived at age three, it was apparent how severely traumatized the kids were. The girls would have these screaming fits, almost daily, that would last for hours. They wouldn't cry; it was more of a guttural scream. The destruction to personal and family property was mind-blowing. At one point in time, the twins could not have beds because they had ripped all of the stuffing out of their mattresses. They had sleeping bags and small tents in their bedroom, but the tents were broken within a few days. My mom would spend hours in their room trying to get them to fall asleep. She would play lullabies, she would sing to them, read to them, and rock them."

STRATEGY #15: STOP ASKING WHY!

John, now 15, (adopted at age three) emptied the batteries from a flashlight. In their place, he put his own feces. He screwed the top back on the flashlight, and put it back in the drawer in the kitchen. Soon the odor of poop began to permeate the kitchen. This was particularly difficult during dinner! Mom and Dad searched and searched for the source of the smell. Mom eventually realized that the stench was strongest in the drawer that contained the flashlight. She removed all the items from the drawer and eventually she came to the flashlight. When she took the top off, she was disgusted and angry! She wanted to know "Why?"

"Why?" This is a word sure to generate a response that can anger a parent. "Why did you lie?" "Why did you break the remote?" "Why are you wearing your sister's shoes?" "Why did you go in your brother's room?" "Why didn't you turn in your homework?" Responses include "I don't know" or "It wasn't me." Some children simply stare at the enraged mother or father. This child's brain is moving into dissociation. The infuriated parent pursues an answer. A lengthy argument ensures. During the conflict, the "why" was never answered, and the child most likely lied numerous times. The typical kids fled to their rooms or a friend's house.

A well-intentioned parent hopes that "If I could comprehend 'why', then I could eliminate this behavior." "Why" is being explained in this chapter. John lacks cause-and-effect thinking. John feels like "crap" about himself because his birth mother placed him in the orphanage. So, ask "Why" no more.

Instead, ask "What?" "What do I want to do about this behavior?"

John's mother, when both were calm, sat down with John. She succinctly let him know that his behavior had created a health hazard and an inconvenience to his family members. She asked him, "How do you think it best to make this up to the family?" After some hemming and hawing, John decided he would clean the kitchen with disinfectant. He would also make a formal apology to the family. Satisfied, John's mom concluded, "I do hope you figure out that you're not crap."

John learned problem solving and he was given a key piece of thinking to help him heal. Attachment was facilitated.

If John didn't want to sanitize the kitchen, Mom and Dad had many other options. John could use money from his savings account to pay his Mom or a sibling to carry out the needed cleaning. John could sell some electronic equipment or games in order to provide payment for a cleaning service.

So give "What?" a try today! "What" you have to lose is anger and conflict. "What" you have to gain is healing and a more peaceful home environment!

Strategy #16: Joining In

Lisa, age 11, was adopted from the foster care system at age three. She was removed from her birth parents as a result of severe neglect. She has always "collected" household items. As a pre-schooler, this included shoe boxes, little pieces of fabric, and bottle caps. Once she entered kindergarten, pencils became her object of choice. She would arrive home with five, six, or more pencils. Fellow students were always looking for their pencils! This has continued through each grade. Her fifth grade teacher, Mrs. Baily, a wise woman, purchased an array of pencils after a consultation with Lisa's mom. Each day she gave Lisa several pencils. The pencils were different colors, some were fat, some were skinny, some had animal-shaped erasers, and some had messages on them such as "Great job." Lisa loved these pencils. She looked forward to getting to school to see what pencils she would receive from Mrs. Baily. This very economical solution ended the disappearance of classmates' pencils. After several months, Lisa, on her own, said, "No, thanks, Mrs. Baily. I think I have enough pencils now."

Mrs. Baily's solution was to "join in" with Lisa. Rather than become angry and dole out detentions, Mrs. Baily realized that Lisa's pencil theft was a way to quell the social anxiety the school setting created for Lisa. Pencils and other trinkets were a way for Lisa to try to make herself feel better. Such self-soothing isn't uncommon. Adults often go shopping when they feel depressed. Kids don't have a credit card!

Here is another example:

Carol arrived in the family from Guatemala. Her self-concept was shattered by her pre-adoptive experiences. As she grew, this issue manifested itself via tattling on her three older sisters. She had to appear better than them. So she liked to point out what she felt they were doing wrong. Her sisters opted to join in by making a chart. Each time Carol tattled, a sticker was placed next to that sibling's name. The sister with the most stickers at the end of the week won a prize! It didn't take Carol long to decide that tattling was no longer for her. Then her kind siblings treated her to an ice cream—a celebration for ending her tattle-tale ways!

Joining in is a powerful tool that the whole family can partake in. It is designed to be fun! Nothing is more the opposite of anger than fun! At the Attachment and Bonding Center of Ohio, we join in with unwanted behaviors every day. We have lots of fun with bizarre behaviors. Your family can too!

As another example:

Peter left a trail of food wrappers, magazines, clothes, toys, papers, magic markers, K'Nex® pieces everywhere he went! Siblings and parents could clearly tell where Peter had been in the house! Yet he always replied, "It wasn't me!" His mom came across a coffee mug online with Peter's exact sentiment. She ordered a pair. Over breakfast, she and her husband could barely contain their giggles as they discussed what could be possibly be happening in their house that such messes were so commonplace. Was someone coming in while they were out? Perhaps, they needed to contact the "mess police"! Throughout the whole conversation, they held their mugs enameled with "It wasn't me!" Peter didn't utter a sound. Yet his standard of housekeeping certainly improved.

Chapter summary

- Behavioral change occurs when the "young" adoptee grows up. Facilitating developmental growth—cause-and-effect thinking, moral development, emotional regulation, emotional expression, problem-solving skills—is an essential component of healing the adoptee, as well as a means to restore a positive home climate. Once your "little" child develops cognitively, emotionally, socially, physically, and physiologically, he will mature into a respectful, responsible family member who is fun to be with (Cline and Fay 2006).

- The nurturing suggestions contribute to forming strong, secure, and healthy attachments. Attachment is essential to human growth and development. With it, humans can navigate relationships in all spheres of their life. As such, their possibilities are endless. Have you nurtured your family today?

- The new arrival's attempts to transfer emotions to mother, fathers, brothers, and sisters must be averted. Parents must demonstrate that chronic conflict is not the way to express feelings. A home environment permeated by anger is unhealthy for each member of the family. Acquiring a toolbox full of new parenting techniques, adjusting expectations, applying skills proven successful in other areas of life, seeking professional help, and education offer the means to keep the family moving forward in a harmonious manner.

- Mirroring peaceful, composed responses enhances the brain functioning of the child who arrives after trauma. A fussy baby is soothed until her crying ceases. Eventually, her brain learns to calm down as needed and when needed. Abused and neglected children did not receive this quality of caregiving. They must learn emotional regulation at later ages and with a brain impacted by horrific early pre-adoptive experiences. This is no small task. The sooner parents learn to settle their emotions, the sooner the whole family will emulate a brighter, optimistic family atmosphere. Children—traumatized and typical—reflect their parents' image.

12

Two of the Toughest Behaviors: Sexual Acting Out and Aggression

ENSURING A SAFE, SECURE HOME ENVIRONMENT

Unfortunately, a portion of newcomers will move in accompanied by behaviors that jeopardize the very sanctity of the meaning of home. This chapter looks at two such behaviors, makes suggestions to curtail these threatening behaviors, and covers ways to protect brothers and sisters and ensure their safety and security.

Ensuring family safety and security: Parenting and healing aggressive adopted children

As a child, I never considered hitting my mother. It didn't even occur to me that I had that option. Even during times when I was particularly angry with her, I accepted her decision with no violence. Yet there are some adopted children—with traumatic beginnings—who daily, hit, kick, bite, slap, push, and shove their parents and siblings, or do damage to the dry wall or break household items! It is simply terrible to live with violence in your own home.

Adoptive families living with an aggressive child feel trapped—held hostage in their own home. Many begin to "walk on eggshells" in an effort to avoid yet another tantrum. In order to reduce or cease the child's aggressive behavior, parents should consider the following instead.

"One time I was babysitting her and she didn't want to dry her hair before bed. It's a rule in our house that you have to dry your hair so you don't go to bed with your hair wet. So I told her she had to go dry it. She told me, 'No.' So I said, 'Okay, I'll dry it for you.' I put her in the bathroom and I took the dryer to dry her hair, and then she just went into a complete tantrum. She started kicking and biting. She got herself down on the floor and tried to kick me. There has been lots of violence and hitting and destroying things in the house."

Cognitive therapies

Professional assistance will be needed to alter the belief system (see Chapter 2) of the child who exhibits aggression and violence in the adoptive home. The pattern of violence is perpetuated by the perceptions the child developed while residing in an environment of domestic violence and/or physical abuse. Or the display of violence resulted from psychological deprivation. Babies who aren't shown love and kindness frequently develop into children and adolescents who don't demonstrate affection and tenderness. This should make sense. Do you remember, at some point in your life, vowing, "When I have children, I'll never say _____ to my own kids!" Then one day you shout, "No dessert until you clean your plate!" "Turn off the lights. Money doesn't grow on trees!" "Close the door! Were you raised in a barn?" You think, "Oh my goodness, I have become my mother!" or "I sound just like my father!"

We all repeat the patterns from our families of origin. Children who have experienced trauma alter the dynamics of the adoptive family in a manner that is referred to as a trauma re-enactment. In essence, the adopted son or daughter can move into an adoptive family and recreate the dynamics he or she experienced in the orphanage or abusive birth family. This compulsive repetition or trauma re-enactment is unconscious. Yet, in most instances, once these kids look at their trauma, they can learn to interrupt the repetitive patterns.

They can begin to live in the present (van der Kolk 1989). They can function in more healthy ways in interactions with brothers, sisters, and parents. Families are encouraged to locate an adoption- and trauma-competent therapist, even if this means traveling. It is often more constructive and cost-effective to seek the help of a specialist, whether a drive or a flight away!

Neurofeedback: Training for the brain

Neurofeedback is a form of therapy proving successful at calming the most disruptive of children. It can be conducted in an office or in the home, by a parent under the supervision of a qualified professional. Neurofeedback is training for the brain. Electrodes are placed on the scalp. Brain activity is monitored on a computer screen. This provides constant feedback to the individual about his brain activity. This feedback is actually presented in the form of a video game or a movie—no hands required. The child uses—trains—his brain to play the video game or favorite film. In turn, brain activity (hyperarousal, dissociation, etc.) is increased or decreased. The end result: new and improved brain function! This calmer state allows the traumatized arrival to access the parts of the brain associated with more rational actions and reactions—there is greater ability to think in a logical manner. In selecting a neurofeedback provider, ensure this professional has the skill in treating traumatized children. One adoptee recently said, "This neurofeedback makes my brain smarter, and it behaves better now!"

Physical restraint

Parents of violent children frequently report using physical restraint as a means of managing the child that slaps, bites, punches, or batters his brother, sister, mom, or dad. Consider this: being roughly managed is often the child's way of seeking physical touch from the parent. That is, children who didn't receive kisses or cuddles pre-adoption or children who have a hard time accepting affection post-adoption seek affection via aggression. Physical restraint is a way to get the touch they so desperately need. Parents are encouraged to avoid restraint. Parents are also urged to utilize the nurturing suggestions offered in Chapter 11. Increasing embraces and pecks on the cheek decreases the drive to get held down by a parent. A wonderful adoptive mom recently commented to me, "I always have my son snuggle in bed with me 15–20 minutes on the morning of a jam-packed day. This nurture is relaxing, and he remains peaceful and pleasant throughout the day."

911: Is this an option?

Calling the police requires the use of common sense. The police can't do much with young children other than talk to them or tell them what might happen in the future. Many children with histories of trauma have no sense of time, so telling them that "down the road" or "at some point in time" or "the next time we get called out here" has little meaning. Frequently, officers arrive, calm everyone down, and then leave. The message this unintentionally sends to the child is that "nothing happened." This validates the aggression. The child thinks, "Even the police didn't do anything, so it must not be that bad." Parents are encouraged to explore the outcome of a police visit—prior to the need for such a visit. Talk with your local police department or juvenile probation officer to understand their perspective and the legal options that exist when you have a violent child in the home. Then make a decision as to whether or not this is a helpful option for your particular situation.

Resist accommodating the violent child

You can't predict what will cause a child to have an aggressive outburst. When you attempt to accommodate the child in order to offset a fit, you are doing the child's work. The child cannot change her behavior if you are working harder to curtail it than she is! Along these same lines, sympathy and aiding the child in keeping the behavior "secret" perpetuate the behavior as well. Mothers and fathers can implement natural and logical consequences and restitution in response to household damage or physical altercations with the resident kids. The adopted son or daughter learns that violence is not the solution to any situation when he or she must repeatedly pay for breakage or when he or she must make amends to the offended family member.

Several months ago, I sustained a large bruise from a kick squarely delivered by a tween-age client. For several sessions after the injury, I limped in order to emphasize to this client the manner in which he hurt me. I made a big deal out of the behavior. Aggression is a big deal—at any age! I made certain that there was also something for him to carry or something I needed from the secretary. He wasn't happy about this restitution. However, he hasn't kicked me again!

Parents are encouraged to follow through with the parenting tools that lend to logical thought, empathy, and remorse. It takes Mother Nature many years to put forth and complete the skills essential for humans to be kind in their interactions with others. Therefore, restitution and natural and logical consequences will need to occur *many* times before you see positive changes in your troubled transplant.

"When my parents told me that we were adopting a baby from China, I was so excited. I expected my new sister to be like a biological baby, but I was so wrong. She ended up not letting anyone hold her except Mom and Dad. She would cry every time someone didn't hold her or even left the room. When she got older, she would pull my hair, kick, and hit me just to make me mad. She acted so different in public. She was like a little angel and everyone thought she was so cute and perfect. When we got in the car or when we got back home, it all changed."

Limit screen time

In homes where no physical or emotional violence is present, children are still bathed in violent images. The average child spends more than three hours a day watching television. Television, videogames, music, and film have become increasingly violent. The average 18-year-old will have viewed 200,000 acts of violence on television. Even with solid emotional, behavioral, cognitive, and social anchors provided by a healthy home and community, this pervasive media violence increases aggression and antisocial behavior (Perry 2004). If you don't like what your children are watching on television, turn it off!

If you don't like the Nintendo DS® game, take it away! You are the parent and this is an area you can control.

When parents need to step in

When sibling conflict escalates into frequent violent interactions, or the physical or mental abuse of a weaker sibling is caused by a stronger sibling, this can be harmful (Cicirelli 1995). In such instances where there is a clear imbalance of power, the parent will need to step in. Joseph Sparrow, co-author of *Understanding Sibling Rivalry*, says:

> When it is necessary for a parent to intervene, it will be important to keep from giving the older or stronger child more to be angry about, more fuel for her fights. Talk with that child about herself, not the other child: "When you get out of control like this, I'll have to help you." And to the victim: "You are going to need to learn to protect yourself. You may have to learn to get away from her for now. But you're going to learn ways to protect yourself." (Brazelton and Sparrow 2005, p.106)

The point to understand is that when there is an aggressive child in the family, she becomes the focus. She receives the bulk of the consequences and the majority of the attention—anger—while the victim receives sympathy. Actually, the victim is engaging in just as poor a pattern of behavior as the aggressor, and so the victim needs to change as well. Seek professional assistance when both the aggressor and the victim persist in their respective patterns of behavior.

Create a "safe spot"

Overall, evacuating the area of conflict is often a good interim solution. Many children, even toddlers, can learn to go to a "safe spot" so as to remove themselves from the destructive sibling's path of fury.

Vikki joined the family when she was 18 months old. She exhibited a "strong will" immediately. As she has aged into a pre-teen, daily loud rampages over chores, which include pushing and shoving, have become commonplace, Catherine, one of her three younger siblings, all birth children, said, "Vikki thinks nothing of getting in Mom's face and yelling! I try to stay by Mom to protect Mom. I'm afraid that Vikki will hurt her."

Catherine was assured that Mom thought it was so kind of her to want to be protective. Yet Mom could handle Vikki; Mom was the parent. Catherine could be a kid! If Mom ever felt the need for help, she would call on Dad or their very good neighbor, Mr. Stewart.

However, Catherine was then given the task of coming up with a "code word." This word or phrase could be anything she wanted—"broccoli" and "cheddar cheese" were her first two picks. She would get to say the code word whenever Vikki started to "lose it." This would be the prompt for all three kids to go—together—to the family room. It was stocked with a "fit bag" which included all kinds of supplies—board games, video games, cards, markers, paper—anything they wanted that would be fun for them! It also included the key to the lock box that was loaded with snacks! They would ride out Vikki's storm by creating a fun time for themselves. They would go on with the business of being kids! Mom would call out another of Catherine's code words when the "coast was clear" and Vikki was back on an even keel. At this time, all the kids—including Vikki—would reconnect with Mom, and Dad if he had arrived home from work.

"The two major things that weighed on my mind every day while my sisters were living at home were the loss of the peaceful household we had and the loss of a sense of safety. We lost a peaceful home because there was constant conflict all the time. I think I can count on one hand the number of days we had in the last four years that were not filled with conflict. My sisters antagonized each other, pitted my parents against each other, or just tried to wreak havoc any way that they could. As for a sense of safety, I think that disappeared after the first conflict we had in the home. Before these children came to our home, my bedroom door was never shut, and I never even had a lock to my room. After they came, I had a lock put on my room and my door was shut nearly all the time, so I could block out some of the conflict and bizarre behavior they often exhibited."

Ensuring family safety and security: Parenting and healing the sexual adopted child

The difficulty of living with a child that sexually acts out is immense! There is the day-to-day stress of supervising the child with sexually reactive behaviors. There is the parental guilt of knowing that your child has the potential to harm/or has already harmed another child. There is the matter of having to come to terms with the fact that your son or daughter is sexual—at ages at which this behavior is not expected. In essence, there is facing that this isn't just a stage. This is a serious problem for which the family must seek help. Certainly, there is also fear associated with seeking help. Will we be believed? Will we be viewed as the source of the sexual behavior? Will our sons and daughters be removed from our home? Religious values, relational values, and ideas about wanting childhood to be an innocent time collide! There is anger for this son or daughter causing such upheaval in the family, as well as sadness in cases in which the child experienced the horrible tragedy of sexual abuse prior to arrival in the adoptive home.

Please note, the ensuing content covers sexual behaviors that have already been deemed abnormal. Certainly, a first step with any sexual behaviors among children is to decide between what is and is not the result of "normal" sexual development. Parents and professionals can find this information on the website of the National Child Traumatic Stress Network (www.nctsn.org).

Again, many adoptees act younger than their chronological age. There is a discord between their social and emotional age and their actual numerical age. So adopted sons and daughters may be "playing doctor" at ages well beyond that considered "normal." The recommendation in this chapter is to keep this fact in mind.

Safety and supervision: The first priority

IMPLEMENT A SAFETY PLAN

On their own, most mothers and fathers increase the level of supervision in their home. In essence, a safety plan—the first priority—is designed and implemented. A basic safety plan includes the ideas already presented in Chapter 5 such as installing door alarms, altering sleeping arrangements if necessary, developing and implementing a sexual safety contract, providing sex education to all children in the family, and engaging in discussions about the relational context in which parents would prefer sexual interactions occur.

"Time in" with Mom or Dad

Mothers and fathers will want to know the whereabouts of the son or daughter with sexually acting-out behavior. In some cases, the sexual child is limited in his freedom within the home. He is kept close to a parent or an older trusted sibling (often paid for this babysitting service). This is not a punishment. This is a way to reduce the odds of the behavior occurring, especially when there are young—infant, toddler, pre-school-age—brothers and sisters in the home. The traumatized arrival can see that she can function in the family without engaging in sexual relations when her opportunities to conduct this behavior are limited. "Time in" with Mom or Dad strengthens the parent–child attachment. Sons and daughters with secure attachment honor the rules, values, and morals of their parents. When possible, place the responsibility for staying in the line of sight of a parent on the child. Many children will voluntarily move about the house in tow of Mom or Dad. This keeps the problem on the sexual child. We do want to help these kids accept responsibility for their sexual behaviors.

Or supervision may look like this example. In this family, Ivan (adopted at age 16 months, now age five) is sexual and aggressive toward the infant daughter, Jessica:

> "Adopting our infant daughter, Jessica, with an unhealthy child already in residence has been a bit challenging. I take special precautions to keep Jessica safe. We just can't trust Ivan to ever be alone with the baby, or the dog for that matter. When I shower, the baby comes with me. I put her in the stroller and push her into the bathroom where I know she'll be safe. Her crib is in our room, and I never leave her out of my sight. I have a child-proof door-knob cover on the outside of our door as a double precaution. If she's napping, he cannot get in, and I do keep an eye on him at all times. He's always needed constant monitoring,

even before the baby. I've never left him unsupervised, so this is really nothing new. Now that the baby is older, she wants to play with him and he does seem to like her. I still keep a very close watch; there's no way I'm taking any chances."

BALANCING TIME "IN" AND "OUT" OF PRIVILEGES

Mothers and fathers must examine privileges. Sexual children need to be involved in life. Yet their participation may only extend to those activities in which supervision is available and adequate. This is unfortunate. With older children (school-age and up), we make them aware that this type of restriction is their choice. When they curb their sexual behavior, they will be allowed the freedom associated with the level of trust that can be extended. We can offer these sexualized children a greater number of opportunities by scheduling periods during which parental supervision is available. That is, the sexual adoptee can have a play date when mom or dad has the time to ensure the safety of the friend. The child can be on the soccer team if the coach is willing to watch over the troubled child. We balance time "in" and "out" of activities as we can.

LEARN THE LAWS IN YOUR GEOGRAPHIC LOCALE

Adoptive families need to gain clarity regarding the laws in their geographic region regarding what types of sexual activity must be reported to the local children's services agency. Various professionals—teachers, school administrators counselors, social workers, psychologists, for example—are "mandated reporters." These professionals must legally report sexual activity to the local children's services agency.

Creating a sexually healing home environment

Once safety and supervision are established, parents need to turn their attention to creating a home environment that is open and honest regarding sex and sexuality. For some families, they must educate their typical children about sexual matters long before the age desired by parents. This suggestion connotes becoming comfortable using direct, anatomically correct language—frequently! Many of us were raised by parents who never mentioned the word "sex" or who gave us the very basic facts. So this can be hard, but it is necessary for healing.

TALKING THE TALK

For example, regarding an adoptee who "gropes" his mother during temper tantrums, we want to state clearly and as matter-of-factly as possible: "I don't like it when you grab my breasts (or vagina). I would prefer you hug me when you need my attention/affection. In this family, we (the parents) don't have sex with the children."

In another case, the youngster "humps" the mother during rages. The statement here would be: "I don't like it when you rub your penis on my leg. I would prefer to offer you a back rub, a hug, or a kiss on the cheek when you need my attention. In this family, Dad and I don't have sex with our children."

When brothers and sisters are exposed to unwanted sexual behaviors—if old enough to talk—we want to sit down with the children involved. Ceasing this behavior becomes a joint family endeavor. Each family member is on the "same page"—working together to help the new addition learn to act in accord with the family's values and morals.

The parent could say, "Touching Betty's vagina is against the rules in this family. Children don't have sex with children in this family. You must apologize to Betty. Betty, you must make it clear to your sister that you don't like it when she touches your vagina."

Betty then states, "I don't like it when you touch my vagina. I do like it when we can play dolls together, or color. Anytime you touch my vagina, I will be letting Mom or Dad know."

Siblings—typical and offending—must understand that anything considered sexually inappropriate definitely gets reported to their mom and dad, just as any other rule violation that jeopardizes safety.

LET'S TALK SPECIFICS

Obviously, such conversations must have the precursor that your children understand what is meant by the words "sex," "penis," "vagina," for example. Children who were sexually abused prior to arrival in the adoptive family are typically familiar with slang—

"pussy," "dick," "cock," "getting it on," "do it like dogs," and so on. Often, they don't understand that such language and sexual acts are disrespectful (to their body and mind)—and criminal.

Adoptive moms and dads may need to practice these statements—for a time period—prior to implementation. Certainly, no parent expected to need to say such things to their children. Yet being concise and direct is important. It has become common practice to utilize "inappropriate" or "appropriate." My perspective is that such language minimizes the severity of this particular behavior. I prefer to tell a child exactly what behavior to cease. I want children to tell me precisely what behavior they are engaging in. This lends to accepting responsibility. Recently, I was evaluating an adolescent.

I asked, "Why are you here for this assessment?"

He stated, "I act inappropriate with my younger sisters."

I asked, "What does that mean?"

He stated, "I do things to them."

I said, "What kind of things?"

He responded, "You know. Things!"

I finally said, "Like, you put your penis in their vaginas?"

He said, "That sounds terrible!"

I said, "It is. In order to return to your family, you must learn to keep your penis in your pants."

Language is an important part of the healing process. It wasn't helping this young man, his sisters, or his parents to allow him to believe that he was doing "things" to his siblings.

Another advantage of clear and direct language—including the statement "Dad and I don't have sex with our children"—is that it lets the adoptee know that he or she is now in a safe place. Children are safe from each other, and children are safe from adults. It may take time for your adopted son or daughter to believe this message.

Teach children the type of affection you prefer

After the discussion is complete, demonstrate the type of affection you would prefer. Practice the hug, cuddle, or snuggle. A "replacement behavior" must be provided. Again, nurture—"good touch"—is offered to the sexual child. We speak much of "good touch" vs. "bad touch" in the child welfare and mental health systems. Applying "good touch" is an essential component of any intervention designed to cease sexual behaviors. Yet very frequently parents are discouraged from offering hugs, kisses, or back rubs—good touch—to the formerly abused child. Instead, it is suggested to "wait" until the child comes forward for affection. In reality, the sexual advances *are* the child coming forward. For many children, sex is the way they have learned to be affectionate or to be valued. I would suggest that we need to offer these children "good touch" immediately upon placement with the adoptive family. Humans seek touch. If we don't offer "good touch," we force children to continue their learned pattern of seeking "bad touch."

I have often wondered how this type of "hands off" philosophy plays out in a home in which there is a combination of traumatized and typically developing children. One or more children are receiving hugs and kisses, and another isn't. What message does this send?

Here is one dad's account of nurturing his four adopted daughters. These siblings all experienced sexual abuse prior to being adopted by this dad and his wife.

> "Parenting daughters who have been sexually abused requires much patience, compassion, creativity, and humility. It requires much patience because all four of my daughters had a complete distrust of me. While I've never hugged a rock, I have a very good idea of what it must be like from hugging my daughters for the first three years of our adoption. This would be a slow process.
>
> "The compassion comes from realizing that the two men they should have been able to trust—their birth dad and birth uncle—consistently abused them. It is illogical for them to trust me, when the only messages they received from their birth dad is that it is fine to be a drunk who both abuses his children and allows them to be abused. Obviously, changing such a deep, pervasive

concept requires time. Understanding their past allowed me not to take the rejection of my daughters personally.

"I knew from the first that appropriate physical touch was essential for my daughters. If they couldn't learn to accept my touch, they would look for physical touch from someone else. So I decided to make a game of it. Often when I was going up or down the stairs and one of my daughters was coming the other way, I'd call out 'cuota' (toll). (Toll booths are extremely common in the country in which we live.) They would have to give me a kiss on the cheek to continue up or down the stairs. Or I'd reverse it and give them a peck on their cheek. I'd also 'accidentally' plow gently into one of my children in the kitchen, and say jokingly, 'Honey, did you walk into me?' and then hug her. With Carley, my oldest, we'd have pushing contests across the hall floor.

"At times, their behavior makes it impossible, or at least seem impossible, to nurture them. Both my wife and I deliberately put forth a hugs, snuggles, a pat on the back, a hand on the shoulder, a gaze, and other gestures regardless of their actions.

"Humility comes from realizing (both my wife and I) that we needed professional help, because the problems of our children were so serious. It is amazing how professional counseling helped our daughters in being able to appreciate me and accept appropriate physical touch."

BE VIGILANT!

There are juvenile perpetrators who threaten their siblings, "If you tell Mom or Dad, I'll hurt you!" Kids do sometimes believe these threats. I have worked many cases in which these sibling sexual relations have been kept secret because of such intimidation. I encourage parents to "check in" with all of their children periodically. Ask, "Has Johnny tried to touch you sexually? If so, I want you to know so that I can protect you, and you need to tell me." Still, there are instances in which the children will not tell. The only advice to offer is to be as vigilant as possible and to know that sexual interactions can and do happen among children. Don't bury your head in the sand!

DEALING WITH SEXUAL BEHAVIOR OF UNKNOWN ORIGINS

There are also children who join their family at very young ages with sexualized behavior of which we don't know the root cause. For example, it could be a self-stimulating behavior, rather than the result of sexual abuse. In any event, it can be handled as already stated.

> Colleen and Roy have two sons and a daughter by birth; Tori, Glenn, and Nathan are ages 11, nine and eight. Colleen and Roy felt very blessed. They had three great children, thriving careers, a lovely home, and wonderful friends and relatives. Rather than having a fourth birth child, they opted to share their good fortune with a child in need of a home. They flew to Belarus and arrived back in America with 22-month-old Aimee.
>
> Aimee presented immediate difficulties. She was unable to sleep for longer than two hours at a time. When awake, she cried constantly. She also masturbated chronically. It was not uncommon to find Aimee in the living room—fully naked—masturbating. It is not known if Aimee was sexually abused during her time in Belarus or if she learned to stimulate herself by masturbating in order to survive the deprivation of the orphanage environment.

In this case, Colleen and Roy had already initiated "sex education" with Tori. Glenn and Nathan were totally surprised by their sister's behavior and asked, "What is Aimee doing?" So Glenn and Nathan needed to know:

> "She is masturbating. Masturbation is a type of sexual behavior in which the person rubs their own penis or vagina. Rubbing her vagina feels good to her. We don't want Aimee masturbating."

Then this conversation needs to continue with the full explanation of sexual behavior, including the difference between Aimee's vagina and Glenn's and Nathan's penis. Subsequently, Glenn, Nathan, and Tori were taught to say to Aimme, "In this family, we don't masturbate. Please put your clothes back on."

Then Mom or Dad was informed of the behavior. Mom or Dad's response is a reiteration:

"Aimee, in this family, children don't masturbate. Please take your hand off your vagina. Let's get your clothes back on. You must be feeling lonely or sad. Sit here on my lap and let's have a hug."

Yes, Aimee is just a toddler and we are talking with her explicitly. We want to! We want her to grow into "normal" sexual language and into the values and morals of the family. The earlier we start this process, the more Aimee should adjust her behavior. We actually do this same process instilling religious tenets, political views, and so on. Parents routinely have conversations about all kinds of topics in front of their children. As kids become school-age, they have internalized their parents' views on a wide array of issues. Sex and sexuality can be treated in this same manner with young and older children alike. When a child arrives sexualized, it is never too early or too late to get started teaching the child the appropriate way to act sexually.

In closing this segment, it is important to reiterate that the large majority of children who arrive after experiencing the atrocity of sexual abuse, or with sexual behaviors of unknown origin, do not go on to be lifelong sexual perpetrators. Children most often learn to stop this behavior when provided with information from and redirection by their adoptive parents and siblings, and perhaps with the assistance of professionals.

Chapter summary

- Sexualized behaviors and aggression are two behaviors that are indeed tough to live with! They undermine the safety of each member of the family. They are in direct conflict with the security that home is supposed to provide.

- The children present in the family at the time of the adoption deserve to feel secure. While healing the violent or sexual adoptee, parents can utilize door alarms, safe spots, code words, safety contracts, frank discourse, time-in supervision, and so on. Parents can also use the advice in previous chapters pertaining to family meetings, reverse respite, nurture and the ripple effect—designed to facilitate the flow of grief caused by the shocking changes that this duo of behaviors surely brings to the family. Overall, parents have an array of options to help the birth and/or adopted children feel protected.

- There are tools and therapeutic interventions that can stop sexualized behavior and aggression in their tracks. The child who arrives and unconsciously elicits a trauma re-enactment can shed this role. He or she can learn to play a healthy part in the family system.

- Brothers or sisters who engage in patterns of being aggressor or victim require parental intervention and/or professional assistance. Neither of these patterns of behavior is healthy. Parents must teach both aggressor and victim to function with self-confidence. Children don't need to bully to obtain wants and needs. Children also don't want to view themselves as powerless, weak, and vulnerable. Each son or daughter needs to grow in self-confidence.

- Nurture, again, is key to healing behaviors. Touch is a critical component of how we humans relate to each other. When we teach the violent or sexual son, daughter, brother, or sister to give and receive loving touch, they will heal. Thus, each member of the family is once again safe and sound.

13

"We Hardly Have Family Game Night Anymore"

RESTORING FAMILY FUN

Nothing facilitates attachment between family members like laughing, joking, teasing, and playing with one another. Yet in families with a child with a history of complex trauma, giggles and chuckles don't always come easily. This is disappointing to everyone, but especially for the typically developing children who expected that their new sibling would be a playmate. Numerous examples of the ways in which fun is impeded because of the complexity of the adoptee's inability to socialize have been shared throughout this book. Chapter 2 made clear the lifelong risks of inadequate social skills.

Helping the newcomer develop social skills is important for his long-term functioning, and it is a way to restore family fun. So this chapter offers up some ideas to facilitate the playful side of your adopted son or daughter.

"Speaking as a kid that was the youngest until our family adopted, I didn't really understand the adoption process. I was six when everything happened, so things at that point didn't really make sense. You know, I had heard of 'biological' and what it meant, so I thought adoption would be the exact same. I was so wrong! The process is very difficult and it takes time, patience, and courage, but it is so worth it! Since my parents had to pay a lot of attention to my new little sister, our lives pretty much changed. We hardly had game night anymore. So much of our family time just blew away!"

Sizing up the adoptee's social skills: Identifying the child's social and emotional age

Expanding the new arrival's repertoire of social skill starts with taking stock—sizing up—the strengths and areas of concerns in the child's day-to-day play and interaction with other kids. In essence, we are once again taking a developmental approach. Just as we learned to "grow" cause-and-effect thinking, moral development, and problem-solving skills earlier in this book, we're now going to learn to "grow" social skills!

A good starting place for identifying your troubled child's actual social and emotional age is to read a good book on "normal" child development such as *Your Baby and Child: From Birth to Age Five* or *Ages and Stages: A Parent's Guide to Normal Child Development*. There are also reliable online sources of child development such as the sites of Zero to Three (www.zerotothree.org), the Child Development Institute (http://childdevelopmentinfo.com), and the Centers for Disease Control and Prevention (www.cdc.gov).

Compare the skills for children ages infant on up to your traumatized son or daughter's chronological age. Yes, I said, "Infant on up." The post-institutionalized baby, toddler, or older child—according to the University of Minnesota's International Adoption Clinic—*loses one month of linear growth for every three months in an orphanage*. This is because lack of stimulation and consistent caregivers, suboptimal nutrition, and abuse all conspire to delay and sometimes preclude normal development, speech acquisition, and attainment of necessary social skills (Johnson 2012).

Thus—frequently—the arrival with a history of deprivation lacks the play skills of even very little children. She may have a hard time imitating faces or playing peek-a-boo. She can't stack, mold, build, sort, string beads, sing nursery rhymes—the list goes on. Using your knowledge of your adoptee, identify the areas she has mastered and those that are underdeveloped.

You can also observe your child in social situations. Visit the park and compare your child to peers. What are they able to do in comparison to your adoptee? Visit the playground at school. What is causing his difficulties on the playground?

If you have parented typically developing children, you have personal knowledge of child development that you can apply to this process as well.

Lastly, you can carry out formal developmental testing, such as the Vineland Adaptive Behavior Scales presented in Chapter 2, via a psychologist, neuropsychologist, a developmental pediatrician, social worker, counselor, or pediatric nurse (depending on state licensing policies). An adoption medical clinic, the school, your family physician, or your health insurance company can help you locate professionals who conduct this type of testing.

I have included some simple charts in the Appendix that overview the types of tasks children ages infant to pre-school carry out when their development is proceeding as it should. Observe your son or daughter in comparison to these charts. Be on particular lookout for the following red flags.

"My friends change frequently"

The traumatized adoptee changes friends constantly. Peer relationships are short-lived. "Billy" comes to play a few times, and then parents don't hear about or see anymore of Billy again. Billy is replaced by Sally, George, Mark, Matthew, and so on! Friendships keep going around like a revolving door. A new playmate is always entering or exiting.

"I flit from toy to toy"

Children with difficult beginnings in life may play with a toy for a few minutes and then move on to the next toy. Sustained interest in one toy or activity is lacking. Pretty soon, every toy available has been looked at and tossed to the floor. Play equals making a mess.

"I prefer to be a couch potato"

Some adopted sons and daughters prefer to sit—chronically! These children can sit among a room full of wonderful toys or arts and crafts supplies and never make a move to sample any of this great stuff!

> Rose was adopted internationally at the age of five and a half. Now age 11, she still hasn't mastered playing outdoors. If seated in front of an Xbox® or holding a Nintendo DS®, she is masterful. Yet ask her to go outside on a beautiful summer day and within minutes she'll be at the screen door begging to come inside. With a back yard full of amazing play equipment, in a neighborhood replete with potential playmates, Rose is totally out of her element.

"I play the same thing over and over and over…"

> Randy is 11. He arrived on American soil at age ten months. To date, his play continues to lag behind his actual age. In fact, toy cars are his only form of entertainment. Each day after school Randy smashes all the cars into each other—repetitively! This destructive play has been going on as long as Randy's parents can remember. The cars are never used to transport people around town, even though he has a lovely carpet imprinted with a Main Street full of shops, a park, a school, and two neighborhoods.

"My play involves no people"

Play lacking people is particularly common among post-institutionalized children or domestically adopted youngsters who experienced neglect prior to their arrival in a healthy family. Actually, in this scenario, animals often dominate the play (i.e. stuffed animals, animal figures). Animals are okay for a while, as they serve as transitional objects in a similar fashion to a favorite "blankie." However, children's play, especially from ages two and up, should contain "people"—dolls, Fisher Price Little People®, imaginary friends, for example. Imaginative play or pretend play in which kids work out feelings and act out all kinds of themes involving people—pretending to be Mom or Dad, launching astronauts in a spaceship made from empty boxes, teaching dolls in a classroom, hiding from "bad guys" in a fort—should be a preferred type of play through age seven.

"My play is all electronic"

> Brian and Bryce, twins, came from Russia at age three and a half. They entered therapy when they were 13 years old. The parents presented a laundry list of behavioral issues and also noted that these boys were totally absorbed with PlayStation®— about 25 hours per week! Board games, card games, arts and crafts, drawing, painting, playing an instrument—anything that required creativity—were snubbed in lieu of screen time!
>
> The PlayStation® was packed up and given to nephews when services were initiated. Mom and Dad replaced the PlayStation with an assortment of activities. For three months, Brian and Bryce sat on the couch looking at the empty table on which the PlayStation® used to sit. They were totally perplexed as to what to do! Finally, about four months into therapy, Mom left a voicemail for the therapist. The sound of laughter could be heard in the background of the message. Mom said, "You'll never believe it! Brian, Bryce, and Marie [the family's birth daughter] are having a good time playing a board game! I can't believe they are actually playing and enjoying themselves! This is the first time I remember the three kids doing anything like this together!"

Traumatized adoptees are perfectly content to let screens be their BFFs! Interacting with machines is far less complicated and hurtful than connecting with people.

"I break my toys"

Parents lament, "Every toy he has is broken! Christmas morning, he'll receive great new toys. By Christmas evening, they'll all be broken or taken apart—the pieces will be scattered everywhere!" Certainly, the child with a history of trauma views himself as "broken." "Shattered" by being abused and abandoned, "destruction" becomes the metaphor for his experiences.

"I re-enact my trauma in my play"

On a tragic evening, four-year-old Kelly witnessed the murder, by physical abuse, of her younger sibling at the hands of her birth father. Once the birth father and birth mother realized the injuries, they placed both Kelly and her sibling in the car and drove to the hospital. En route, they concocted a story of innocence. Kelly, scared, was unable to speak to the police. However, the event was ingrained in her memory, as was her last moment with her sibling—connected to life support. Eventually police arrested the murderer. Kelly was placed in foster care. Subsequently, at age five and a half, she was adopted. Once in her adoptive home, Kelly relayed the details of the murder verbally and through play. All of her dolls were named after her deceased sibling. She would sit for long periods of time meticulously bandaging their wounds. If she played house, the "mom" and "dad" fought violently. The pretend "family" scenarios ended with the police arriving. Kelly's drawings were morbid funeral scenes. The doll play and the drawings Kelly created were shocking to her brothers and sisters who had lived a life enveloped by safe and loving parents.

Once you have all of your information gathered, identify the earliest skills the child is missing. Start filling in your troubled arrival's social gaps with the tips that follow.

Putting the horse and cart in the correct order: Parenting sons and daughters at their social and emotional age

There is a common belief that the ability to play and develop social skills will simply happen if we place children in activities comprised of same-age peers. This will work with some children who have experienced trauma. Certainly, if the adoptee can play baseball, enjoy gymnastics, and sing in the church choir, do continue their participation in these extracurricular activities. Always keep what is working. However, if you have tried several different endeavors and there has been limited or no social movement forward, it is time to try a new approach.

Play and social skills have their root in parent–child interactions (Chapter 2). Children gain their social skills foundation via their first playmates—Mom and Dad. Siblings influence social development as well. Most parents teach their children to play without really thinking about it. For example, a young toddler is sitting in the living room with some blocks. Mom or Dad, passing by, stops for a few minutes and stacks the blocks. Soon, the toddler is stacking her blocks on her own. The skill of building has been learned. By age four or five, the child is with friends building with Lego™. The skills learned from parents, brothers, and sisters are transferred to peer relationships.

Thus, placing the traumatized child in a group activity may not advance his social skills because it places the cart before the horse. We are attempting peer play prior to the child having learned to play with parents, and we are attempting complex group play before the child has mastered solitary play—the child plays alone—and parallel play—the child plays side-by-side other kids. In these instances, parents may want to consider *parenting at the child's social and emotional age.*

Becky and Cole parent four children, three by birth and their son, Gabe, by adoption from Guatemala. Gabe arrived at 18 months, and is now age six. His social and emotional age is quite infantile:

> "First, we elicited the assistance of our three daughters, Jennifer, Jessica, and Mary, ages eight, 11 and 14. We assigned each girl ways to be helpful. We held a family meeting and asked each girl to play with Gabe 20 minutes each week. Then we stopped at the local thrift store, where we purchased a set of stacking rings, large blocks, a shape sorter, some small plastic containers, and a mirror. We also obtained a CD of nursery rhymes and a few bathtub toys.
>
> Jennifer went first. She spread a blanket on the floor. She gathered Gabe and the shape sorter. She sat with Gabe, demonstrating what she wanted him to do. He kept moving off the blanket. She would wait a few seconds and then gently guide him back to the blanket and the shape sorter. Mary worked in the same manner with the blocks and Jessica opted to teach Gabe to sing nursery rhymes.
>
> "Gabe was shifted from an evening shower to a bath. Cole has many memories of getting quite wet during his efforts to

help Gabe dump water from one plastic container to another. I, Becky, spent much time playing face games and peek-a-boo which, to my total surprise, absolutely delighted Gabe.

"About a year late, our successes included that Gabe has learned to sit and play by himself for periods lasting about 15 minutes! We now have small windows of calmness! We expanded his toys as he made progress. Gabe graduated from the blocks to Lego™. He had peg puzzles, Play-Doh™, a toddler-age xylophone, a Little People® car and garage set, a Fisher Price The Farmer Says™, and many more toys designed for toddlers ages 12 to 24 months. Gabe is currently moving on to learn Candy Land™ and Chutes and Ladders™.

"A year of consistently working with Gabe has paid off. Gabe is developing social skills critical to being a fun little brother and a friend to other children in our neighborhood and school!"

Gabe and his family demonstrate that parenting a child at her social and emotional age is an effective way to facilitate the growth of social skills. We must keep in mind that the child who previously resided in an orphanage or a neglectful and abusive birth home had little opportunity to play and most likely access to few toys. Many parents have a difficult time allowing their adoptees to act like "little" kids. Parents are often heard saying, "Grow up!" "Act your age!" "Those are the baby's toys. Leave them alone!" The next time you find yourself making any of these statements, stop! If your 11-year-old son wants to play with your three-year-old daughter's toy kitchen set, let him. If you find your 14-year-old digging in your toddler's sandbox, join in. If your nine-year-old is baby-talking, give him a hug and some lap time just as you would lavish on a toddler. If your 12-year-old plays with the younger kids in the neighborhood safely, this is fine as well. The more you allow the child to be "younger," the more the child will actually "grow up."

Certainly there will be children, especially tweens and teens, who may find the thought of playing with "baby toys" embarrassing. In these cases, creativity is called for.

Colleen lived in an abusive birth family for five years and then a South American orphanage for the next five years. Adopted by Sue and Howard, at age ten, she exhibited the social and emotional age of a youngster age two:

"We belonged to a church with a large congregation and so there were many Sunday school classes. We made arrangements for Colleen to be a 'helper' in the classes with children ranging in age from toddler through pre-school. We simply presented the idea to Colleen in terms of the teachers needing some assistance. Colleen received the benefit of playing with children who helped her social skills mature, and the Sunday school teachers appreciated having a reliable assistant. Colleen was proud of her contributions to the church. Over this past year, Colleen has mastered many social tasks and so has now moved on to be the volunteer helper in classes for five- and six-year olds."

Adrianne and Craig adopted Jeremy from a Bulgarian orphanage as an infant. Now, at age 13, his social skills continue to be delayed. He remains stuck in solitary play. He has not advanced to parallel or group play in spite of years of social skills training programs, sports participation, scouting, and so on. Adrianne said:

"My sister has four young children—a daughter, Eliza, age two, and a new set of triplets. My mother, my sisters, my sisters-in-laws, and I have been taking turns helping out with the new babies.

"I decided to take Jeremy along. I asked him if he could please play with Eliza because she needed some attention—the babies were taking up a lot of time! Jeremy did well in this role. He sat with Eliza for hours. He giggled as much as Eliza over her Laugh and Learn 2-in-1 Learning Kitchen™. Eliza was very happy to have a playmate. Jeremy takes pride in his role as the 'fun Uncle.'

"Jeremy's social skills are growing as fast as my nieces and nephews are growing! This summer he actually joined in with kids who were playing water tag at the community pool. This is the first time Jeremy has played with neighborhood kids!"

Carrying out chores at the appropriate social and emotional age

Parenting the child at his actual social and emotional age is important when striving to develop cognitive, emotional, and social skills. It can also be important in other ways. For example, would you expect a two- or three-year-old to be able to clean his room? Most likely, you would work jointly with the young child to clean his room. If you have a 12-year-old who is actually three in social and emotional age, assisting him in picking up his clothes, vacuuming the carpet, and making his bed will most likely reduce the power struggles that frequently accompany trying to get him to carry out chores on his own. As he matures, he will be able to clean his room, handle privileges, and do lots of other things appropriate for children of his chronological age.

The family that eats together...

The popular after-school childhood question "What's for dinner?" is often replaced with "Which drive-through do you want to do?" or "Who should we have deliver tonight?" The demands of the after-school and after-work hours are so great that meal preparation goes by the wayside. Athletics, math club, spelling bee practice, and so on demand such a quantity of time that they interfere with the ability of the entire family to sit down at the table—*together*.

Yet there is clear evidence that family dinner has many benefits. Adults and children are less likely to snack and are more likely to eat fruits, vegetables, and whole grains. Kids who are given time to connect with their parents and siblings are *less* likely to smoke, drink alcohol, use drugs, get depressed, and be overweight. They are also *more* likely to do well in school (Davis 2007)—these are all things that make moms and dads smile!

Homework or Monopoly?

It is quite common in families including a traumatized child that reading, writing, and arithmetic consume an inordinate amount of after-school time. Traumatized children are easily frustrated, lack recognition of the benefits of education, have various learning difficulties or disabilities, and have a hard time accepting help. Parental tempers flare, evenings become a battleground, the typical kids flee, and little fun occurs!

Homework battles require some rethinking. As we learned in Chapter 2, the best childhood predictor of adult adaptation is not school grades. It is the ability with which children are able to get along with other children—brothers, sisters, and friends (Hartup 1992).

Mothers and fathers may want to consider setting the timer when it comes to homework. Give the child an adequate period of time to complete her assignments. Then, *calmly* pack up the homework and move on. (Actually, most kids, after about three months, will begin to comply with this time period.) Parents can also consider various accommodations via special education services. Mothers and fathers are encouraged to talk with teachers about ways to reduce the work coming home. Striking a better balance between academics and social skills development is critical. Giggling, joking, teasing, and playing are as essential as the three Rs to your children's futures— this includes the birth and/or previously adopted children and the newcomers!

Practice social skills

"The way he grew up, he had to learn to pass it off as 'If I sit down and cross my legs like her, then I'll fit in.' He was good at reading how to behave in certain social situations. Yet it wasn't genuine. He could only mimic."

Children practice the piano, catching a ball, shooting hoops, math facts, and so on. Children can also practice social skills. Conversation can be improved by asking open-ended questions. A common close-ended conversation with a child who has experienced trauma goes like this:

Parent: "How was school today?"

Adoptee: "Good."

Parent: "How did you do on your math test?"

Adoptee: "Not good."

Or there is the opposite: the adoptee who chatters incessantly about things that have very little meaning.

Either way, getting some of these kids to converse can be difficult. Their inability to communicate makes forming relationships, in the family and outside of the family, difficult. Alter the questions you ask: "What was your favorite part of school today?" "What is it about that you like?" "Who did you play with today?" "Tell me about those kids."

Ask questions that require an answer longer than one word. If you did something special over the weekend, ask your child to recap the event. Mention that he could share this fun family time with his classmates on Monday—give some specific ideas about the words he can actually use.

Usually, the first response to a child who is talking on and on is to say, "How many times have I told you to quit interrupting?" Rather, redirect the child: "Mary, your brother is talking about his baseball game. It's your turn to listen. Then you can have a turn talking." Practicing, modeling, suggesting, and helping children find the words to talk are all ways to practice the art of making conversation.

Look over the following list of skills that help children succeed socially and think about what *practice* activities will improve relationships inside and outside of your home.

Skills that help children succeed socially

- Taking turns.

- Making conversation.

- Formulating and communicating opinions.

- Greeting.

- Maintaining appropriate personal space.

- Being able to read faces and tone of voice.

- Giving and receiving compliments.

- Really listening to what others are saying.

- Developing a sense of humor.

- Sharing.

- Making eye contact.

- Negotiating and compromising.

- Being able to enter a group to join a discussion or an activity.

- Demonstrating problem-solving skills.

- Following directions.

Parties, play dates, vacations, and more

A trip to the zoo, a vacation to Florida, going next door to play with the neighbors, family game night, birthday parties, and holidays are all events that can present challenges in families built by adoption. Often the adoptee struggles to handle such situations. The child with a history of trauma views herself as "bad." She thinks, "I don't deserve fun or presents." While she may enjoy the company of her family during outings, subsequently the family becomes the brunt of poor behavior. Scared that she found herself attaching to the family, she feels she must go into rejection mode. Family fun may trigger the lack of pleasure in her birth family or her few good memories of her birth family or orphanage mates. Her grief surfaces. Unable to express her emotions, the feelings are manifested though negative behaviors.

In response to such behavior, the family may scale down or stop having fun. Instead, let's look at some options to enhance the outcomes of family fun times.

Practice can be helpful. Traumatized children may need you to practice—review—what will be happening at the birthday party. How many kids are coming? What games will be played? Yes, your brother will get presents. How does this make you feel? How long will the party be? Children, given an idea of what to expect, can often make it through an event on an even keel.

Parenting at the child's actual social and emotional age is also helpful in this area. What would you expect of a three-, four- or five-year-old at a museum? In Disney World? At holiday gatherings? Overall, mothers and fathers may want to expect that their "little" newcomer may become overwhelmed when there is a flurry of activity. Expect the child with Sensory Dysfunction Disorder to become over-stimulated at the zoo. Build in breaks just as you would with a younger child. One parent may have to sit on a bench with the adoptee, while the other family members move on to the lion and tiger display. Have an ice cream while you are resting—this isn't a punishment. Later, you can meet back up at the rain forest and proceed on your way.

Add, reduce, and remove toys as necessary

We met 11-year-old Randy earlier in this chapter. He smashed his toy cars day after day, year after year! Fisher Price Little People® were added to his car collection. Dad began making statements like "Cars need drivers," "People go on vacation in their cars," "People go shopping in their cars," "People like to take drives to view scenery." Eventually, Randy's cars and people intermingled in the ways Dad suggested. Simply, Dad facilitated a dramatic, positive shift in Randy's play!

Don't be afraid to remove or reduce electronics. I believe kids need some electronic play or they wind up out of the loop with their peers. Play that fosters imagination and creativity needs to be the dominant form of play.

If your child is over-focused on animals or anything else you find concerning, remove or reduce these too; this can be done gradually over a period of weeks or months. Simultaneously, add toys, people figures, props, crayons, paints, arts and craft kits, clay, beads, blocks, and so on! Provide directions like Randy's Dad: "Why don't you draw a house for me?" "Let's make some Christmas ornaments as gifts this year," "I would love to see you build an airplane with your Legos." Continue this until you have success. Realize this may take time. Unfortunately, reversing the ravage of trauma doesn't happen overnight. However, the sooner you get started, the sooner you will find your child's playful side!

Interrupt and provide corrective play experiences

We also met Kelly who re-enacted the murder of her sibling. Kelly's play was full of violent themes in her adoptive home. Kelly's mom and her older sisters, Linda and Sally, made sure to interrupt Kelly's play as needed. When Kelly's dolls were beating each other, Linda or Sally would sit down with Kelly and say, "In our family, dolls don't hit each other. They play nicely. Let's have the dolls make dinner." Gradually, Kelly's play shifted from chaos to calm!

Set the timer

Patty and Rich, ages seven and eight, are a birth child and an adopted child respectively. They were able to play well for only about 15 minutes. After that, shouting, bickering, and a cry of "Mom, he won't play fair!" ruined the fun.

Joyce, their mom, eventually decided to set a timer for 15 minutes. At that point, she would casually call one of the children to the kitchen to help her "for a minute" or she would arrive in the play area with a candy kiss. She provided enough of an interruption to offset the argument that was certain to occur. Patty and Rich continued playing for another 15 minutes. By that time, dinner was ready.

Joyce gives us a nice way to promote a positive ending to a situation that could easily conclude in an ugly manner. Families can also use this idea when the family sits down to play a card or board game. Announce at the start, "I have 15 minutes; let's play cards." When time is up, the parent concludes, "Wow! That was fun! I have to go do the laundry." This style of play also offsets having a winner and a loser. You are playing for 15 or 20 minutes rather than until the game is over. The son or daughter with a traumatic past may be a "poor loser." So playing for fun, instead of playing until there is a winner, can end a game on a positive note.

To go or not to go

Liv and Bill parent two children by birth, Peggy and Martha, ages ten and 11. They also parent their son, Roger, age 12 whom they adopted. The family was to go to a science center on Saturday. Liv and Bill knew this outing could be difficult. Roger would grumble, lag behind, and want to see different displays to the rest of the family. Peggy and Martha were already asking, "Why does he have to go?"

Hmmm... How does the parent respond? Sometimes with "He has to go because he is part of the family, and he needs to learn to enjoy family fun." However, there are instances in which he doesn't need to go. Below, an adoptive father illustrates this point:

> "If the situation warrants it, consider taking your family vacation without your adopted child. One year we were to take our vacation in a place where the kids could easily get away from us and get lost. That same year, our troubled son, age nine, had run away from us at retail stores two or three times and my wife had recently had surgery so she was in no condition to chase after anyone. We decided that the only way we and our other two children would enjoy ourselves was to leave our troubled son at his grandparents' for the week. He wasn't being punished. He had a great time with his grandparents, and we called him every day. Everyone had a good time that week."

The answer as to whether the sibling who arrived by adoption should go or not actually hinges on how the family carries out activities as a whole. If you are always only excluding the adoptee, this isn't acceptable. If being excluded from family fun is a frequent consequence, this isn't acceptable. If you carry this out with an attitude of "In this family, each child gets special time with Mom and Dad, and each child gets time with Mom alone and Dad alone, and there are times the whole family is together," this is acceptable. Again, it is all about what adoptive parents want to mirror. The latter reflects that each family member gets what he or she needs from the family.

"Mom and Dad spend too much time with my brother. I don't have anything to myself anymore. It's been crazy around here and I never get to have friends over because he always messes things up for me."

No batteries needed

As you can see, many of the suggestions regarding restoring family fun require rethinking family fun a bit. Until the adoptee is able to play for a longer period of time, family game night may consist of one short game. Or family fun may require returning to a "no batteries needed" approach. A few minutes of collecting lightening bugs or blowing bubbles, or playing hide and seek, musical chairs, Ring-around-the-Rosie, or other such "old-fashioned" games keeps fun shorter and less complicated. Overall, parents of a family that includes a socially or emotionally delayed child may need to think about fun in terms of short, frequent increments instead of day-long or longer outings.

Family fun may also mean rethinking screen time. Computer games, hand-held video games, game systems, and television promote interacting with machines. If you want to improve relationships in your family, you actually need to interact! Certainly, there are times when a hand-held video game makes a long trip in the car more pleasant or gives a parent at the end of her rope a break. In these situations, do what is necessary.

Overall, play is an activity. Play involves *unstructured* time in which children can explore their environment, use their imagination, learn to negotiate, compromise, and problem-solve amongst their siblings and peers. Today, we structure most aspects of children's life. We organize play dates and sports. For many children, athletic practice and homework consume after-school hours and portions of their weekends. Youngsters, tweens, and teens are allowed little spontaneity and free time—two essential ingredients that go into making the play that lends to the development of social skills and other critical life skills! Parents are encouraged to reflect on what family fun means. Prioritize what your children need, rather than give in to the pressures of what your neighbors or the school expect, or what is being advertised as the toy or device that is a "must have."

Fun is the parents' choice

Frequently, the child with difficulties winds up in charge of the family fun (Keck and Kupecky 2009). It goes like this. The parent says, "If you are good all week, Saturday we'll go to the mall." Faithfully, by

Friday evening some rule violation has occurred and the trip to the mall is taken away. Or, because punitive consequences have piled up all week, the family decides to stay home so Billy can wash the kitchen floor, rake the leaves, vacuum, and carry out all kinds of other chores. The troubled child has determined the family's weekend plans.

Whom does this benefit? A now angry family is stuck at home together. Or the typical kids go off to their friends' homes. The family is separated. If you want to go to the mall on Saturday, then go! Chores can wait. "Good" isn't likely going to happen for a long time. "Good" won't happen if parents and brothers and sisters are always mad at their sibling. Fun is the best way to navigate new relationships. So, go! Find the playful side of yourself, your typical kids, and your adoptee!

Siblings may need separate time for their own development (especially younger siblings)

Brothers and sisters influence each other's development. Mothers and fathers must ensure that each child is able to grow and develop. This means that the appropriately developing children need ample opportunities to play with developmentally equal peers in order that their cognitive, emotional, physical, and social skills proceed within normal parameters. Let's further exemplify the idea that siblings need time for their own development.

> Adam and Laurel adopted twins, Reanna and Hal, age six at arrival, presently nine. The twins had experienced pre-natal drug exposure, neglect, and physical abuse, and they had moved through seven foster homes before being placed with Adam and Laurel. Reanna had the social and emotional age of a 14-month old, while Hal exhibited social skills similar to a two-year-old.
>
> Alyson, their infant birth sister, arrived one year later. Now age three, her development is typical. Socially, then, she is surpassing her siblings. She is moving on to using her imagination. She loves her play telephone and her medical kit. She likes to dress up and take care of her baby dolls. She tries to engage Reanna and Hal, but their delays don't allow them to participate in a reciprocal manner. They can do only what Alyson tells them to do.

Certainly, this is good interaction for Reanna and Hal. However, Alyson needs the company of healthy peers in order to ensure that her development progresses as it should. Laurel makes sure that Alyson has play dates and she is enrolled in pre-school three mornings per week. Laurel monitors her skills to make sure she is doing all of the things a three-year-old should do.

I cannot stress enough the need to protect your youngest sons' and daughters' development. I have personally encountered many boys and girls whose growth has been delayed because their closest playmates are their brothers and sisters with histories of complex trauma. Certainly, this occurs because parents are uninformed about this matter. It is easier to keep age-appropriate cognitive, social, physical, and emotional skills on track than it is to rebuild the skills.

Chapter summary

- Parenting at the child's social and emotional age is a concept worth understanding and using. When you can see your adoptee for the "little" child he actually is, healing will occur. You and the resident children won't be so frustrated by his behaviors or his lack of abilities.

- The typical children can be assigned ways to be helpful when it comes to advancing the social skills of the brother or sister who arrived with fractured social development. Mothers and fathers can organize the birth and/or previously adopted children into a concerted effort to interlock puzzle pieces, belt out "Old McDonald," blow bubbles, make mud pies, weave pot holders, and so much more! There is pride for all when the newcomer "grows." There is also the subsequent benefit of a sibling who can more fully participate in family fun.

- The child with a history of complex trauma can enjoy fun separately from her mother, father, brothers, and sisters. She may go to Grandma's house during a birthday party, a family trip to a museum, or when her brothers and sisters are entertaining friends. Other times, she is included because she is a family member.

- Restoring family fun implies prioritizing. There must be time to conduct the important activity of play. Parents, brothers, and sisters need to create opportunities to be together. Sitting down for family meals and partaking in enjoyable activities is as important as academics and organized extracurricular activities. Decide how to strike a balance in all of these areas of family life.

- When the youngest children are appropriately developing, it is imperative that mothers and fathers take steps to protect their health. Read, monitor, and supervise! Create opportunities for these typical kids to socialize with developmentally equal peers. Keep these boys and girls on track!

- Fun is the best way to attach, to navigate new relationships. Carry out your plans regardless of behavior or consequences. All kids need to enjoy life! As for the typically developing children, when they are adults, what do you want them to remember about their family—conflict or joy? It bears repeating: parents are the mirrors. Your children notice you and reflect you. Show them your playful side—they'll return the fun!

14

"Yes, I have Experienced Positives!"

BROTHERS, SISTERS, AND ADOPTEES SPEAK ABOUT THE BENEFITS OF ADOPTION

Brothers and sisters: The benefits of sharing my home

From very practical sentiments such as, "We got a bigger house" or "I didn't have anyone to play with and now I do" to more principled thoughts, brothers and sisters express many positives of sharing "home."

In my clinical experience, the teenage and young adulthood years are the time when these well-developing siblings—most likely as abstract thought and identity development are more advanced—can begin to fully integrate the experiences that adoption brought into their lives. They see the pros and the cons. They begin to apply the lessons learned from being a brother or sister to an adoptee who presented challenges.

Overall, six main positives emerge from living within a family raising a combination of typical and traumatized children. These six positive factors are identified on the following pages. Mixed in are the reports of actual brothers and sisters. These birth and/or previously adopted siblings range in age now from 15 to 25. They were between the ages of seven and 16 at the time their families adopted. Their families adopted children ages ten months old to

13 years old. The adoptees have now been a part of the family for between six and twelve years.

"I developed greater compassion for people"

Our resident sons and daughters develop a compassion for those less fortunate from having lived with a sibling afflicted by abuse, neglect, and abandonment. They are able to realize that adversity strikes many—young and old alike. They listen and strive to see beyond the outside of a person. They acknowledge that there are individuals who require help. Compassion supports the development of tolerance, insight, and empathy.

> "As a whole, I believe that our family has had to make numerous sacrifices since my sister's adoption, but we have gained from it. Spending time as a family was more difficult, and the household was definitely less peaceful. However, I now find it much easier to relate to children with differences and the families of those children. Before, when I saw a badly behaved child, it was easy to attribute that to bad parenting. Now I realize that other factors may be involved. Even with a loss of family time, I feel that we have become closer as a family because taking care of my sister brought us together."

"I have grown in my capacity to be appreciative"

There is an understanding of the fact that they are well-off to have been born to (or adopted by) and raised by healthy, loving parents (Smith, Greenberg and Mailick 2007). On one level, the typical children tend to appreciate fun times and quiet moments. On a different level, they acknowledge that they are fortunate to have escaped the often horrendous long-term effects of early childhood trauma.

> "I think a positive experience for me is that this has made me become a stronger person. I look at my brother and see what a horrible past he had with his foster mom (very neglectful). I look at my past and think, wow, I was really lucky to have a foster mom as good as I did. She treated me good and gave me food and all that. My brother grew up in a whole different situation."

"I have matured"

Maturity develops as a result of the knowledge that life can be unfair, things might not get better, and bad things do not always happen only to others. This maturity produces children who are well adjusted and more responsible than most same-age peers (Meyer and Vadasy 1994).

> "I think it's been a positive experience just in the fact that it opened my eyes to other issues that are out there. Like in school, my French teacher would always talk about students who would trash the desks—write on them and stuff—and that it was the parents' fault. The parents didn't care about their children. Bringing in disruptive children, whom we have tried to help as much as possible, let me see that, no, that's not always the case. There are parents who actually try to help and do whatever they can. This child, in her own mind, doesn't want to follow it and chooses not to do what the parents want. So it opened my eyes to the fact that it's not always the parents who are causing the problem. It may be the child herself."

"I think about my actions. I am aware of consequences"

In setting their own life courses, brothers and sisters into whose life arrived a child fractured by early experiences may have a heightened awareness of the consequences of various actions. For example, regarding drinking and pregnancy, they know first-hand how drinking while pregnant can condemn a child to brain damage and a lifetime of challenges (Olesen 2004).

"I learned how to solve problems"

> "We found a way to occupy our time with making the best out of the situation. You learn how to work with what you got. This is good."

In essence, we all have to learn to "work with what you got." This process helps to develop problem-solving skills. The resident children become quite creative in making life with a sibling with mental health issues work to their advantage. It is not uncommon that they negotiate, with Mom and Dad, to earn money for comforts such as a television, an iPod®, a smart phone, and so on. These supplies allow a comfortable escape during major family storms. They learn to be heard when absolutely necessary—demonstrating improved communication skills. Certainly, enhanced problem-solving, communication, and negotiating skills will serve them well throughout their lives.

Vocational opportunities

Brothers and sisters frequently gravitate toward the helping professions. These young adults are more certain of their own futures and about personal and vocational goals than comparable young adults without similar experiences.

I have conducted therapy with brothers, sisters, and adoptees for 15 years now. So I have encountered a lot of kids! I now know practicing or on-the-way-to-becoming social workers, psychologists, psychiatrists, pediatricians, counselors, teachers, and more! All of these fine young professionals or students are brothers and sisters in adoption-built families. Each has a genuine desire to make the adoption journey smoother for those entering or amidst their adoption endeavor.

Parents agree with the positive sentiments of their sons and daughters:

> "I think that one of the main positives is that we've taught our children by what they've seen through our lives—you just persevere. I think, in our society, too many people give up and bag out. Our kids have learned that we're not the type who are ever going to give up, and we hope that will be something that they're going to take on in the real world. I think all of the kids have learned compassion, and that doesn't come naturally to people. So, they've learned because of what's happened at home that there are people who just don't have life as good, and that they can do something at a young age to reach out to others."

> "The positive aspects of adopting far outweigh the negatives from my own perspective. Our birth children have been exposed to a broader view of life through fostering and adoption. If we

had not adopted or fostered, our children would have had a very marshmallow life. Things would have been ordinary, easy, and pretty predictable. With new children in our family, our girls have learned compassion and understanding for other people that might have developed otherwise, but not in such an intense manner."

The adoptees: The benefits of having a place to call "home"

Adoption means that a child waits no longer for a home. A family wants to care for her and offer her all of life's opportunities. Who can deny the positive aspects of having a family? Certainly, it is great to have someone with whom to share excitement about a job promotion, to eat with on holidays, to pet-sit, to make an emergency trip to the doctor, to help choose a first car, or to phone when the car breaks down. A parent is available to help out with a new baby, a marital problem, or a move to new place. The best part is that this family is available lifelong to share the ups and the downs! The adoptee always has a place to call "home."

Below, adoptees, ages eight to 18, comment on the benefits of being adopted:

"Adoption, to me, means being accepted, taken into a new family, receiving things you never had—I receive love and help. Before I was adopted, I was beaten and sexually abused."

"Adoption is joining a new family, the beginning of a new life, comfort, love, safety—no hitting! You don't get rejected. You get fed. You get privileges. You get to learn new things. You don't get hit or abused and you get safety. It was hard leaving my birth mom. It has also been hard forgiving my birth parents. They told me things like, 'You are dumb! You are fat and ugly! You are not worth anything!' I only wish my adoptive family had more of the Mexican dishes I love so much!"

"Adoption is the willingness of a family to be the kind of parents you need. My parents love me and are always there for me. They give me what I've missed. I got a whole new way of living and freedom to grow up the right way. I learned to speak, think, and write in a different language. I can catch up with school."

"Adoption means that you are in an orphanage and a mom and dad come to get you and bring you home. It is good because I get to be with a mom and dad that take care of me the best."

"The positives about being adopted have been numerous. First, I have a permanent family who will always be there for me no matter what. I've been able to do things that I wouldn't have been able to do in foster care such as playing the clarinet, having the ability to make lifelong friends, and I've been able to travel. I've been able to trust my family and learn to love them. I stopped having to continually pack my things."

"One of the positives about being adopted is that you have someone who you can ask for help in life. You can count on them to be on your side through good or bad. I was put in one of the best homes, I think, because my mom loves me for who I am."

"I am staying with my adoptive family forever. It is good to have a lot of siblings (ten). I feel safety and love. I am with a Christian family and don't have to go through fighting every day. We do lots of activities together like games, movies, Bible studies, art projects, and go to the library. It is good to have a family you can trust. I miss my bio parents and my one birth sister who still lives with them. I miss my bio grandparents (even though I get to see them sometimes) and other people who were important to me."

"The positives about being adopted are way too numerous to put on paper. I have a family that is all mine. I know that I'm not going anywhere just because I'm not what they were looking for. I know what it means to be loved and in turn to love. I understand that trust is something valuable that I had to give to my parents. I feel safe. I don't have to worry about waking up in the morning and thinking that I'm going to die."

"To me, living in an adopted family is a blessing beyond all others. When I was just a baby, I was abused and neglected by my birth mom and came close to death on a few occasions. Because of the situation I was in, I needed to be adopted as soon as possible. Luckily for me, there was a very nice and loving family looking to adopt a baby about my age. Once I was in a stable family who loved me, I was given the chance to grow up in a normal family with a normal life. As I grew up, I gradually found out that I was adopted. At first I didn't really think about being adopted, but gradually hate and love stirred up inside of me. My family helped me a lot in this part of my life because they were always there for me and gave me the chance to go to therapy to figure my problems out. To me, therapy was and still is a struggle. Most of the time I find it hard to cooperate and share my feelings with my therapist. But through much patience my therapist gradually helped me to be more comfortable with the fact that I am adopted and helped me to accept who I am as a person and who I want to be as an adult. I still am in therapy, but because of therapy I now can share my feelings openly with others and I have accepted the fact that my adoptive family *is* my family and I am not going back to my birth family. All in all I live in a wonderful family who loves me very much and I could not hope for anything better."

Plentiful research supports the positive aspects of adoption expressed by the kids above. Table 14.1 compares foster children who "age out" of the child welfare system between ages 18 to 21 with no permanent family with their peers who were adopted.

If these are outcomes for American foster children, what must be the end result for children leaving orphanages in less developed countries with fewer social programs?

TABLE 14.1 COMPARISON OF FOSTER CHILDREN
WHO "AGE OUT" OF THE CHILD WELFARE SYSTEM
WITH CHILDREN WHO ARE ADOPTED

Foster children	Adopted children
Poor educational outcomes; more than one-third have not completed high school. Considerably more mental health issues than others in the same age group. Much more likely to have been pregnant and to carry the pregnancy to term. Within 18 months of discharge from foster care: More than one-third have been physically or sexually victimized, incarcerated, or are homeless. One in five has lived in four or more places. Only 61% were employed, earning a median wage of $4.60 per hour.	More likely to complete high school or the equivalent. More likely to attend and complete college. Less likely to become teen parents. Less likely to abuse drugs and alcohol. Less likely to have mental health problems. Less likely to be arrested and incarcerated. More likely to be employed. More likely to have adequate incomes. More likely to have health insurance.

Sources: Courtney *et al.* 2007; Courtney
et al. 2001; Freundlich *et al.* 2008

Ava: "Just look at me now!"

Ava finally found her "forever" family at age 13 after abuse, neglect, a series of foster homes, two residential treatment placements, and two psychiatric hospitalizations. Her adoptive family was a single mom. Mom has since married. The marriage was actually the merger of two adoptive families. Now Ava has 12 brothers and sisters—two are birth children and the rest adopted.

Ava is 20 years old now, and she has grown into a beautiful young woman in all ways possible. She wrote her story for the readers of this book. It is a story that truly captures the essence of adoption in all its facets. It is a story that truly captures the essence of adoption in all its facets. It offers a thought provoking perspective from the adoptee. The traumatized adoptee's voice has been touched upon only lightly in this book because this book's emphasis is the typical brothers and sisters. Yet I think it critical, in the day-to-day challenges that adoption may bring to your family, to keep in mind that underneath the negative behaviors lays a deep pool of thoughts and feelings. Once brought to the surface, healing can occur.

"Adoption is the hardest thing to define, because it means so very much to me. How do you define being redefined as a person? How can I explain what it means to have a mother who loves me for no reason at all? She didn't give birth to me, and she didn't raise me as a small child and watch me grow into an honest, loving, and caring adult.

"She was given a cold, undesirable, manipulative, unruly teen, and she loved me unconditionally. I can say most people would've given up on me because they had all given up on me. She is the greatest person I will ever know, and I am so honored to say she's my mother.

"Adoption, to me, means acceptance—acceptance of peers, acceptance of family, and acceptance of society. The thing that case workers, foster parents, and counselors don't understand is that no one accepts a foster child. I can truly say that's how it felt. I felt like an outcast for so long, like no one could really understand me.

"Okay, so even if my foster parents could accept the fact that I wasn't their blood relation, and that I had behavioral problems, they would never understand my secrets. The case workers could explain that I had been sexually abused, or that my birth mother was on drugs and I was beaten, but they couldn't explain how I felt about it. Even after the rape, the abandonment, drugs, neglect, and abuse, I still loved my birth mother like any other nine-year-old girl would. I thought the world of her. In fact, when I was 11, and my case worker told me that she wasn't coming back, I wanted to die. I was even hospitalized for attempted suicide. I thought to myself, 'If she didn't want me, who would?' I felt even more isolated. As if this wasn't hard enough, there was something I had to face every day that was much worse—school.

"I must say that school was one of the hardest parts of being a foster child. You know that kid, in school, who had a really runny nose that was so gross? Or the girl who was just plain fat? Or the kid in the wheelchair you always felt bad for? I felt as if I was all of them rolled into one. The kids at school were vicious. Because they so badly wanted to fit in, they'd prey on the weak and different. I was all kinds of different. I was so out of the norm that kids that weren't making fun of me or questioning me pitied me. The ironic thing was that as many questions as they had for me, I had for them. What's it like to have the same mom, same school, same house and family your whole life? What's it like to come first in your parents' eyes? These things were all as foreign to me as foster care was to them. With so much emotion running bottled up inside my adolescent mind, school work just wasn't a priority.

"At this point, I had learned to block myself from feeling almost all emotion. I still had anger, though. I flew through foster homes until I was placed in residential treatment. Imagine being 11 years old and rooming with 15-year-old girls who had just been released from jail. I learned a lot of new traits, like how to get a male's attention, how to dance, how to fight, and how to play cards. I believe this placement was one of the system's biggest mistakes. I mean, what were they thinking? I was 11! Most of these girls had records and some had children.

"But, in a sense, I felt at home. Sure, it was scary as hell, but everyone was different and had behavioral problems—not just me! It was easier than some of the foster homes, because next to those girls, I looked like an angel.

"My next residential placement was an experience also. Living in a children's home is like having an around-the-clock parent who would never want you as their child. But at least I knew that up front. No one there wanted me. I knew that the other undesired, unloved, dysfunctional kids and myself were alone.

"Quiet time was the worst. Basically, it was an hour in your room every day with nothing to do. It felt like I was being punished for something I didn't even do. An hour felt like days in my room. Consumed with only my thoughts, I thought I was going crazy. Nights were hard, too. I was somewhat of an insomniac, because in my past, at night when everyone was asleep, was when I was raped, so sleep just didn't seem important to me. Plus, the night shift staff was male, which contributed to my anxiety. Although Mr. Jefferson helped me to trust men a little. He'd sit up with me and talk, laugh, play games on the computer, watch television, and he'd tell me about his family life. He had a wife and two daughters—family, something which I knew nothing about. Nights became easier than the days. And then there were weekends. The weekend staff was bitter. You weren't their child, you were their job. Your enjoyment of life wasn't their concern. They just wanted quiet. I'd sit in my room and cry. I was very lonely. Eventually, they found me a home, but I didn't know that.

"When I first met my mom, she was the same as any other mother I'd ever had—temporary. Little did I know, she wasn't willing to give up on me. It started out the same, the honeymoon. This was short. I was determined to push her away, but she wouldn't budge. I lied, cheated, and did drugs. I must say, she caught me by surprise when she took me to see Arleta.

"Arleta was like no other counselor I'd met. She made me angrier than I thought possible. See, with other counselors, it was easy to play mind games, to persuade them I was sad, when I had actually cut myself off from my feelings. Aside from anger, I was numb. Arleta was a new breed of counselor. I tried everything to show her that I was making an effort, but she saw through it. Unlike me, she let her feelings be known. She just wasn't going to take any of my crap. She wanted me to deal with my pain. It took a long time to get me to open up. I felt as though if I let my feelings out they'd judge me like so many others before them had. It was hard, but I did it. They didn't hate me or judge me! I was vulnerable and they didn't hurt me. I was sure this was a fluke! They couldn't really love me!

"So, I decided to push harder. I yelled louder and stayed out later. I was bad. I got moved back to residential treatment. This time I was lonelier, because I thought it was going to be my last home. I was shocked when my mom started visiting me again! Was she crazy? I put her through hell! I tried so hard to keep this woman from loving me and to keep myself from loving her. Yet she still wouldn't give up on me.

"Eventually, I went back to live with her. I was on my best behavior just long enough to get her to adopt me. Then I broke her heart again. I didn't mean to hurt her. I mean, this woman wanted nothing but for me to love her, but instead I put her though a lot of pain.

"I moved to my boyfriend's home. He was 21 and I was 16. He was a real winner: high school dropout, drug dealer, drug user, had no car and no job. He was my birth mother's dream man. I think this was one of the toughest times in my life. I skipped school every day and I partied all the time. I hated myself. I was my birth mother.

"But then one day I woke up, looked in the mirror, and decided I was done. I was going home. I called my mom and asked if I could come home. She was hesitant at first, but even through all the pain, hurt, and trouble I had caused, she said, 'Yes.' I started counseling with Arleta again. It was hard. It was knowing I was dealt a shitty hand for no reason. It was picking up and moving forward, gluing back together the pieces of a broken child. One thing I've learned to accept is the fact that I am different, and I always will be. I am strong but fragile, wise but still learning, all grown up but still so young, but most of all I am blessed—I am adopted.

"It's so hard to put into words what it is like to come from the gutter and feel as if this world is a cruel, shallow, evil place. Now I am a good person. I thrive on the thought of what the world has to offer, when I once shunned any form of compassion. I've worked so hard to get to where I am today, and knowing that I have this amazing woman who loves me, no matter what, and who is so proud of me makes every day worth living. I am moved. I have been shaken to the core. I know in my heart that God has watched over me every step of my life.

"There used to be a show on television called *Touched by an Angel*. It was about these people who were going through tough times. God would send them an angel to help them through their pain. Well, that's my life. I was given an angel. She's helped me in so many ways to become the person I am today. You could only be so lucky to meet her. She is everything I hope to be. I am headed off to college now. I have the world ahead of me. I also have a crazy, weird, heaven-sent family, with a saint for a mother and a rock for a father. I am truly blessed."

Chapter summary

- Brothers and sisters in adoption experience a multitude of benefits, in spite of the common challenges. Compassion, maturity, awareness of the outcome of choices, developing a fulfilling career path, advanced problem-solving skills—and the list could go on! The positive aspects of sharing one's home with a child in need contribute to deeply honing the types of skills that lead to success in all areas of life.

- The adoptee, upon joining the family he or she can now call home, receives innumerable and untold benefits! In the day-to-day life with the adopted son, daughter, brother, or sister, it is sometimes difficult to believe that they do appreciate their family. Yet their totally original comments, presented in this chapter, make clear that they are happy to have arrived home!

Appendix

Tables A1–4 are provided to demonstrate the developmental tasks accomplished by infants, toddlers, and young pre-school children when they proceed along a path of "normal" child development. Adoptive mothers and fathers may use this information to compare and contrast the development of young adoptees joining the family post-institutionalization or post-life with a dysfunctional birth family. The social and emotional age of the newcomer can be determined, and parents can initiate the process of "growing" their son or daughter via parenting at the child's social and emotional age.

TABLE A1 DEVELOPMENT OF INFANTS AGE 0–12 MONTHS

Physical	Cognitive	Social/emotional
• Movement: 2–3 months lifts head when on stomach; 4–6 months control of head and arm movements, purposive grasping, rolls over; around 7 months control of trunk and hands and can sit alone; 9–10 months crawls; 10–11 months pulls to a stand and cruises while holding on. • Vision: by 6 months infants can scan, track, and focus on objects. They can see in color, see more clearly, perceive depth, and adjust to different distances. Especially enjoy looking at caregiver's face. • Sound: will turn to the sound of the caregiver's voice when only a few days old. Infants are amazingly interested in the basic speech sounds of language.	• Language: 2–3 months includes cries, coos, and grunts; 4–6 months babbling; 10–12 months one or two words, imitates sounds, responds to simple commands. • 0–2 months simple reflex activity such as grasping or sucking. • 2–4 months stereotyped behaviors such as opening or closing fingers. • 4–8 months repeats actions that resulted in a consequence of interest such as kicking feet to move a mobile suspended over the crib. • 8–12 months actions become intentional such as reaching for a specific object.	• Moves from being asocial to visually fixating on faces and smiling at faces, to recognizing the primary caregiver and being able to distinguish between familiar persons and strangers. In essence, has formed a specific emotional attachment to the primary caregiver. • Moves from a state of generalized tension, to expressing emotions such as delight, distress, anger. • Touch: infants especially responsive to touch around the mouth, the palms of the hands, and bottom of feet. 2–4 months begins to particularly enjoy rocking and being cuddled; 7–9 months enjoys peek-a-boo; around 10–12 months, responsive to own name, waves bye-bye, plays pat-a-cake, gives and takes objects.

TABLE A2 DEVELOPMENT OF TODDLERS AGE 12–18 MONTHS

Physical	Cognitive	Social/emotional
• The brain has grown to two-thirds of the adult size. • Birth weight has tripled. • Takes first independent steps. • Creeps up stairs. • Climbs on objects such as chairs. • Able to throw and grasp objects. • Able to put objects together and take objects apart, such as stacking blocks or putting objects in and out of a bucket.	• Begins to see the relationship between actions and consequences and as such, begins to act in a way that causes something to happen. • Deliberately uses an adult to achieve a goal—such as dropping a spoon over and over for the adult to keep retrieving. • Begins linking events. Puts a doll in a stroller and pushes the stroller. • Begins pretend play. • Mimics observations and sounds. • Desires to do chores. • Achieves object permanence—the knowledge that something continues to exist even when out of sight. • Language: uses 50 words and understands many more than 50. Makes two-word sentences. • As a result of language, become very interested in books. • Sorts objects into rudimentary categories—for example, all snacks are called "cookies."	• Securely and firmly attached to a small number of adults. • Will experience separation anxiety when separated from primary caregiver. • Use the caregiver as a base. That is, they explore their environment but return to the caregiver at frequent intervals. • The ability to delay gratification increases. • Develops a favorite blanket or stuffed animal as a transitional object. • Growing interest in toys and other inanimate objects. • Variety of emotions are expressed—joy, frustration, pride, fear, anger. • Play offers an outlet for emotions. • Play promotes increased growth of cause and effect thinking. • Play is "onlooker" (watching others play but not interacting) or "parallel" (sitting next to another toddler but not playing with the other toddler). • "Me do it" becomes a favorite expression.

TABLE A3 DEVELOPMENT OF TODDLERS AGE 18–30 MONTHS

Physical	Cognitive	Social/emotional
• At 18 months can back up, sit on a low chair, run stiffly, jump down from a step, walk up stairs with assistance, creep backwards down stairs, turn pages of a book. • At 30 months has mastered running, jumping with both feet, walking up and down stairs, kicking a ball, throwing overhand, holding large objects, stringing large beads, folding paper, building a tower with large blocks, and unbottoning large buttons.	• Consistent schedules become important. This provides a basis for understanding time schedules. • Rudimentary problem-solving skills develop. For example, the toddler can devise a way to get to a cookie sitting on a kitchen counter. • Curiosity peaks and children very actively explore their environment. • "No" and "Mine" become favorite words. • Can follow a two-step direction such as "go to your room and get your pajamas." • Play takes on themes. For example, the child may drive a truck, pretend to load and unload, reload, and park. • Vocabulary increases to 300 words. • Can identify body parts. • Can answer "Who, What, Where" questions.	• Alternates between independence and dependence. Fluctuates between seeking the caregiver's affection and testing the limits. • Primary caregiver still the essential base of support especially when tired, frustrated or fatigued. • Refers to oneself by name and recognizes oneself in photos. • Parallel play remains dominant. • Possessiveness, rather than sharing, is prevalent. • The roots of conscience begin to develop. Remorse may be expressed. Or the toddler may reach for something and then state "no, no" indicating the start of learning right from wrong. • Brief temper tantrums are a common way of expressing frustration or anger, or getting attention.

TABLE A4 DEVELOPMENT OF TODDLERS AGE 30–36 MONTHS

Physical	Cognitive	Social/emotional
• Can run around objects and turn corners. • Hops on one foot for a few steps. • Draws horizontal and vertical lines and circles. • Walks up and down stairs with alternating feet. • Catches a ball against the chest. • Uses a forearm rotation to turn objects such as door knobs. • Puts on socks. • Zips and snaps. • Cuts with a child's scissors.	• Uses symbols to represent objects—for example, a block might be a car, or a doll may be mommy. • While the concept of past and future remains confusing, they can use yesterday to represent anything past, and tomorrow to represent anything future. • Match objects that go together such as shoe and sock, coat and mitten. • Able to remember and follow three-step commands. • Language now includes possessives, verbs, and adjectives. • Categorization improves—for example, truck now describes a variety of trucks. But understands that trucks are different from buses.	• Now has a mental image of the caregiver and feels safe and protected even during brief separations. • Temper tantrums decrease as language increases and the child can verbally express feelings. • Begins to play with rather than next to peers. Possessiveness decreases. • Recognizes gender and racial differences.

Permission for the information contained in these charts was obtained from Zero to Three: National Center for Infants, Toddlers, and Families (www.zerotothree.org), the Child Development Institute (http://childdevelopmentinfo.com) and *Toddler Adoption: The Weaver's Craft*, by Mary Hopkins-Best. (London: Jessica Kingsley Publishers, 2012.)

References

Balk, D. (1990) "The self-concepts of bereaved adolescents: Sibling death and its aftermath." *Journal of Adolescent Research 5*, 1, 112–132.

Bank, S.P. and Kahn, M.D. (1997) *The Sibling Bond*. New York, NY: Basic Books.

Belsky, J. (1984) "The determinants of parenting: A process model." *Child Development 55*, 83–96.

Belsky, J. and Kelly, J. (1994) *The Transition to Parenthood: How a First Child Changes a Marriage*. New York, NY: Delacorte.

Bower, J.W. (2012) *Transracial Parenting Self-Awareness Tool*. St. Paul, MN: North American Council on Adoptable Children. Available at www.nacac.org/postadopt/transracialWilling.html, accessed on October 24, 2012.

Bowlby, J. (1980) *Attachment and Loss, Volume III. Loss: Sadness and Depression*. New York, NY: Basic Books.

Brazelton, T.B. and Sparrow, J.D. (2005) *Understanding Sibling Rivalry: The Brazelton Way*. Cambridge, MA: Da Capo Press.

Buehler, C., Rhodes, K., Orme, J., and Cuddeback, G. (2006) "The potential for successful family foster care: Conceptualizing competency domains for foster parents." *Child Welfare 85*, 523–558.

Campbell, D. (2000) *The Mozart Effect for Children: Awakening Your Child's Mind, Health, and Creativity with Music*. New York, NY: Black Thistle Press.

Casas, P. (2001) *Toward the ABCs: Building a Healthy Social and Emotional Foundation for Learning and Living*. Chicago, IL: Ounce of Prevention Fund. Available at www.ounceofprevention.org/research/pdfs/Towards_the_ABCs.pdf, accessed on October 24, 2012.

Child Welfare Information Gateway (2001) *Understanding the Effects of Maltreatment on Early Brain Development: A Bulletin for Professionals*. Washington, DC: U.S. Department of Health and Human Services. Available at http://dcfs.co.la.ca.us/katieA/docs/Maltreatmnet%20on%20Early%20Brain%20Development.pdf, accessed on October 24, 2012.

Cicirelli, V.G. (1995) *Sibling Relationships across the Life Span*. New York, NY: Plenum Press.

Cline, F. and Fay, J. (2006) *Parenting with Love and Logic*. Colorado Springs, CO: NavPress.

College Entrance Examination Board (2001) *College-Bound Seniors National Report: Profile of SAT Program Test Takers*. Princeton, NJ: NJAEP Resources.

Cook, A., Blaustein, M., Spinazzola, J., and van der Kolk, B. (eds) (2003) *Complex Trauma in Children and Adolescents*. National Child Traumatic Stress Network, white paper. Available to download from www.NCTSNet.org.

Courtney, M.E., Dworsky, A., Cusick, G.R., Havlicek, J., Perez, A., and Keller, T. (2007) *Midwest Evaluation of the Adult Functioning of Former Foster Youth: Outcomes at Age 21*. Chicago, IL: Chapin Hall Center for Children, University of Chicago.

Courtney, M.E., Piliavin, I., Grogan-Kaylor, A., and Nesmith, A. (2001) "Foster youth transitions to adulthood: A longitudinal view of youth leaving care." *Child Welfare 80*, 6, 685–717.

Crumbley, J. (1999) *Transracial Adoption and Foster Care: Practice Issues for Professionals*. Washington, DC: Child Welfare League of America.

Cummings, E.M. and O'Reilly, A.W. (1997) "Fathers in Family Context: Effects of Marital Quality on Child Adjustment." In M.E. Lamb (ed.) *The Role of the Father in Child Development* (Third Edition). New York, NY: John Wiley and Sons.

Davies, P. and Cummings, M. (1994) "Marital conflict and child adjustment: An emotional security hypothesis." *Psychological Bulletin 116*, 3, 387–411.

Davis, J.L. (2007) *Family Dinners are Important: 10 Reasons Why, and 10 Shortcuts to Help Get the Family to the Table.* Available at www.webmd.com/a-to-z-guides/features/family-dinners-are-important, accessed January 26, 2013.

Duehn, W. (2009) "Creating Sexual Safety and Promoting Recovery in Adoption and Foster Care." North American Council on Adoptable Children (NACAC) conference.

Evan B. Donaldson Institute (2012) *Openness in Adoption: From Secrecy and Stigma to Knowledge and Connections.* Available at http://adoptioninstitute.org/research/2012_03_openness.php, accessed on October 24, 2012.

Freundlich, M. and North American Council on Adoptable Children (NACAC) (2008) *The Value of Adoption Subsidies: Helping Children Find Permanent Homes.* Available at www.nacac.org/adoptionsubsidy/valueofsubsidies.pdf, accessed on October 24, 2012.

Ginther, N., Keefer, B., and Beeler, N. (2003) *Keeping Your Adult Relationship Happy in Adoption.* Columbus, OH: Institute for Human Services for the Ohio Child Welfare Training Program.

Goetting, A. (1986) "The developmental tasks of siblingship over the life cycle." *Journal of Marriage and the Family 48*, 703–714.

Gray, D. (2012) *Attaching in Adoption: Practical Tools for Today's Parents.* London: Jessica Kingsley Publishers.

Hartup, W. (1992) "Having friends, making friends, and keeping friends: Relationships as educational contexts." *ERIC Digest*, ED345854. Urbana, IL: ERIC Clearinghouse on Elementary and Early Childhood Education. Available at www.eric.ed.gov/PDFS/ED345854.pdf, accessed on October 24, 2012.

Hogan, N. and Greenfield, D. (1991) "Adolescent sibling bereavement symptomatology in a large community sample." *Journal of Adolescent Research 6*, 1, 97–112.

Hopkins-Best, M. (2012) *Toddler Adoption: The Weaver's Craft* (Revised Edition). London: Jessica Kingsley Publishers.

Ingels, S.J. (1992) "National Education Longitudinal Study (NELS): 88 first follow up." *ERIC Digest*, ED354257. Urbana, IL: ERIC Clearinghouse on Elementary and Early Childhood Education.

Jernberg, A. and Booth, P. (1999) *Theraplay: Helping Parents and Children Build Better Relationships Through Attachment-Based Play.* San Francisco: Jossey-Bass.

Johnson, D.E. (2012) *A Letter from Dr. Dana Johnson.* University of Minnesota, International Adoption Clinic. Available at www.peds.umn.edu/iac/topics/letter/home.html, accessed on October 24, 2012.

Judge, K. (1994) "Serving Children, Siblings and Spouses: Understanding the Needs of Other Family Members." In H.P. Lefley and M. Wasow (eds) *Helping Families Cope with Mental Illness.* Chur, Switzerland: Harwood Academic Publishers.

Katz, L. and McClellan, D. (1991) *The Teacher's Role in the Social Development of Young Children.* Urbana, IL: ERIC Clearinghouse on Elementary and Early Childhood Education. Urbana, Illinois, 1991. Available at www.eric.ed.gov/PDFS/ED331642.pdf, accessed on October 24, 2012.

Kaye, K. (1990) "Acknowledgement or Rejection of Differences?" In D.M. Brodzinsky and M.D. Schechter (eds) *The Psychology of Adoption.* New York, NY: Oxford University Press.

Keck, G.C. and Kupecky, R.M. (2002) *Parenting the Hurt Child: Helping Adoptive Families Heal and Grow.* Colorado Springs, CO: NavPress.

Keck, G.C. and Kupecky, R.M. (2009) *Adopting the Hurt Child: Hope for Families with Special-Needs Kids.* Colorado Springs, CO: NavPress.

KidSource (1996) *What Is Early Intervention?* Available at www.kidsource.com/kidsource/content/early.intervention.html, accessed on October 24, 2012.

Kübler-Ross, E. (1969) *On Death and Dying: What the Dying Have to Teach Doctors, Nurses, Clergy and their Own Families.* New York, NY: Scribner.

Kübler-Ross, E. and Kessler, D. (2005) *On Grief and Grieving: Finding the Meaning of Grief through the Five Stages of Loss.* New York, NY: Scribner.

Lindeman, L., Kemp, G., and Segal, J. (2012 *Laughter is the Best Medicine.* Available at www.helpguide.org/life/humor_laughter_health.htm, accessed on October 24, 2012.

Lobato, D. (1990) *Brothers, Sisters, and Special Needs: Information and Activities for Helping Young Siblings of Children with Chronic Illnesses and Developmental Disabilities.* Baltimore, MD: Paul H. Brooks Publishing.

McClellan, D. and Katz, L. (1993) "Young children's social development: A checklist." *ERIC Digest,* ED356100. Urbana, IL: ERIC Clearinghouse on Elementary and Early Childhood Education. Available at www.ericdigests.org/1993/young.htm, accessed on 12 February 2013.

Mental Health America (2007) *10-Year Retrospective Study Shows Progress in American Attitudes about Depression and Other Mental Health Issues.* Available at www.mentalhealthamerica.net/index.cfm?objectid=FD502854-1372-4D20-C89C30F0DEE68035, accessed on October 24, 2012.

Meyer, D.J. and Vadasy, P.F. (1994) *Sibshops: Workshops for Siblings of Children with Special Needs.* Baltimore, MD: Paul H. Brooks Publishing.

Miller, F., Dworkin, J., Ward, M., and Barone, D. (1990) "A Preliminary Study of Unresolved Grief in Families of Seriously Mentally Ill Patients." In H.P. Lefley and M. Wasow (eds) *Helping Families Cope with Mental Illness.* Chur, Switzerland: Harwood Academic Publishers.

Olesen, M. (2004) "How siblings fare in difficult adoptions." *Adoptalk,* Summer 2004.

Perry, B. (1997) "Incubated in Terror: Neurodevelopmental Factors in the Cycle of Violence." In J. Osofsky (ed.) *Children, Youth and Violence: The Search for Solutions.* New York, NY: Guilford Press.

Perry, B.D. (2004) *Understanding Traumatized and Maltreated Children: The Core Concepts. Violence and Childhood.* Available at www.lfcc.on.ca/Perry_Core_Concepts_Violence_and_Childhood.pdf, accessed on October 24, 2012.

Perry, B. and Szalavitz, M. (2006) *The Boy Who Was Raised as a Dog and Other Stories from a Child Psychiatrist's Notebook: What Traumatized Children Can Teach Us about Loss, Love, and Healing.* New York, NY: Basic Books.

Peth-Pierce, R. (2000) *Good Beginning: Sending America's Children to School with the Social and Emotional Competence They Need to Succeed.* Bethesda, MD: The Child Mental Health Foundations and Agencies Network (FAN). Available at http://casel.org/wp-content/uploads/goodbeginning.pdf, accessed on October 24, 2012.

Pinderhughes, E.E. and Rosenberg, K.F. (1990) "Family bonding with high risk placements: A therapy model that promotes the process of becoming a family." *Journal of Children in Contemporary Society 21,* 204–230.

Poland, D. and Groze, V. (1993) "Effects of foster care placement on biological children in the home." *Child and Adolescent Social Work Journal 10,* 153–164.

Powell, T.H. and Gallagher, P.A. (1993) *Brothers and Sisters: A Special Part of Exceptional Families* (Second Edition). Baltimore, MD: Paul H. Brooks Publishing.

Ratey, J.J. (2001) *A User's Guide to the Brain: Perception, Attention, and the Four Theaters of the Brain.* New York, NY: Pantheon Books.

Santrock, J.W. (1995) *Life-Span Development.* Dubuque, IA: William C. Brown Communications.

Seigel, D.J. (2001) *The Developing Mind: How Relationships and the Brain Interact to Shape Who We Are.* New York, NY: Guilford Press.

Smith, M.J., Greenberg, J.S., and Mailick, S.M. (2007) "The effect of the quality of sibling relationships on the life satisfaction of adults with schizophrenia." *Psychiatric Services 58,* 9, 1222–1224.

Sparrow, S.S., Cicchetti, D.V., and Balla, D.A. (2005) *Vineland Adaptive Behavior Scale* (Second Edition, *Vineland-II*). San Antonio, TX: Pearson.

Trout, M. (1986) *The Awakening and Growth of the Human, Unit IV: The Newborn, the Family, and the Dance* (VHS/DVD). Champaign, IL: The Infant-Parent Institute.

van der Kolk, B. (1989) "The compulsion to repeat the trauma: Re-enactment, revictimization, and masochism." *Psychiatric Clinics of North America 12,* 2, 389–411.

Ward, M. and Lewko, J. (1988) "Problems experienced by adolescents already in families that adopt older children." *Adolescence 23,* 89, 221–8.

Wooten, P. (1996) "Humor: An antidote for stress." *Holistic Nursing Practice 10,* 2, 49–55.

Resources

Books and websites for parents
Adoption

Davenport, D. (2006) *The Complete Book of International Adoption: A Step-by-Step Guide to Finding Your Child.* New York, NY: Three Rivers Press.

Eldridge, S. (1999) *Twenty Things Adopted Kids Wish Their Adoptive Parents Knew.* New York, NY: Delta Trade Paperbacks.

Eldridge, S. (2009) *20 Things Adoptive Parents Need to Succeed: Discover the Unique Needs of Your Adopted Child and Become the Best Parent You Can.* New York, NY: Delta Trade Paperbacks.

Hopkins-Best (2012) *Toddler Adoption: The Weaver's Craft* (Revised Edition). London: Jessica Kingsley Publishers.

Keck, G.C. and Kupecky, R.M. (2009) *Adopting the Hurt Child: Hope for Families with Special-Needs Kids. A Guide for Parents and Professionals.* Colorado Springs, CO: NavPress.

Maskew, T. (2003) *Our Own: Adopting and Parenting the Older Child.* Morton Grove, IL: Snowcap Press.

Adoption Learning Partners (ALP)

www.adoptionlearningpartners.org

ALP, founded by The Cradle, seeks to improve adoption outcomes for all members of the adoption circle. ALP offers valuable, timely, web-based educational resources for adoptive parents, adopted individuals, birth parents, and the families who love them.

Child Welfare Information Gateway

www.childwelfare.gov

The Child Welfare Information Gateway is a service of the Children's Bureau, the Administration for Children and Families, and the Department of Health and Human Services. This website is sated with articles on all aspects of adoption and trauma.

Attachment

Cogen, P. (2008) *Parenting Your Internationally Adopted Child: From Your First Hours Together to the Teen Years.* Boston, MA: Harvard Common Press.

Gray, D.D. (2012) *Attaching in Adoption: Practical Tools for Today's Parents.* London: Jessica Kingsley Publishers.

Golding, K.S. and Hughes, D.A. (2012) *Creating Loving Attachments: Parenting with PACE to Nurture Confidence and Security in the Troubled Child.* London: Jessica Kingsley Publishers.

Hughes, D.A. and Baylin, J. (2012) *Brain-Based Parenting: The Neuroscience of Caregiving for Healthy Attachment.* New York, NY: W.W. Norton and Company.

Purvis, K., Cross, D., and Sunshine, W. (2007) *The Connected Child: Bring Hope and Healing to Your Adoptive Family.* New York, NY: McGraw-Hill.

Association for Treatment and Training in the Attachment of Children (ATTACh)

www.attach.org

ATTACh is an international coalition of professionals and families dedicated to helping families experiencing attachment difficulties. ATTACh puts forth a quarterly newsletter, sponsors an annual conference, and maintains a directory of attachment-focused clinicians.

The Theraplay® Institute

www.theraplay.org

Theraplay® is a structured play therapy for children and their parents. Its goal is to enhance attachment, self-esteem, trust in others, and joyful engagement. Because of its focus on attachment and relationship development, Theraplay® has been used successfully for many years with foster and adoptive families.

Parenting

Brazelton, T.B. and Sparrow, J.D. (2005) *Sibling Rivalry: The Brazelton Way.* Cambridge, MA: Da Capo Press.

Gardner, J.W. and Mazlish, E. (2012) *Siblings without Rivalry: How to Help Your Children Live Together So You Can Live Too.* New York, NY: W.W. Norton and Company.

Keck, G.C. and Kupecky, R.M. (2009) *Parenting the Hurt Child: Helping Adoptive Families Heal and Grow.* Colorado Springs, CO: NavPress.

McKay, G. and Dinkmeyer, D. (2002) *How You Feel Is Up to You: The Power of Emotional Choice.* Atascadero, CA: Impact Publishers.

MacLeod, J. and Macrae, S. (eds) (2006) *Adoption Parenting: Creating a Toolbox, Building Connections.* Warren, NJ: EMK Press.

Siegel, D.J. and Bryson, T.P. (2011) *The Whole-Brain Child: 12 Revolutionary Strategies to Nurture Your Child's Developing Mind.* New York, NY: Delacorte Press.

Siegel, D.J. and Hartzell, M. (2003) *Parenting from the Inside Out: How a Deeper Self-Understanding Can Help You Raise Children Who Thrive.* New York, NY: Jeremy P. Tarcher/Penguin.

KidsHealth

www.kidshealth.org

KidsHealth is the largest and most-visited site on the Internet. Created by the Nemours Foundation's Center for Children's Health Media, KidsHealth provides families with accurate, up-to-date, and jargon-free health information. There are separate areas for kids, teens, and parents—each with its own design, age-appropriate content, and tone. There are literally thousands of in-depth features about medical illnesses, mental health issues, school issues, child development, and more!

Love and Logic
www.loveandlogic.com
The Love and Logic Institute is dedicated to making parenting and teaching fun and rewarding, instead of stressful and chaotic. They provide practical tools and techniques to help adults achieve respectful, healthy relationships with their children.

Culture

Alperson, M. (2001) *Dim Sum, Bagels, and Grits: A Sourcebook for Multicultural Families.* New York, NY: Farrar, Strauss and Giroux.

Coughlin, A. and Abramowitz, C. (2004) *Cross-Cultural Adoption: How to Answer Questions from Family, Friends, and Community.* Washington, DC: Lifeline Press.

Evans, K. (2008) *The Lost Daughters of China: Adopted Girls, Their Journey to America, and the Search for a Missing Past.* New York, NY: Jeremy P. Tarcher/Putnam.

Nakazawa, D.J. (2003) *Does Anybody Else Look Like Me? A Parent's Guide to Raising Multiracial Children.* Cambridge, MA: Da Capo Lifelong.

Steinberg, G. and Hall, B. (2012) *Inside Transracial Adoption: Strength-Based, Culture-Sensitizing Parenting Strategies for Inter-Country or Domestic Adoptive Families that Don't "Match"* (Second Edition). London: Jessica Kingsley Publishers.

Wright, M. (1998) *I'm Chocolate, You're Vanilla: Raising Healthy Black and Biracial Children in a Race-Conscious World.* New York, NY: Jossey-Bass.

North American Council on Adoptable Children (NACAC)
www.nacac.org
NACAC promotes and supports permanent families for children and youth in the US and Canada who have been in care. The NACAC website contains articles covering all aspects of transcultural adoption as well as all other facets of adoption.

Pact—An Adoption Alliance
www.pactadopt.org
Pact is a non-profit organization with a primary mission to serve children of color in need of adoption or who are growing up in adoptive families. If you are looking for information related to any transcultural adoption issue, you are sure to find it on the Pact website!

Child development

Borba, M. (2002) *Building Moral Intelligence: The Seven Essential Virtues that Teach Kids to Do the Right Thing.* Hoboken, NJ: Jossey-Bass.

Leach, P. (1997) *Your Baby and Child: From Birth to Age Five*. New York, NY: Alfred A. Knopf.

Schaefer, C.E. and DiGeronimo, T.F. (2000) *Ages and Stages: A Parent's Guide to Normal Childhood Development*. New York, NY: John Wiley and Sons.

Child Development Institute (CDI)

http://childdevelopmentinfo.com

CDI was founded by Robert Myers, PhD, a clinical child psychologist with 25 years of experience working with children, adolescents, families, and parents. This website is packed with information about child development and play.

Zero to Three

www.zerotothree.org

Zero to Three's mission is to support the healthy development and well-being of infants, toddlers, and their families. This organization advances this mission by informing, educating, and supporting adults who influence the lives of infants and toddlers.

Talking with kids about adoption and trauma

Lacher, D.B., Nicholas, T., and May, J.C. (2012) *Connecting with Kids through Stories: Using Narratives to Facilitate Attachment in Adopted Children* (Second Edition). London: Jessica Kingsley Publishers.

O'Melley, B. (2011) *Lifebooks: Creating a Treasure for the Adopted Child*. Winthrop, MA: Adoption Works Press.

Schooler, J.E. and Keefer, B.E. (2000) *Telling the Truth to Your Adopted or Foster Child: Making Sense of the Past*. Santa Barbara, CA: Praeger Publishers.

Trauma and other special issues

Bell, T.J. (2003) *When the Brain Can't Hear: Unraveling the Mystery of Auditory Processing Disorder*. New York, NY: Atria.

Johnson, T.C. (2007) *Helping Children with Sexual Behavior Problems: A Guidebook for Professionals and Caregivers*. San Diego, CA: Institute on Violence, Abuse and Trauma.

Johnson, T.C. (2007) *Understanding Children's Sexual Behaviors: What's Natural and Healthy*. San Diego, CA: Institute on Violence, Abuse and Trauma.

Meese, R.L. (2002) *Children of Intercountry Adoption in School: A Primer for Parents and Professionals*. Westport, CT: Bergin and Garvey.

Miller, L.J. (2006) *Sensational Kids: Hope and Help for Children with Sensory Processing Disorder*. New York, NY: Penguin Books.

Papolos, D. and Papolos, J. (2002) *The Bipolar Child: The Definitive and Reassuring Guide to Childhood's Most Misunderstood Disorder*. New York, NY: Broadway Books.

Children and Adults with Attention Deficit/Hyperactivity Disorder (CHADD)

www.chadd.org

CHADD is a national non-profit organization providing education, advocacy, and support for individuals with ADHD. This website contains abundant information pertaining to ADHD and special education services.

Child Trauma Academy (CTA)

www.childtrauma.org

CTA recognizes the crucial importance of childhood experiences in shaping the health of the individual and, ultimately, society. This site contains articles and online courses related to attachment, trauma, and grief and loss.

National Child Traumatic Stress Network (NCTSN)

www.nctsn.org

NCTSN is a unique collaboration of academic and community-based service centers whose mission is to raise the standard of care and increase access to services for traumatized children and their families across the United States. Via articles and videos, there is coverage of the impact of all types of trauma on children's development.

National Institute of Mental Health (NIMH)

www.nimh.nih.gov

NIMH is the largest scientific organization in the world dedicated to research focused on the understanding, treatment, and prevention of mental disorders and the promotion of mental health. The website provides thorough descriptions and treatment options for all mental health diagnoses. Treatment recommendations are included for each disorder.

The National Organization on Fetal Alcohol Syndrome (NOFAS)

www.nofas.org

NOFAS is the leading voice and resource of the Fetal Alcohol Spectrum Disorders (FASD) community. This website provides articles and additional resources for those parenting or working with children with FASD.

Books and websites for children and adolescents

Adoption

Blomquist, G.M. and Blomquist, P.B. (1990) *Zachary's New Home: A Story for Foster and Adopted Children.* Washington, DC: Magination Press.

Brodzinsky, A.B. (2012) *The Mulberry Bird: An Adoption Story.* London: Jessica Kingsley Publishers.

Gabel, S. (1988) *Filling in the Blanks: A Guided Look at Growing Up Adopted*. Indianapolis, IN: Perspectives Press/St. Paul, MN: Koryo Press.

Grossnickle, M. (2004) *A Place in My Heart*. Available from www.speakingofadoption.com.

Kasza, K. (1992) *A Mother for Choco*. New York, NY: Puffin Books.

Koehler, P. (1990) *The Day We Met You*. New York, NY: Aladdin Paperbacks.

McCreight, B. (2010) *Help! I've Been Adopted*. Mount Hermon, CA: Adoption Press.

MacLeod, J. (2003) *At Home in this World: A China Adoption Story*. Warren, NJ: EMK Press.

Mitchell, C. (2006) *Welcome Home, Forever Child: A Celebration of Children Adopted as Toddlers, Preschoolers, and Beyond*. Bloomington, IN: Author House.

Parr, T. (2007) *We Belong Together: A Book about Adoption and Families*. New York, NY: Little, Brown Books for Young Readers.

Peacock, C.A. (2000) *Mommy Far, Mommy Near: An Adoption Story*. Morton Grove, IN: Albert Whitman and Co.

Adoption Clubhouse

www.adoptionclubhouse.org

The Adoption Clubhouse is a program of the National Adoption Center, whose mission is to expand adoption opportunities throughout the United States, particularly for children with special needs and those from minority cultures. Through the activities and information on this site children can experience a sense of belonging to a wider adoption community of peers.

Attachment

Chara, K.A. and Chara, P.J., Jr. (2005) *A Safe Place for Caleb: An Interactive Book for Kids, Teens and Adults with Issues of Attachment, Grief and Loss, or Early Trauma*. London: Jessica Kingsley Publishers.

Collodi, C. (2001) *Pinocchio: A Classic Illustrated Edition*. San Francisco, CA: Chronical Books.

Munsch, R. (1986) *Love You Forever*. Richmond Hill, ON: Firefly Books.

Penn, A. (2007) *The Kissing Hand*. Terre Haute, IN: Tanglewood Press.

Pryor, J.E. and Hafer, T. (ed.) (2007) *Stuck on You: 100 Wam, Witty, Wonderful Ways to say, You're Special*. Kansas City, Missouri: Andrews MeMeel Publishing.

Rath, T. and Reckmeyer, M. (2009) *How Full is Your Bucket? For Kids*. Washington, DC: Gallup Press.

Wise, M.B. (1977) *The Runaway Bunny*. New York, NY: Harper Trophy.

Culture

Ballard, R. (2009) *Pieces of Me: Who Do I Want to Be? Voices for and by Adopted Teens*. Warren, NJ: EMK Press.

Burnett, K. (2001) *If the World Were Blind... A Book About Judgment and Prejudice*. Felton, CA: GR Publishing.

Katz, K. (2007) *The Colors of Us*. New York, NY: Henry Holt and Company/BYR Paperbacks.

Payne, L.M. (1997) *We Can Get Along: A Child's Book of Choices*. Minneapolis, MN: Free Spirit Publishing.

Becoming a sibling/being a sibling

Alley, R.W. (2007) *Bratty Brothers and Selfish Sisters: All about Sibling Rivalry.* St. Meinrad, IN: One Caring Place.

Cole, J. (2010) *I'm a Big Brother.* New York, NY: Harper Festival Publishers.

Cole, J. (2010) *I'm a Big Sister.* New York, NY: Harper Festival Publishers.

Coville, B. (1997) *The Lapsnatcher.* Mahwah, NJ: BridgeWater Books.

Crist, J.J. and Verdick, E. (2010) *Siblings: You're Stuck with Each Other, So Stick Together.*

Little, J. (2001) *Emma's Yucky Brother.* New York, NY: Harper Trophy.

Penn, A. (2004) *A Pocket Full of Kisses.* Terre Haute, IN: Tanglewood Press.

Petertyl, M.E. (1997) *Seeds of Love: For Brothers and Sisters of International Adoption.* Grand Rapids, MI: Folio One Publishing.

Sheldon, A. (2006) *Big Sister Now: A Story about Me and Our New Baby.* Washington, DC: Magination Press.

Stoeke, J.M. (2005) *Waiting for May.* New York, NY: Dutton Children's Books.

Sugarman, B.O. (2006) *Rebecca's Journey Home.* Minneapolis, MN: Kar-Ben Publishing.

Winokur, M.R. (2009) *My Invisible World: Life with My Brother, His Disability and His Service Dog.* Brooklyn Park, MN: Better Endings New Beginnings.

Coping

Huebner, D. (2007) *What to Do When Your Temper Flares: A Kids' Guide to Overcoming Problems with Anger.* Washington, DC: Magination Press.

Lamia, M. (2010) *Understanding Myself: A Kids' Guide to Intense and Strong Feelings.* Washington, DC: Magination Press.

Lamia, M. (2012) *Emotions: Making Sense of Your Feelings.* Washington, DC: Magination Press.

Moss, W. (2010) *Being Me: A Kids' Guide to Boosting Confidence and Self-Esteem.* Washington, DC: Magination Press.

Spelman, C.M. (2000) *When I Feel Angry.* Morton Grove, IL: Albert Whitman and Co.

Spelman, C.M. (2002) *When I Feel Sad.* Morton Grove, IL: Albert Whitman and Co.

Spelman, C.M. (2002) *When I Feel Scared.* Morton Grove, IL: Albert Whitman and Co.

Spelman, C.M. (2003) *When I Feel Jealous.* Morton Grove, IL: Albert Whitman and Co.

Verdick, E. and Lisovskis, M. (2002) *How to Take the Grrr Out of Anger.* Minneapolis, MN: Free Spirit Publishing.

Coping Skills for Kids

www.copingskills4kids.net

Kids who are prepared for dealing with coping challenges in early adolescence are more confident of dealing with these upsetting experiences during their early teenage years. This site explains a brain-based method of coping in an interesting and hands-on manner.

Trauma and other issues

Bernstein, S.C. (1991) *A Family that Fights.* Morton Grove, Illinois IL: Albert Whitman and Co.

Bobula, J. and Bobula, K. (2009) *Forgetful Frankie, The World's Greatest Rock Skipper: Fetal Alcohol Spectrum Disorder.* Ottawa, ON: Wildberry Productions.

Bobula, J. and Bobula, K. (2011) *Sad, Sad Seth, The World's Greatest Writer: Depression*. Ottawa, ON: Wildberry Productions.

Clark, T. (1992) *The House that Crack Built*. San Francisco, CA: Chronicle Books.

Fisher, A.Q. and Rivas, M.E. (2002) *Finding Fish: A Memoir*. New York, NY: Harper Torch.

Harrie, R. (2004) *It's So Amazing: A Book about Eggs, Sperm, Birth, Babies, and Families*. Somerville, MA: Candlewick.

Huebner, D. (2008) *What to Do When You Dread Your Bed: A Kid's Guide to Overcoming Problems with Sleep*. Washington, DC: Magination Press.

Lance, J. (1997) *It's Not Your Fault: A Guide for Children to Tell if They're Abused*. Indianapolis, IN: Kidsrights.

Lewis, B.A. (2005) *What Do You Stand For? For Teens: A Guide to Building Character*. Minneapolis, MN: Free Spirit Publishing.

Loftis, C. (1997) *The Words Hurt: Helping Children Cope with Verbal Abuse*. Far Hills, NJ: New Horizon Press.

Ludwig, T. (2006) *Sorry!* New York, NY: Tricycle Press.

McLain, P. (2004) *Like Family: Growing up in Other People's Houses, a Memoir*. New York, NY: Back Bay Books.

McNamara, J. (2005) *Borya and the Burps: An Eastern European Adoption Story*. Indianapolis, IN: Perspectives Press/St. Paul, MN: Koryo Press.

Rashkin, R. (2005) *Feeling Better: A Kid's Book about Therapy*. Washington, DC: Magination Press.

Seuss, T.G. (1960) *One Fish, Two Fish, Red Fish, Blue Fish*. New York, NY: Random House Books for Young Readers.

Spelman, C.M. (1997) *Your Body Belongs to You*. Morton Grove, IL: Albert Whitman and Co.

Welton, J. (2003) *Can I Tell You about Asperger's Syndrome? A Guide for Family and Friends*. London: Jessica Kingsley Publishers.

Organizations

International

Adoption Today (digital magazine devoted to international and transracial adoption)

www.adoptinfo.net

La Leche League International

www.llli.org

UNICEF (agency of the United Nations to improve the lives of children worldwide)

www.unicef.org

United Kingdom

Action for Children

www.actionforchildren.org.uk

Adoption Information Line
www.adoption.org.uk/information/default.html

Adoption Matters Northwest
www.adoptionmattersnw.org

Adoption UK
www.adoptionuk.org

After Adoption Yorkshire
www.afteradoptionyorkshire.org.uk

BAAF Adoption and Fostering
www.baaf.org.uk

Catchpoint (adoptive family support)
www.catchpoint.org

Child Bereavement Charity
www.childbereavement.org.uk

Childhood Bereavement Network
www.childhoodbereavementnetwork.org.uk

Contact a Family
www.cafamily.org.uk

Cruse Bereavement Care
www.crusebereavementcare.org.uk

Every Norfolk Child Matters
www.everynorfolkchildmatters.org

Family Futures
www.familyfutures.co.uk

The Family Hub
www.thefamilyhubleeds.org

InterCountry Adoption Centre
www.icacentre.org.uk

Leeds Safeguarding Children Board
www.leedslscb.org.uk

MENCAP (support and education for individuals with learning disabilities)
www.mencap.org.uk

RD4U (bereavement site for children)
www.rd4u.org.uk

TACT Fostering & Adoption (foster and adoptive family charity)
www.tactcare.org.uk/pages/en/childrens_champions.html

Winston's Wish (childhood bereavement charity)
www.winstonswish.org.uk

Young Minds
www.youngminds.org.uk

United States

Adoptive Families
www.adoptivefamilies.com

American Adoption Congress (Education, advocacy and support group)
www.americanadoptioncongress.org

Attachment Parenting International (non-profit education and support organization)
www.attachmentparenting.org

Focus on the Family
www.focusonthefamily.com

Kids Aid (grief and loss support group)
http://kidsaid.com

LD Online (learning disability and attention disorder resource organization)
www.ldonline.org

National Foster Care and Adoption Directory (United States, by state)
www.childwelfare.gov/nfcad

Canada

Adoption Council of Canada
www.adoption.ca

Attachment parenting
www.attachmentparenting.ca

Canadian Children's Rights Council
www.canadiancrc.com/default.aspx

Australia

Adoption Australia
www.adoptionaustralia.com.au

Adoption-Related Movies and Documentaries

Ann of Green Gables (2006) Sullivan Studios.

First Person Plural (2000) Information about this film is available at www.pbs.org/pov/firstpersonplural, accessed 27 January 2013.

"I Wonder..." Families Adopting in Response. Available at www.fairfamilies.org/2012/index.php?option=com_content&view=article&id=80, accessed 27 January 2013.

Martian Child (2008) New Line Cinema.

Supporting Brothers and Sisters in Adoption. Available at www.arletajames.com, accessed January 27 2013.

The Blind Side (2009) Warner Home Studio.

The Lion King (1994) Walt Disney Studios Home Entertainment.

The Lost and Found Family (2009) Sony Home Pictures Entertainment.

Toy Story 3 (2010) Disney Pixar.

Wo Ai Ni Mommy (2010) Information about this film is available at   www.pbs.org/pov/woainimommy, accessed 27 January 2013.

Index